BASIC TEXTS IN COUNSELLING AND

Series Editors: Arlene Vetere and Rudi Dallos

This series introduces readers to the theory and across a wide range of topic areas. The books appeal to anyone wishing to use counselling and psychotherapeutic skills and are particularly relevant to workers in health, education, social work and related settings. The books are unusual in being rooted in psychodynamic and systemic ideas, yet being written at an accessible, readable and introductory level. Each text offers theoretical background and guidance for practice, with creative use of clinical examples.

Published

Jenny Altschuler
COUNSELLING AND PSYCHOTHERAPY FOR FAMILIES IN TIMES OF ILLNESS AND DEATH
2nd Edition

Bill Barnes, Sheila Ernst and Keith Hyde
AN INTRODUCTION TO GROUPWORK

Stephen Briggs
WORKING WITH ADOLESCENTS AND YOUNG ADULTS 2nd Edition

Alex Coren
SHORT-TERM PSYCHOTHERAPY 2nd Edition

Jim Crawley and Jan Grant
COUPLE THERAPY

Emilia Dowling and Gill Gorell Barnes
WORKING WITH CHILDREN AND PARENTS THROUGH SEPARATION AND DIVORCE

Loretta Franklin
AN INTRODUCTION TO WORKPLACE COUNSELLING

Gill Gorell Barnes
FAMILY THERAPY IN CHANGING TIMES 2nd Edition

Fran Hedges
AN INTRODUCTION TO SYSTEMATIC THERAPY WITH INDIVIDUALS

Fran Hedges
REFLEXIVITY IN THERAPEUTIC PRACTICE

John Hills
INTRODUCTION TO SYSTEMIC AND FAMILY THERAPY

Sally Hodges
COUNSELLING ADULTS WITH LEARNING DISABILITIES

Linda Hopper
COUNSELLING AND PSYCHOTHERAPY WITH CHILDREN AND ADOLESCENTS

Sue Kegerreis
PSYCHODYNAMIC COUNSELLING WITH CHILDREN AND YOUNG PEOPLE

Liz Omand
SUPERVISION IN COUNSELLING AND PSYCHOTHERAPY

Ravi Rana
COUNSELLING STUDENTS

Tricia Scott
INTEGRATIVE PSYCHOTHERAPY IN HEALTHCARE

Geraldine Shipton
WORKING WITH EATING DISORDERS

Gerrilyn Smith
WORKING WITH TRAUMA

Laurence Spurling
AN INTRODUCTION TO PSYCHODYNAMIC COUNSELLING 2nd Edition

Laurence Spurling
THE PSYCHOANALYTIC CRAFT

Paul Terry
COUNSELLING AND PSYCHOTHERAPY WITH OLDER PEOPLE 2nd Edition

Steven Walker
CULTURALLY COMPETENT THERAPY

Jenny Walters
WORKING WITH FATHERS

Jan Wiener and Mannie Sher
COUNSELLING AND PSYCHOTHERAPY IN PRIMARY HEALTH CARE

Shula Wilson
DISABILITY, COUNSELLING AND PSYCHOTHERAPY

Jessica Yakeley
WORKING WITH VIOLENCE

Invitation to authors
The series editors welcome proposals for new books within the Basic Texts in Counselling and Psychotherapy series. These should be sent to Arlene Vetere at the University of Surrey (email a.vetere@surrey.ac.uk) or Rudi Dallos at Plymouth University (email R.Dallos@plymouth.ac.uk)

Basic Texts in Counselling and Psychotherapy
Series Standing Order ISBN 978–0–333–69330–8
(outside North America only)

You can receive future titles in this series as they are published by placing a standing order. Please contact your bookseller or, in case of difficulty, write to us at the address below with your name and address, the title of the series and the ISBN quoted above.

Customer Services Department, Macmillan Distribution Ltd, Houndmills, Basingstoke, Hampshire RG21 6XS, UK

THE PSYCHOANALYTIC CRAFT

How to Develop as a Psychoanalytic Practitioner

LAURENCE SPURLING

 palgrave

First published 2015 by
PALGRAVE

Palgrave in the UK is an imprint of Macmillan Publishers Limited, registered in England, company number 785998, of 4 Crinan Street, London N1 9XW.

Palgrave Macmillan in the US is a division of St Martin's Press LLC, 175 Fifth Avenue, New York, NY 10010.

Palgrave is a global imprint of the above companies and is represented throughout the world.

Palgrave® and Macmillan® are registered trademarks in the United States, the United Kingdom, Europe and other countries.

ISBN 978–1–137–37710–4

This book is printed on paper suitable for recycling and made from fully managed and sustained forest sources. Logging, pulping and manufacturing processes are expected to conform to the environmental regulations of the country of origin.

A catalogue record for this book is available from the British Library.

A catalog record for this book is available from the Library of Congress.

Printed in China

To Lesley, Daniel, Eleanor and Pearl

CONTENTS

TABLES AND FIGURES

Tables

Figures

ACKNOWLEDGEMENTS

It is well known that in order to develop as a psychoanalytic practitioner, one has to become dependent on one's teachers and supervisors. What is less widely acknowledged is that teachers and supervisors, in order to develop further, are also dependent on their students. This is evidently the case in this book, as a substantial part of it could not have been written without the active participation and collaboration of all my students and supervisees. Some of their work appears in this book and I would like to thank the following for allowing me to use their contributions: Gina Campbell-Harris, Dorota Jagielska-Hall, Anne Kane, Kiran Kaur, Jane Langley, Sara Macgregor, Jan Mckenzie, Carolyn Nicholson, Bola Shonobi, Susan Stevens and Maha White.

ACKNOWLEDGEMENTS

INTRODUCTION

What this book is about

By common consent, it takes a long time to become a competent psychoanalytic practitioner. Comparing his experience of learning to become a psychoanalyst to his time as a medical student in a neurology hospital, Ronald Britten describes how his medical chief assured him that "the complexity of the clinical picture and the laboriousness of anatomical diagnoses would, through familiarity, become easily recognized patterns" (2003, p.x). And within just a few months of seeing a large number of different patients each week, this is what Britton found. By contrast, learning to become a psychoanalyst involved a far longer timescale:

> The patterns in analysis that eventually become familiar are those of the transference-countertransference relationship. It takes many years, however, to see enough patients and hear about more for these patterns to become very familiar. (Ibid. p.x)

"In the meantime," Britton adds, "the authority of the teacher/manual is relied on" (ibid. p.x).

But what happens if the teachers and manuals that are the source of authority for so long convey a picture of ordinary psychoanalytic practice that gives a partial or even misleading view of how this work is actually done? What if this picture glosses over or misses out some important features of this work? Or, if these features are included, what if they are presented as things a "proper" analytic practitioner should not be doing, as deviations from a model of how analytic practice "ought" to be done? Then one is likely to find trainees, students and even experienced practitioners struggling to match these accounts with the work they are actually doing, and therefore concluding that there must be something wrong with the way they are working.

1

This lack of confidence in one's own ability is a common experience in learning to do anything new. But it is likely to be made worse and last longer if it is reinforced by the presentation of good analytic work as an ideal that can never be attained. The only remedy to this state of affairs seems to be that of gaining sufficient experiences of one's own of conducting successful pieces of analytic work, of patients or clients getting better and improving the quality of their life. This at least has been what has happened with me. Only when I attained a critical mass of successful outcomes could I start to connect up how I was conducting a therapy with improvements, or setbacks, in my patients and clients, and thereby develop sufficient confidence in my own judgement of when I thought I was doing good work and when not.

But with the development of a more solid sense of my own competence, something happened that I had not expected. I saw that a good deal of what I could see as an essential part of my normal way of working did not figure in the way analytic work is usually described in the literature and manuals of analytic practice. I seemed for much of the time in my normal work to be much more actively thinking, making clinical judgements and trying to "do" things in my interventions than would be seen as constituting "proper" analytic practice.

The prevailing view of analytic practice

In this prevailing view of good or correct practice, what is emphasized is how the analytic therapist needs to give up on their wish to structure the therapy according to some pre-determined pattern. Instead the therapist learns to take their lead from the patient, and in particular from what the patient may be communicating unconsciously. This is normally described as the acquisition of an "analytic attitude", characterized by a "receptiveness to the client's unconscious communications and to the unfolding of the transference" (Lemma, Roth and Pilling, 2010, p.16). In order to be receptive to these unconscious communications and the transference, the therapist is taught to develop a relatively unfocused and free-floating state of mind. Much of the technical discussion in the literature is then about how the therapist can foster and protect this state of mind, which is seen as under threat from a constant pull, from both patient and therapist, to avoid facing the most difficult or painful areas in the patient's experience and behaviour. "Doing" something then gets associated with acting in accord with this pull, and so the emphasis becomes one of not doing rather than doing. This emphasis on refraining from doing as the key element of analytic practice goes back to Freud and his original recommendations on analytic technique:

For my recommendations on technique which I gave back then were essentially negative. I considered the most important thing to emphasize what one should not do, to demonstrate the temptations that work against analysis. Almost everything that is positive that one should do I left to "tact." (Freud's letter to Ferenczi, 1928, quoted in Jimenez, 2008, p.581)

In this view of analytic practice, theory and techniques should be brought into play only after the "data" from the patient's unconscious has been received or registered by the therapist, in order to render this data meaningful and a basis for intervention. If theoretical ideas are brought in too soon, they are viewed as prematurely introducing a pre-determined meaning and reference point, thereby interfering with and spoiling the unfocused and receptive nature of the analytic attitude.

It is clear to me that this description of analytic practice, which puts the acquisition of the analytic attitude and the capacity to listen in a receptive way at its heart, captures an essential and distinctive feature of the analytic approach. Without an analytic attitude, there can be no analytic practice. The analytic attitude describes a state of mind that many practitioners find difficult to attain, and for most takes a long time to develop. For myself, it was only when I came to rely less on teachers and supervisors and more on my patients and clients to guide me in my day-to-day work that this attitude started to come more naturally to me.

Clinical thinking

But with my increasing sense of competence, I found that this view of analytic work, although necessary, was not sufficient to describe what I was doing most of the time. I could not help but notice that I was doing a lot more purposeful thinking, and playing a much more active part in determining how any given session might end up, than would corre-spond to this picture of proper analytic work, or be easily incorporated into what Freud described as "tact". In any particular session, along-side this receptive attitude, I also found myself engaged in a constant dialogue with myself about how I was conducting the session, what I thought I was trying to do, how I might do it and how I would know whether what I was doing was working or not. This dialogue might well be in the background most of the time, and would not normally inter-fere with my attempt to tune in to the unconscious communications from the patient. As it often operated below the level of consciousness, it was easy to overlook. However, with growing experience and confi-dence, I found this form of internal conversation with myself, which can be called my ordinary clinical thinking, to be a part of the work no less important than that of the receptive attempt needed to register the patient's unconscious communications.

So, for instance, I would normally wait for my patient to begin a session, to see what might be uppermost in their mind, and thus serve as a bridge to or pointer towards what they may be trying unconsciously to communicate to me. In this sense, I could be seen as adopting a receptive attitude by allowing my patient to determine the course of the session. However, if I shifted my attention to my own internal dialogue, to what was going through my mind in the few first minutes of a session, it would then seem to be the case that I had a no less decisive part to play in how the session began and how it unfolded. Somewhere in the back of my mind, I would normally be weighing up whether to respond to what my patient might say, or whether it might be better to remain silent. Once I did speak I would be registering how my patient responded, and, while continuing to listen to what they had to say, I would at the same time be engaged in some sort of evaluative process; that is, trying to judge whether what the patient said (or did not say) could be seen as suggesting that my particular intervention, or way of conducting the session so far, was on the right track or not. If I chose to remain silent and continue to listen to the patient before intervening, I might still be trying to tune in to how my silence might be affecting my patient and the progress of the session.

I came to realize that the image of myself as a receiver of what my patient was unconsciously communicating to me was useful, but only up to a point. Some of the time the image fitted well, particularly when I felt puzzled or stuck and needed my patient to "guide" me as to how to understand this and what to do next. But if I reflected on my ordinary, day-to-day practice, I could see that much of the time I was not listening in this way. I found instead that what I was doing for each of my patients was constructing a kind of internal picture or model of them. This internal model consisted of what I took to be their typical range of affects and states of mind, their internal objects and patterns of relationships and their normal manner of conducting themselves in the therapy with me. Whatever they told me about their experiences, relationships, past or current life, and what they made of the therapy would be heard by me through the filter of this internal model or models (it was likely that there would be more than one such model in my mind). It was this model which alerted me to when the patient said something that did not fit what I expected or anticipated, and it was on these occasions that I was aware of trying to put my internal model to one side and listen in a more open and unfocused way.

Theory and practice

Once I paid more attention to these tacit processes of constructing and listening through internal models, composing interventions and making on-the-spot evaluations to help me judge how to conduct the session, I was led to re-think the way I thought about the relationship between psychoanalytic theory and practice. It was clear to me that my practice was inextricably tied in with my theoretical understanding. As my theoretical ideas changed, so did my practice. However, I found it very difficult to pin down exactly in what way my practice changed in accord with my theoretical ideas. Furthermore, as my theoretical and clinical repertoire increased, I suspected that any new ideas or practices I had incorporated were indelibly marked with the previous ones I had accumulated and still found useful. When I tried to look at the theory I was using in any particular session, it seemed to make less sense to speak of "theory" as a distinctive entity, and more sense to speak of "bits" of theory which I might use for specific purposes with each particular patient. These fragments of my own theorizing, probably borrowed and adapted from a number of different theoretical frameworks and ideas, seemed to be bound up with, although not the same as, the clinical thinking that was going on all the time in my mind. So although, if I had to, I could give an account of myself as a practitioner of such-and-such a theoretical orientation, applying or making use of this or that particular theoretical framework, I came increasingly to feel that such abstract and general accounts failed to describe much of what was specific and unique to my own way of working.

In short, I had been taught, and was trying to teach my students, to "apply" theory to practice, but I was finding it harder and harder to detect this pure theory in my own work and that of my students. I have found the work of a number of recent commentators of help in finding a way out of this puzzle. Peter Fonagy, for instance, argues that in actual practice theory no longer serves to provide "generalized, absolute, grand, omnibus accounts", but functions much more as "a working, living, tightly organized but flexible set of assumptions that is not sharply separated from other bodies of knowledge". He adds that this change in the way we think of theory – no longer a domain separated from practice but consisting primarily of "local, differentiated, specific rules used to guide action" – "has not yet taken place within the public theory of psychoanalysis" (Fonagy, 2006, p.83). In the course of the book, I draw on these and other recent attempts to re-think the relationship between theory and practice.

The craft metaphor

But for some time I felt I lacked a focal point, an overall framework or overarching metaphor within which I could incorporate these aspects of practice which I have called the ever-present and background processes of "clinical thinking". Then I came across a book by the sociologist Richard Sennett called *The Craftsman* (2008). In this book, he looked at a wide range of practices – incorporating professional, technical, intellectual and artistic activities and pursuits – and found in all of them that the exercise of skill was the outcome of a host of tacit procedures, judgements and evaluations; that is, the same kinds of operations I was doing in my clinical thinking. Applying this metaphor to analytic practice not only confirmed for me the importance of this dimension of the work, it also deepened my understanding of it in several ways. Firstly, all of these accounts made clear that all craft practices involve an initial design or structure in the mind of the practitioner or artist. I knew this to be the case in my own work and could see it in the work of my students, but could not square this with the way psychoanalytic practice is described in the prevailing view. Secondly, in the craft literature there is an emphasis on skill and how skill comes to be embedded in competent practice. It is striking how most contemporary accounts of psychoanalytic practice make little or no reference to skill. I think this is because it does not fit so easily with a way of thinking that puts the acquisition of a certain attitude or stance as the key element, with the implication that once this is achieved, skilful practice will flow automatically. In my experience, this is simply not the case; skills need to be learnt, practised and their intrinsic logic understood. Finally, the descriptions emphasize that skilled work is the outcome of a constant dialogue with the material, and that it is this feedback which allows the artist/artisan/craftsman to constantly evaluate the methods and tools used and their effectiveness. This dialogue with the material produces a distinctive rhythm of work, which moves between the poles of routine problem-solving punctuated with periods of more discursive thinking and reasoning when something new or puzzling is encountered. I now see this rhythm and the continual on-the-spot evaluations made as a key part of analytic practice.

The basic argument of the book

So the basic argument of the book can be summed up as follows. Most accounts of analytic practice minimize or miss out a fundamental part of ordinary analytic work, namely the tacit clinical thinking that operates below the surface. By contrast, this dimension of skilled practice is well described in the literature on craft. If we then think of psychoanalytic practice as a form of craft, as employing the same fundamental processes that are essential to any skilled practice, we may then end up with a description of analytic work which is closer to actual analytic practice than that conveyed in most accounts. The task I have set myself in this book is to produce such descriptions. These will be of value to all analytic practitioners, but especially to those who are still developing their competence. In so doing, my hope is that by reading this book the "persecutory misery" that is too often part of many students' experience of analytic development can be converted into the "common unhappiness" that is inevitably part of learning to do something well.

Who is this book for?

This is not a book for the beginner. It is written for those who have already achieved a foothold in analytic theory and practice and have started out on their clinical career. It is intended as a sequel to my book *An Introduction to Psychodynamic Counselling* (Spurling, 2009), which is a primer or introductory text for those starting out as psychoanalytic practitioners. The present book is primarily aimed at a different readership, those who have passed the beginning phase and are now seeking to develop their understanding and skill as practitioners.

The book addresses the question, how best to develop as a psychoanalytic practitioner? It gives a simple answer: think of psychoanalytic practice as a form of craft. If you adopt that metaphor, you will learn to pay attention to your own clinical thinking, to how you structure your work and design and evaluate your interventions. Looking at both practice and development in this way involves a critical re-appraisal of a host of assumptions and concepts which form the basis of how we normally think about psychoanalytic practice. As such, this book will be of interest to any analytic practitioner, at any stage of their career, as well as those more generally interested in psychotherapeutic practice.

How this book is organized

The book is divided into four parts. Part I seeks to make sense of the degree of anxiety of many analytic practitioners by looking at the way practice is currently conceptualized within conventional analytic think-ing. In Chapter 1, the nature of this persecutory anxiety felt by many analytic students is described and explored. I argue that some of this is simply the consequence of the position of the developing analytic prac-titioner who for a long time inhabits a kind of limbo in their career, where they habitually feel they are neither competent nor incompetent. In Chapter 2, I explore how this in-between state can be made worse for students when they try to match their own work with authoritative accounts of analytic practice which miss out important aspects of what goes on in ordinary analytic work. I illustrate this by looking in detail at one such account.

In order to produce skilled analytic work, the practitioner needs to have found a way of applying or integrating theory into their practice. But here the developing practitioner comes up against a major prob-lem. With the development of a plurality of psychoanalytic schools and orientations, a host of theoretical ideas, concepts, frameworks and metaphors have developed which are used by different theoreticians and practitioners in different ways, usually without spelling out the dif-ferences or similarities between these concepts. This has led to what has been called the "babelization" of psychoanalytic language. This phenomenon and its consequences for development are explored in Chapter 3.

In Chapter 4, the relationship between theory and practice is explored. Whereas the "inseparable link" between theory and practice is often espoused as a key part of analytic practice, what is actu-ally meant by this is often not clear. The current "babelization" of psychoanalytic language has led to a situation where the "theory" that practitioners think they draw on no longer seems to inform their prac-tice. In re-thinking how theory is actually used in practice, I draw on some recent developments in psychoanalytic thinking about the way ordinary practice is organized by a series of clinical assumptions and models (an "internal clinical template") together with a host of tacit the-oretical assumptions which form a reservoir of "private" theories ("map of implicit theory").

Part II further develops this way of thinking about analytic prac-tice by drawing on the craft metaphor and craft literature, which sees practice in terms of skills and how these become embedded. Chapter 5 argues that a craft perspective can illuminate certain key aspects of ana-lytic practice that would otherwise remain obscured: how good practice involves the employment of an initial design which is gradually modi-fied over the course of the work, how a distinctive rhythm of working becomes established and how interventions are routinely evaluated.

Thinking of analytic practice as a form of craft in this way leads to a re-evaluation of some familiar psychoanalytic concepts in terms of the kinds of craft skills they can be seen to be describing. Chapter 6 looks at the concepts of evenly suspended attention, the "rules" of neutrality and abstinence and the principle of "not-knowing", and Chapter 7 revisits the notions of countertransference and containment.

Part III addresses the question, how would we describe ordinary analytic practice if we think of it as a form of craft, and so brought in the elements that are normally left out of analytic accounts? Two extended examples are given, one from an intensive therapy (Chapter 8) and one from a brief therapy (Chapter 9). The aim of these examples is to reconstruct the implicit clinical thinking of the practitioner which can be seen to inform the "choice" of strategy adopted and interventions made. These two chapters form the heart of the book. They attempt to describe ordinary analytic work from a perspective different from that normally employed. The focus is not on the patient but on the practitioner. The basic question asked is, how can we account for the particular way each practitioner conducted the session described? What kinds of models, clinical assumptions, metaphors, theoretical segments, etc., were employed which "produced" the actual work?

Part IV considers the implications of thinking of practice in this way for supervision and teaching. Chapter 10 describes how a specific intervention is explored in a clinical discussion group, Chapter 11 gives an example from a supervision session and Chapter 12 shows a group of students trying to articulate their own developing sense of how they work. The focus shifts from inculcating a tradition and a "correct" way of working to one of finding ways of helping the supervisee or student become more aware of their implicit clinical thinking, helping them articulate it and, in so doing, make them more aware of the basis of their own practice. Only when they know what they are doing and why they are doing it can developing practitioners learn to both appreciate and critique their own practice – the key developmental task in learning to become an analytic practitioner.

A note on confidentiality

In the clinical examples given in the book, all identifying details have been changed or disguised. However, accounts of clinical sessions, apart from changes made to further protect confidentiality, have been presented without change.

A note on terminology

One of the consequences of the division of psychoanalytic practice into different types – psychoanalysis, psychoanalytic psychotherapy, psychodynamic psychotherapy, psychodynamic counselling – is that there exists no one word to describe analytic practice, or an analytic practitioner. If one uses one of the normal words – analyst, therapist, counsellor – one is forced to buy into this division. However, this book is about analytic practice as a whole, carried out by any competent analytic practitioner, whether counsellor, therapist or analyst. So I have needed to come up with a generic term, where none exists. I have made most use of the rather clumsy term "psychoanalytic practitioner" as my general term. At other times, I have used the term "clinician". Where the context requires, I have stuck with the terms "therapist" or "analyst", but these terms should always be taken as standing for the more general term "psychoanalytic practitioner".

PART I

Obstacles to Development

THE DEVELOPING PRACTITIONER

From pervasive to acute anxiety

Writing this book has been the outcome of something that has puzzled me for a long time. As an experienced teacher and supervisor of psychoanalytic practitioners of various types, it has been no surprise to find that students starting out in their learning and practice typically feel deskilled and incompetent. This is well known in the literature on how psychotherapy students develop. For example, in an extensive research study of over 100 psychotherapy practitioners of different orientations and at different levels of development, the authors found the beginning stage characterized by a state of mind they termed "pervasive anxiety". They accounted for this as follows:

> In our research study … we noticed the large theory-practice gulf experienced by the student. The student is immediately exposed to extensive new theoretical and empirical information and is then expected to perform adequately in practicum. The student at this level naturally lacks the competency to perform professionally and is generally painfully aware of it, even though much energy is invested in concealing it. (Ronnestad and Skovholt, 1993, p.398)

I expected this profound and sometimes debilitating sense of shame to gradually diminish as my students' level of training increased, and particularly when they gained some clinical experience. And to some extent this did happen. What the authors note as "the external orientation and rigidity in role and working style that we found in our student sample" (ibid. p.398), which is characteristic of the beginner, started to give way to pockets of understanding and competent practice, giving the developing student some sense of starting to internalize their own way of working. However, this did not seem to result in a significant lessening of the student's anxiety. What seemed to happen instead was that the nature of the anxiety changed. Instead of the global and pervasive anxiety of the beginner, a new form of anxiety made its appearance, more circumscribed, but also more acute.

Instead of the more diffuse sense of shame identified by Ronnestad and Skovholt, the painful awareness of incompetence which the beginner tries to conceal, the state of mind I encountered in my developing students, now became focused on a constant sense of "getting it wrong". That is, they felt they *should* know what to do, but for some reason, they didn't. There was still shame, but now more mixed with more depressed feelings of guilt. I noticed for example how often students or trainees adopted an apologetic or self-abasing tone, using the qualifiers "only" or "just", as in, "I thought it was enough to just contain the patient." Containment means a capacity to tolerate a high level of tension and pressure in the work, and if done well, is the mark of a considerable level of skill (see Chapter 7). But in presenting their work as so devoid of skill or quality, the idea seemed to be that "someone else" – the representative of an ideal compared to whom the practitioner feels inadequate and inferior – would be doing something "more analytic", which seemed to mean something "deeper" like making an interpretation or exploring the transference.

It seemed to me as if this "someone else" – the ideal figure, writer or perhaps institution who is taken as the embodiment of true, proper or legitimate analytic conduct and practice – comes to constitute a form of harsh, internal analytic superego, and this gives the depressed state of mind a persecutory quality. This often comes out in situations which call for the student or supervisee to make a clinical judgement, particularly over boundary issues. For instance, if the patient asks a question, or makes a demand of the student, or wants to change the time of the session, or if the student says something which seems to reassure the patient, many students are prone to describe their response or rejoinder to this in the form of "I know I shouldn't have done this, but..." On being asked why they think they should not have acted as they did, the typical reply is that it is not analytic. But if this is explored further, as often as not the student is able to bring forward reasons for their actions which, as far as I could judge, were based on sound clinical judgement, in terms of their view of what the client or patient was able to tolerate at this point in the work, or what was most likely to sustain the therapeutic process.

In this state of mind, students seem to experience themselves as constantly in danger of breaking the "rules" of analytic practice. Consequently, they will have a much better sense of what they are not meant to be doing rather than of what they should, can or might try to do. Furthermore, when they do feel they are doing what they are supposed to be doing, if asked why they are doing it or what they are trying to achieve, they are often at a loss to know how to reply.

This difficulty in articulating what they are doing and why they are doing it is reflected in a study of candidates of American psychoanalytic institutes who were the subjects of an empirical study published in 2003. The study found that the candidates were often unclear about what they needed to master to qualify as analysts. They did know they should avoid serious disagreements with their supervisors and should keep their patients in treatment. While they reported a belief that what mattered was to establish a psychoanalytic process, they found themselves mostly unable to define the meaning of psychoanalytic process or to state what their supervisors would say it meant (Tuckett, 2006, p.169).

This inability or unwillingness to articulate what one is doing can be particularly striking when it comes to speaking about the transference. Writing about her experience of conducting seminars on transference, Alessandra Lemma observes that "I have been frequently struck by group members' difficulties in describing why they interpret the transference and, by implication, why they did not do something else" (2012, p.463). In my experience, if making a transference interpretation, many students are bewildered if I ask them to explain why they are doing so. They seem to adopt the position that "this is what I am meant to be doing as an analytic practitioner", and to question this would constitute a heretical attack on the very basis of their practice. It is of course true that the ability to make an appropriate transference interpretation is a mark of great progress in one's development, often signalling a developmental leap in one's learning. But the difference between a beginner and a more experienced practitioner is not only in knowing how to do something, but also when it is appropriate to do so, and when it might be more advisable not to do it. And in order to make these judgements, one needs to know the purpose of what one is doing. This means thinking of a transference interpretation as a particular kind of intervention, designed to achieve certain aims in the therapy, such as deepening the working alliance, addressing a hidden feeling or thought, or circumventing a therapeutic impasse. As such, making a transference interpretation is the outcome of a clinical judgement, namely that it is likely to be the most effective form of intervention at that point compared to any other kind of intervention.

If, however, one thinks of making a transference interpretation as the purest embodiment of analytic practice, as the closest one will ever get to silencing the incessant demands of one's internal analytic superego, then it is likely to prove very difficult to think more critically about the pros and cons of making such an interpretation, or indeed, of any clinical intervention.

Neither beginner nor experienced

In considering the position of the advanced student or developing practitioner, Ronnestad and Skovholt argue that it is characterized by a particular conflictual state of mind. While no longer being subject to the pervasive anxiety of the beginner, they describe the more advanced student as subject to "a particular tension" in their position. This tension is a function of the advanced student or developing practitioner being neither a beginner nor a senior, neither inexperienced nor experienced enough to feel some sense of mastery. So he or she will characteristically experience a sense of confidence that is variable, which they describe as "the duality of feeling confident and professionally uncertain at the same time" (Ronnestad and Skovholt, 1993, p.399). The developing practitioner is in danger of feeling lost in what Ronnestad and Skovholt describe as the "major gulf" that exists between the way the beginner and the experienced practitioner go about their work:

> The beginner uses context-free concrete and specific techniques that he or she has been taught, whereas the senior practitioner operates out of an embedded and internalized gyroscope that we have labelled "experience-based generalizations" and "accumulated wisdom". These internalized data may be hard to articulate or explain. (Ibid. p.399)

The point they are making is that it is not only that developing students and practitioners lack an adequate conceptual framework within which to describe their own practice and its underlying assumptions and rationale. It is also, and more importantly, that it is precisely this articulation of the basis of their practice that they look for in their teachers and supervisors. But some teachers and supervisors, even the most experienced ones, do not necessarily see the need for this, and, even if they do, they do not find it easy to do. In view of this difficulty, Ronnestad and Skovholt note that students at this stage of development sometimes become frustrated in their supervision or learning. "The student has now actively assimilated information from many sources but has still not had enough time to accommodate and find her or his own way of behaving professionally" (ibid. p.399). This leads to a different expectation from teachers and supervisors. Unlike the beginner, who is looking for instruction, the developing student is looking for a dialogue with their teachers, together with more of an opportunity to challenge them as they seek to make sense of the different ways of working and develop their own style. So for many students at this stage of development, there can be a tension around learning, "a tension usually more intense than at any other stage of development" (ibid. p.399), where there is more likely to be conflict and disappointment.

This book is about this stage of development. Or, rather, it is about features of analytic thinking and practice that become most evident at this stage of development. So in this book, I will be using the term "developing practitioner" rather loosely, as my interest is less in delineating a specific developmental phase in learning psychoanalytic practice and more in exploring what it is about psychoanalysis that makes development so difficult.

Learning to negotiate the logics of different practices

The key moment in the transition from beginner to developing practitioner is often described as the point when the student takes on his or her first clinical case. This is when the accumulated theoretical knowledge and technical generalizations and precepts have to be put into practice. No longer can the student imagine themselves to be a practitioner, putting themselves in the place of the author of a case study or clinical presentation, or play the part of a therapist in a role-play. Now he or she gets to work with a real person and has to shoulder the responsibility that comes with this.

Some light can be thrown on this stage in the development of the psychoanalytic practitioner by comparing their position with that of the medical student.

In a study of how doctors manage the transition from medical student to newly qualified doctor, the authors found that newly qualified doctors feel "unprepared" for actual practice, in the sense that their previous training, however well delivered, could never prepare them for the "situational and contextual factors" (Kilminster et al., 2011, p.1006) of the actual clinical situation. For instance, when it came to prescribing medicines and drugs, newly qualified doctors found that the protocols they had learnt in their medical training, although essential in understanding what medicines to prescribe, were not sufficient by themselves to guide them in actual practice. They discovered that practices inevitably varied between different consultants and that "sometimes a particular consultant's preferences carried more weight than formal regulation" (ibid. p.1012).

The authors called this transition from learning in medical school to actual practice on the ward a "critically intense learning period". What they mean by this is that the newly qualified doctor has to learn not only to apply their learning, but to apply it in accord with the contingencies of the particular team or ward culture in which they were based. "Trainees' and health professionals' accounts of their actual experiences of work showed how performance is dependent on the local learning environment" (ibid. p.1006). This means the newly qualified doctor has to learn "to negotiate different pragmatic regimes, different logics of practices, and different conceptions of responsibility/accountability" (ibid. p.1006) that are part of the culture of each different team they work with. The authors' interest was in how doctors learn to develop a sense of clinical responsibility and, in particular, the responsibility of managing risk. They argue that it is precisely in learning to recognize and negotiate the shifts in the prescribing regime of each team and ward, its logic of practice, that such learning takes place.

The conclusion they draw from their study is that "practice, performance and learning are so interlinked that they are inseparable and dependent on the specific setting" (ibid. p.1006). This means that the more aware the doctors are that their learning is contingent and dependent on them recognizing and learning about the context-specific nature of practice, and the more aware their teachers are that this is how doctors learn, the more likely it is that the transition from newly qualified to more experienced doctor will be manageable. As the authors put it:

> Institutions and wards have their own learning cultures which may or may not recognize that transitions are CILPS [critically intense learning periods]. The extent to which these cultures take account of transitions as CILPs will contribute to the performance of new doctors. (Ibid. p.1014)

If we apply this way of thinking to the psychoanalytic student who is starting out on their clinical practice, either as a trainee in an agency or taking on their first training case, it has always been known that the particular ways of thinking and working of one's supervisors and teachers play a part in how psychoanalytic knowledge and skill is learnt.

But if we take seriously what Kilminster et al. found in their study of trainee doctors, we would have to conclude that the "objective criteria" of academic progress or technical competence in learning psychoanalytic practice cannot be separated from the specific setting, or "local learning environment" of the agency or institution in which that learning takes place. If follows, then, that an essential part of learning to become an analytic practitioner, and to take the kind of clinical responsibility described by Kilminster et al., involves precisely how to negotiate between the "particular analytic trend" of one's supervisors, teachers and all those who exercise an influence over the student. These differences and conflicts are well known, but usually seen as an unfortunate complication in the student's training. But if we think of each supervisor and teacher as conveying a particular logic of practice, then what the psychoanalytic student needs to learn is not a way of glossing over these differences, but of finding ways of articulating them.

The progression from beginner to experienced practitioner can be seen as an extended "critically intense learning period", one in which the analytic practitioner gradually moves away from reliance on the authority of teachers to the development of confidence in their own ability. This study shows us how important it is in this process if teachers and writers can be as clear as possible about their own "logic of practice", so that the student can learn to articulate the basis of their own work. But how well do our existing analytic concepts, and the descriptions of analytic work we find in the literature, help both the developing student and the supervisor or teacher in this task? This will be the topic of the next chapter.

2

What Gets Missed Out in Analytic Accounts

In order to look at the kinds of accounts of analytic work that developing practitioners rely on, I have taken an example of practice from a textbook called *A Short Introduction to Psychoanalysis* by Jane Milton, Caroline Polmear and Julia Fabricius (2011). I have chosen this book as it gives a coherent and authoritative description of the psychoanalytic method, with particularly vivid clinical examples of good psychoanalytic work.

Description of the psychoanalytic method

In order to understand the way of working in the clinical example I shall describe, it is useful to see how the authors (whom I shall from now on refer to by the name of the first author, Milton) describe the psychoanalytic method. Milton describes the psychoanalytic method as the creation and maintenance of a reliable setting, which is designed "to allow both analyst and patient to focus on the patient's inner world, with minimal interference from outside" (2011, p.6). She uses the analogy of a "controlled experiment" in chemistry, "in which you can examine a reaction between chemicals in a test tube by making sure temperature, pressure and pH are controlled and that there are no contaminating chemicals around" (ibid. p.6). She describes the "stance" of the analyst as one of "overall non-intrusiveness":

> Although the analyst's personality is bound to come across in many ways, he or she aims as far as possible to stay in the background and let the patient take the foreground. Thus analysts avoid wearing very loud or provocative clothes or giving political opinions, or talking about themselves. Ordinary social chat is avoided. (Ibid. p.6)

In this, she compares the analytic stance to that of other psychotherapies, which involve "a more ordinary supportive relationship between therapist and patient" (ibid. pp.6–7).

Milton describes how the psychoanalytic setting is designed to foster free association, with the patient asked to simply say whatever comes to mind and to also report on their difficulties in following this "rule". She then goes on to describe "the psychoanalytic process". The key element in this process is the analyst's ability to pick up the "unconscious communications" of the patient and find a way of conveying them. The analyst's job is to listen to the patient, but at the same time to listen "beyond the words to what is being hinted at or evaded" (ibid. p.9). This type of listening, beyond the words, can reveal "startling patterns and links in the mind that the patient doesn't know about" (ibid. p.9). These patterns often involve the patient's experience of the analyst; that is, the transference. "There are always little hooks to hang transference on, real features of the analyst's appearance, tastes and personality, but sometimes it involves a huge misrepresentation of the other" (ibid. p.8). Whereas in ordinary life our customary transferences are modified by responses and interactions which allow us to judge whether we are right or wrong in our expectations of others, in the analytic situation this is taken away. Milton points out that the transference is a major source of resistance to free association, with patients becoming hesitant or ashamed in admitting to some of their feelings about the analyst. But unlike other therapies, "the analytic setting is unique in deliberately existing to concentrate, observe and make sense of transference, rather than modify and dispel it" (ibid. p.9).

In order to make sense of the patient's transference experience, the analyst needs to be able to be receptive to it. So although the primary task of the analyst is to observe, this does not mean remaining a neutral observer, but instead having the capacity "to really take in what the patient is saying, and become affected and involved, all the while trying to keep on observing and thinking" (ibid. p.9); that is, to be open to one's countertransference. She then gives an example of the "subtle interplay of transference and countertransference" (ibid. p.9) by describing two sessions with a patient she calls "Doug" in a five-times-a-week analysis.

An example of analytic practice: Two sessions with "Doug"

In the first session, Doug reacted in an angry and upset way when his analyst informed him that she would be taking a week's break. Milton describes how the analyst was aware of feeling "guilty but also defensive" when he first reproached her angrily at the news. "She has to be able to feel the strength and particular quality of his rage directed towards her personally, over something real in the analysis" (ibid. p.9). She has to do this "so she can make proper sense of it". It allows her to wonder: why this particular reaction and why at this point in the analysis? On the basis of what she knows about Doug, and what the present situation feels like, she tries to identify with him, and wonders what kind of internal image of the analyst he is reacting to – a parental figure who leaves him, or one who enrages him by reminding him he is not the centre of the universe, or one of a couple flaunting her coupleness? "If she can pinpoint the image and feelings accurately and make a suggestion to Doug about what is going on and why, she may engage his interest and curiosity about his upset and furious reaction, giving him some relief and new understanding" (ibid. p.10).

The key elements here are containment and interpretation. By containment, Milton means "bearing the way the patient is feeling and seeing one, while one finds a helpful way of talking to the patient about it" (ibid. p.10), which will then form the basis for making an interpretation. She defines interpretation as "the process of making a link in the analysis which invites the patient to think about it" (ibid. p.10). Interpretations aim to bring out the unconscious meaning of behaviour and experience, and often link past and present. She describes the most potent form of interpretation as a transference interpretation, one which addresses the patient's live experience in the consulting room with the analyst, and which can thereby capture and express something "emotionally 'hot' and immediate in the relationship" (ibid. p.10).

In the subsequent session, Doug arrived late. He gave plausible reasons for his lateness. The analyst notes, but does not comment to the patient, that "there was a slightly sulky nonchalance in his manner, suggesting 'so what if I'm late, what is it to you?'" (ibid. p.11). Doug then reported on a situation at work where his female boss had let him and his team down badly by rejecting a project he was working on and accepting a project from another client. The analyst is aware from previous material that Doug cared deeply about this project, as "it would have given him a chance to show what he could do". Doug continued to describe this situation with his boss, sounding furious and impotent, "almost like a child unable to affect his situation". The analyst describes her thinking at this point:

Listening to his distress and complaints his analyst became aware of Doug's fantasy that his boss, a powerful woman, was secretly pursuing her own interests. There was even a suggestion that she had a flirtatious relationship with the other client. (Ibid. p.11)

Doug spoke at length about this situation and other related ones. The analyst noted that he left her no space in which to speak. Half an hour passed. The analyst, although silent, had used this time to take stock of the situation:

> Recognizing his hurt, his rage and his humiliation at work, she felt sure that he also felt those things towards her at the moment. It was unlike him to come late and not to be interested in what she had to say. She had to stop herself from defending herself; she wished she could tell him that she didn't want to have to take the week off either. She found herself wondering what it might have been like for Doug as a small boy when his father had left and his mother had protected herself from her grief with a string of brief affairs, often leaving him in the care of her sister.

> She found a moment when Doug paused to think, and said she thought that he was letting her know how upset and angry he felt with her today, about the unexpected week's break. Doug was in no mood for this and expostulated, "huh, you always think about you, don't you!" She suggested that he felt very humiliated by her high-handed decision as if he was unimportant, and as if she didn't recognize how important all that was going on in his analysis at the moment really is. He listened intently. She continued that she had the impression that he was experiencing her like a mother figure who loses interest in him when there is an interesting man on the scene. (Ibid. p.11)

Following this interpretation, Doug was noticeably calmer, and in a softer, more reflective voice, he told her that the day before, he had noticed a man outside the analyst's house, and wondered whether he was coming to see her. He went on to speak of a difficulty with his girl-friend, and then, after a long silence, said movingly that "he wished his father had stayed around, he could have got on with things without having to keep an eye on his mum, looking out for what she was getting up to all the time" (ibid. p.12).

Milton comments on this session that the patient had been enabled to have a new experience: of someone who could really know about and bear his distress, and his anger towards her, and still go on trying to understand and help him. The session has added a new object to his internal world, "another kind of maternal figure who, while having a life of her own, also has concern for how that affects him" (ibid. p.12).

What picture of analytic work is conveyed in this account?

I have chosen this example because it is a particularly clear and vivid example of skilled analytic work. It shows how making a transference interpretation can shift a session and enable the patient to both understand and experience something new about himself. It demonstrates how an effective interpretation is the outcome of a series of complex steps on the part of the analyst. The reader is shown how the analyst noted the patient's behaviour, distress and anger over the news of the break and his denial of its effect on him through his nonchalant manner. The analyst used his account of what was going on in his life outside to map out a particular set of feelings, notably humiliation and disappointment, and a scenario she felt was being repeated, that of a female figure in authority passing him over for someone else. She made use of her countertransference feelings, namely hurt and guilt, to help get her in touch with Doug's feelings that were driving the rage. She brought in her knowledge of salient facts from his past, about the time his father left and his mother was too preoccupied with her own grief to be of help to him. Furthermore, she alludes to her theoretical knowledge, notably in wondering what kind of object she has become for the patient (abandoning, excluding, flaunting, deflating?) and how she might understand his reaction of rage and subsequent hurt. She was then able to gather together these disparate elements into a direct and potent interpretation. The power of the interpretation lies in its linking together in a clear and vivid way the disparate domains of the patient's experience: in the here-and-now with the analyst, his current life outside and salient features from his past life.

The question I now want to pose is what kind of picture of analytic practice does this example convey? If we go back to the description of the experienced practitioner given by Ronnestad and Skovholt in Chapter 1 – "the senior practitioner operates out of an embedded and internalized gyroscope that we have labelled 'experience-based generalizations' and 'accumulated wisdom'" – we can ask how much of this "internalized gyroscope" is made evident, or at least is indicated as operating somewhere in the background in this account?

One way of answering this question would be to note the lack of articulation about the particular interpretation itself, what kinds of elements it consists of and how the analyst judges the effectiveness of these elements. So, after the initial part of the interpretation, that Doug was letting the analyst know how hurt and angry he felt by the week's break, Doug accused her of talking about herself again. The author does not comment on her thinking here, but we can infer that she took this quick rejection of her comment as a further demonstration of his anger and hurt, and so as evidence that she was on the right track. Furthermore, his reaction supports her understanding of the scenario he had created, namely that of a woman (boss, mother, analyst) too preoccupied with herself to care about him.

The analyst then went on to spell out her understanding of the transference situation, that Doug was experiencing her as a mother figure who has found a more interesting man, thereby linking the here-and-now experience with his internal world and with his past experiences. Doug's change of mood, from anger and resistance to softer reflection, was implicitly taken as further confirmation of the correctness of the interpretation, as were his responses to the interpretation: telling her of the male patient he had seen leaving her consulting room, bringing in material from his life outside with his girlfriend and then recounting a memory from a period in his life he found very painful. As Freud first argued in his paper "Constructions in Analysis" (1937), one learns to hear the correctness or otherwise of one's interpretations, not by eliciting agreement on the part of the patient, but by whether they produce deeply felt associations and memories.

The final outcome of the session is described as the patient having a new experience of containment and of a new object in his internal world, that of a maternal figure who can bear his hurt, rage and humiliation. This new development was clearly taken as further confirmation of the correctness of the whole interpretation.

If one wanted to, there is much more one can ponder over about how this interpretation has been put together: for instance, the order in which it is presented, or whether all the different elements – reference to the patient's affective state, the internal scenario in his mind and to the here-and-now in the session – were of equal importance, etc. The point is that none of this has been made explicit by the authors. We are simply given the interpretation with Doug's reactions, without any commentary.

This lack of articulation about how the analyst has gone about constructing her interpretation and judging its effectiveness is very common in the analytic literature. For the developing practitioner, this is a significant omission, because he or she needs to know not simply the outcome of the analyst's thinking, but how this thinking was carried out. However, it is well known that any skilled performer will struggle to spell out the inner logic of their art. Based on his experience of studying how experienced analysts describe their work, David Tuckett observes:

> Although in practice a given session can be rationalized in a post-hoc account, very little of what even a highly articulate analyst does in a session is explicit in the sense that he or she can easily outline it or answer direct questions about it. They feel they have internalized their clinical method and feel their way with a patient, so to speak. (2008, p.158)

However, although these features of the analyst's own thinking are not described in this account, one could say that this is because this is not the aim of the clinical example, which is simply to illustrate the basic concepts described above. Moreover, the example is written in such a vivid and open way – particularly in the attention to detail in giving us the exact words spoken by analyst and patient (rather than the bland précis one often gets in clinical accounts of "the analyst interpreted that...") – that these features are *potentially* retrievable. Indeed, without the traces of such thinking on the part of the analyst, I could not have carried out the reconstruction I have just made.

However, there are points in the writings of the case example where what can be seen as more deeply unarticulated and embedded is not made potentially available. At the beginning of the session, Milton tells us that she noted Doug's "sulky nonchalance", but does not comment on it. Indeed, the analyst does not speak for over half an hour. This silence on her part seemed to have worked well, giving her more material for her interpretation, perhaps allowing Doug to build up a head of steam and so making him more receptive to an intervention later on. We do know what the analyst was doing in the silence ("although silent, [she] was working hard ... "), so perhaps the analyst felt she needed time to do this thinking and deal with her countertransference. Perhaps she felt he would not be in a state of mind to listen to her at this point. But we don't know because the author does not consider her decision to remain silent worthy of comment. Every practitioner knows that from the moment he or she first speaks to the patient, the session will take on a specific direction, and once the first words on the part of the clinician have been spoken, the nature of the session will have changed irrevocably. But in this account, we are given no access to the author's thinking on this matter.

Indeed, in terms of how the case example is written, it is not clear whether we can speak of her remaining silent as a decision. Nor is it clear that we can describe her breaking the silence when she did as something she chose to do. She describes this moment as: "she *found* a moment when Doug paused to think, and said…" (Milton, 2011, p.11, italics added). Saying she "found" a moment might suggest she was on the lookout for such a moment, which again suggests that by this time in the session, she had formulated an interpretation. Perhaps there had been other moments which had presented themselves earlier but she had judged were not suitable, or she was not yet ready to say what she wanted to say. Or perhaps she was not so consciously on the lookout for an appropriate moment; maybe it was because Doug paused to think, perhaps as opposed to ranting on, that led her to seize that opportunity. We can only speculate because the writer not only does not say, but does not consider it something she needs to comment on. Instead the writing conveys a rather seamless process, in that the moment presented matched her readiness to speak. This is indeed how such clinical moments will seem to an experienced practitioner, unlike the beginner, who has little idea what will constitute an "appropriate moment" for an interpretation.

Where is theory in this account?

If we are trying to map out or put together what we take to be the author's clinical thinking, we might look to the kinds of psychoanalytic theory or theories that are being used to help us in our quest. But one of the most striking things about this account is the absence of any obvious theoretical framework. This is partly why it reads so well, as the practice is so well integrated with the theory and there is evidently no particular theoretical axe to grind. As we saw in the quotation from David Tuckett, it is a feature of highly skilled work that the practitioner is often unable to articulate how the work is carried out. But this can make it difficult to locate the theoretical assumptions and ideas that are operative in this account. The closest the author comes to explicit theoretical thinking is when she wonders what kind of phantasy or scenario is driving the patient's rage and hurt over the cancelled sessions, which would tell her what kind of transference object she had become. It is possible to a certain extent to see what theoretical ideas are in play by the choice of scenarios considered. A couple flaunting their coupleness suggests an Oedipal scenario, whereas a parental figure who reminds him he is not the centre of the universe might also indicate narcissistic features in play. It is likely these theoretical ideas have influenced her interpretation, and, indeed, the whole way the session has been conducted. So one might wonder whether some of the descriptions of Doug's behaviour, such as his "sulky nonchalance", are informed or influenced by a point of view that "sees" the operation of childlike or infantile dynamics in the behaviour of an adult. But this remains speculative, as theoretical understanding and clinical practice are put together in such a way that it is very difficult to see how one might be influencing the other.

However, theoretical ideas are evident in a more specific way when it comes to the author's thinking about how she understands her patient and his behaviour. So in thinking about Doug's strong reaction to her telling him she was taking a week's break, the author reports that she wondered what it might have been like for Doug when his father left and his mother tried to deal with her grief by having affairs. Here it looks as if a more localized theoretical framework or idea is being used, "seeing" Doug's present behaviour and experience through the lens of this past event. We might wonder why this particular event was chosen and not any other, and one would imagine that some kind of internal selection or matching of ideas was going on so that the analyst made the "decision" that this particular scenario fitted best with the material being presented.

But in Milton's account, although there are several references to the analyst's thinking, it is not described as something she is doing, but as something called up in her by what is happening in the session. For instance, Milton writes "She *found herself wondering* what it might have been like for Doug as a small boy" (ibid. p.11, italics added). Describing her thinking in this way is in accord with the way Milton describes the method she employs. It is one which puts the reception of the patient's unconscious communications as the main part of the work. So if one is able to listen to these communications, startling patterns in the patient's material will be "revealed". This suggests these patterns are waiting to be found. Again, Milton writes, "his analyst *became aware* of Doug's fantasy that his boss, a powerful woman, was secretly pursuing her own interests" (ibid. p.11, italics added). This way of putting it suggests that the analyst's main task is to be a kind of receiver or screen onto which the contents of the patient's unconscious communications can be displayed, and then conveyed back to the patient in the form of an interpretation. It follows then that a large part of the analyst's work is to *refrain* from doing anything or bringing anything in which might interfere with or "contaminate" this process.

The place of insight and the role of supportive techniques

In Milton's description of the psychoanalytic method, she describes one such contaminant as supportive interventions. She states that a clear demarcation can be made between psychoanalysis and all other therapies which offer "a more ordinary supportive relationship between therapist and patient" (ibid. pp.6–7). Such a relationship would not contribute to and might get in the way of the analyst's primary, if not sole, task, which is to offer understanding and insight: "If [the analyst] can pinpoint the image and feelings accurately and make a suggestion to Doug about what is going on and why, she may engage his interest and curiosity about his upset and furious reaction, giving him some relief and new understanding" (ibid. p.10). And this is what the analyst is described as doing, biding her time in the second session before she is ready to give an interpretation and refraining from offering the patient any comments or observations that might be seen as reassuring.

There is no indication in Milton's description of psychoanalysis that she is describing one version of it, that other analysts might have a different view. But one can find other accounts of psychoanalysis which not only offer a different conception of the psychoanalytic method, but also do so in the context that there are now a number of different ideas on what constitutes the psychoanalytic method. This is how two analysts, Glen Gabbard and Drew Westen, introduce their 2003 paper "Rethinking Therapeutic Action":

> Contemporary psychoanalysis is marked by a pluralism unknown in any prior era, and this extends to theories of therapeutic action. We no longer practice in an era in which interpretation is viewed as the exclusive therapeutic arrow in the analyst's quiver. Yet precisely what role insight, toppled off its prior pedestal, retains among the range of interpretive and non-interpretive mechanisms of therapeutic action, remains unclear. (p.825)

In looking at the range of interventions that go to make up "therapeutic action", Gabbard and Westen found supportive interventions, which had as their aim changing more conscious behaviour, to be just as important as interpretations, which were directed more at unconscious processes and designed to provide insight. They quote from the results of the Menninger Psychotherapy Research Project, which, they claim, point to "multiple mutative pathways" in psychoanalytic work. In the study, which examined the psychoanalytic therapy or treatment of 42

Table 2.1: Treatment goals or targets

1. Changing unconscious associational networks	2. Changing conscious processes
a) between affects and representations	a) of thought
b) of unconscious wishes	b) of affect states
c) of pathogenic beliefs	c) conscious strategies to regulate affect
d) of defences and compromise formations	d) conscious motives

Source: Based on Gabbard and Westen (2003).

patients, the researchers found that "supportive strategies resulted in structural changes just as durable as those brought about by interpretive approaches", and that "interpretive and supportive elements are always intertwined, and supportive or relationship aspects of the treatment should not be denigrated" (ibid. p.825).

In looking at the different forms of therapeutic action, the authors found it most useful to think in terms of the goals of the treatment and the strategies involved in achieving those goals. I have summarized their recommendations in Tables 2.1 and 2.2.

Different versions of psychoanalytic practice

This is evidently a quite different version of psychoanalytic practice. It incorporates the key elements of psychoanalysis as defined by Milton, namely the use of free association and interpretation. It includes the identification of prominent transference-countertransference patterns and makes the therapeutic relationship a key aspect in the fostering of therapeutic change. But what counts as the "therapeutic relationship" in Gabbard and Westen's account is clearly much wider than in Milton's, incorporating aspects such as "internalization of therapeutic function" (e.g. self-soothing) and the internalization of conscious attitudes of self-reflection. Furthermore, they introduce conscious aspects of thinking and feelings, both in terms of goals and strategies, which are quite absent in Milton's version of psychoanalytic practice. Indeed, thinking in terms of "treatment goals", "interventions" and "strategies" introduces a language of therapeutic practice which is at odds with Milton's account. In her version of psychoanalysis, one can discern a broad sense of the aims of psychoanalysis – that of conveying insight

Table 2.2: Technical strategies for fostering therapeutic change

1. Interventions aimed at fostering insight	2. Interventions that flow from aspects of the therapeutic relationship	3. Secondary therapeutic strategies
a) facilitating free association	a) creating a new/different experience	a) confrontations that imply change
b) making interpretations	b) internalization of therapeutic function (e.g. self-soothing)	b) confrontations of dysfunctional beliefs
	c) internalization of therapeutic attitude (e.g. tempering severe superego)	c) strategies that address patient's problem-solving and decision-making process
	d) internalization of conscious strategies of self-reflection	d) encouraging exposing to feared situations
	e) identification of prominent transference-countertransference patterns	e) self-disclosure (e.g. sharing feelings)
		f) affirmation
		g) facilitative strategies to help patient collaborate (e.g. humour, use of social niceties)

Source: Based on Gabbard and Westen (2003).

and giving the patient a new experience, allowing for the development of a new internal object. But the idea of the analyst having more specific treatment goals and adopting strategies to achieve such goals would be seen as an interference with the analyst's ability to remain open to the patient's unconscious communications.

But perhaps the differences between these two versions are not as great as they might seem. Milton's interpretation, which is designed to foster insight, initiates a profound change in her patient which enables him to have a new experience of having an object in his mind which can be separate but still be concerned and able to tolerate his distress. So the term "insight" is being used in a particular way, which ties it together with the development of new cognitive capacities alongside the development of a greater range and tolerance of emotions. So when Milton observes that providing a "new understanding" brings "relief" (2011, p.10), it may be that what she means by relief incorporates some of the features Gabbard and Westen describe under "regulating affect" or "self-soothing". In order to compare these two accounts of psycho-analysis and see how far they are really different, or whether they are using the same terms in different ways, we would need an overarching framework. But there is no indication in Milton's description of psycho-analysis of the need for such a framework or, if there is a need, where it might be found.

We can now make some sense as to why developing analytic practi-tioners often seem beset with anxiety. In the Milton case example, we have a description of good, if not exemplary analytic practice, written in a lively and elegant way. This account illuminates some features of good practice, in particular what an effective interpretation looks like. It also gives a vivid description of how the analyst processes and makes use of her countertransference feelings. But it pays little attention to what else might be going on in the analyst's mind, in particular to more cognitive processes of clinical thinking – for instance, what pro-cesses of selection were used in deciding which element of her thinking were of most use in composing her interpretation, how its different ele-ments were put together, how the judgement was made that they were effective or not and so on. In other words, we find little or no trace of the clinical and theoretical assumptions that underlay and in some sense "produced" her way of working. Indeed the account is written as though it was Doug's behaviour and experience which determined her approach, as Milton portrays herself primarily as a receiver of his unconscious communications. We only get a sense that there must be underlying assumptions as to what constitutes good analytic practice when we compare her account with another version of psychoanalysis where some of these assumptions are clearly not shared.

In short, in this clinical example from an authoritative textbook, we are given an inspiring and elegant picture of skilled analytic work, but only a partial or even misleading picture of how this analytic work was produced. Furthermore, the account is written in a way that con-veys a sense that this is the "proper" way to do analytic work, but in so doing, glosses over the fact that there are competing versions of psychoanalytic practice. How can we understand this state of affairs within psychoanalysis and how has it come about? Are there other kinds of descriptions we can give of good analytic work which might pay more attention to the clinical thinking that informs this work and which are more attuned to the different ways of thinking of the psychoanalytic method? These are the questions which are addressed in the next two chapters.

THE BABELIZATION OF PSYCHOANALYTIC LANGUAGE

Psychoanalysis since Freud

We saw in the previous chapter how Gabbard and Westen, in their account of the therapeutic action of psychoanalytic therapy, referred to a "pluralism unknown in any prior era". Tracing the development of psychoanalytic theory and practice since Freud is an intrinsic part of any psychoanalytic training. All beginners learn to construct a genealogy of the main psychoanalytic schools, with their key ideas and figures, and their relationship with each other. This map can be drawn in many ways. My own version is shown in Figure 3.1.

All such maps are inevitably over-simplified and arbitrary. My map could be put together in many different ways (e.g. including attachment theory, putting Kleinian theory in the second level, omitting mentalization-based theory and so on). But my concern here is not about how this map is best drawn, nor in describing what each of these approaches involves (see e.g. Lemma, 1993 or Frosh, 2012 for descriptions of the different approaches), but the consequences of this pluralism of schools for the psychoanalytic discipline as a whole, and particularly for those learning to become psychoanalytic practitioners.

For the beginner, the differences between these schools is simply taken as part of the psychoanalytic landscape. Most beginning students learn by gaining a foothold in at least one of these schools, and probably become familiar with one or two more in order to have a basic idea of how to distinguish them from each other. At the beginning level of practice, one can get by with constructing a version of psychoanalysis which contains the main elements of a number of different approaches, but where the differences between these elements

Figure 3.1: The main theoretical schools since Freud

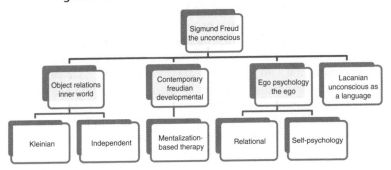

does not become too much of a problem. Indeed, my own introductory textbook, *An Introduction to Psychodynamic Counselling* (Spurling, 2009), was written in a way which emphasized the similarities between the different schools and minimized the differences between them, as I wanted to give as coherent a picture as I could of the basic elements of psychoanalytic theory and practice.

But for the developing practitioner, the situation is more critical. As they develop, they will inevitably be exposed – through training, supervision, personal therapy – to some of these different orientations, so the task of negotiating a way through them becomes of vital importance. The student is faced with difficult choices. Is it better to aim to stay within one orientation, so that one's thinking and practice remain coherent? Or is there a case to be made for "borrowing" theoretical ideas or clinical principles from other orientations? But if one does, the balance and coherence of one's original approach will be disturbed. Furthermore, one will come up against something we have identified in the previous chapter, that there is no overall framework or yardstick in terms of which the different schools can be compared.

This has meant that, historically, psychoanalytic schools have developed side by side, making it unclear how similar or different their basic ideas are to each other. This was already the case with Freud, who started using one model, the topographical one of unconscious/preconscious/conscious areas of the mind, and then developed another one, the structural model of ego/superego/id. However, the structural model did not simply replace the topographical one. Freud continued throughout his life to use both models. The development of the different psychoanalytic schools has tended to follow the same pattern, with new ideas, concepts and models coming into existence alongside those already in existence.

For instance, a major innovation within psychoanalytic thinking was the introduction of the concept by Melanie Klein of an inner world of object-relationships, which has become one of the defining ideas of the whole object-relations school. The notion of an internal world sounds similar to that of the unconscious mind. But as Juliet Mitchell points out in her commentary on Klein, they are quite different concepts. Freud's unconscious describes a system of thinking and psychic mechanisms, whereas Klein's inner world refers to a place, a world of inner objects animated by feelings and moods, which exists as a complementary world to the external world. Mitchell argues that the Kleinian unconscious is thus quite different to the Freudian one; it is a "container full of contents", not "another system of thought" which operates according to certain laws (1986, p.24). This has important consequences for what the clinician will be looking for in their work:

> Klein's unconscious phantasy and Freud's unconscious as a mental area utterly distinct in its laws of operation from consciousness are different concepts. All Klein's interest, therapeutically and theoretically, is directed to finding the unconscious content of the phantasies and the work of the unconscious ego…Klein is not concerned with how the unconscious as a mode of thought works. The content not the dream-work is central to her interpretation of dreams. (Ibid. p.24)

So it remains open as to whether the Kleinian concept of an internal world is meant to replace the Freudian unconscious, or whether it is meant to supplement it, so that both conceptions exist side by side.

Undisciplined pluralism

Those who have studied the nature and consequences of this plurality of concepts have presented a picture of dogmatism and confusion. For example, in 1993 Victoria Hamilton conducted a series of systematic interviews with 68 British and American psychoanalysts about how they worked:

> In pursuing a comparative investigation of analysts' approaches to transference interpretation, I soon encountered daunting problems of translation between alternative schools and "language-games" of different psychoanalytic cultures. For instance, the concepts of

"projective identification", "self-object tie", "containment", "therapeutic alliance" were particularly difficult to discuss with analysts for
whom they had no currency. (p.67)

In her study, Hamilton also noted how analysts used the perceived
differences between different analytic orientations as a way of defining and legitimizing their own way of working. She wrote, "I was
struck by the frequency with which analysts articulated their own
point of view by contrasting this with what seemed to me to be a
caricature or stereotype of an analyst of another school" (ibid. p.67).
She was also struck by "the opposite tendency, manifested by a number of analysts, towards the equation of concepts from quite different
analytic orientations" (for instance, British analysts tended to differ-
entiate Winnicott's concept of "holding" from Bion's "containment",
whereas American analysts equated "containment" with "the real relationship", the "treatment alliance", Sandler's "background of safety"
and "empathic responsiveness").

In 2001, the European Psychoanalytic Federation (EPF) established
two working parties to investigate the clinical and theoretical differences
between the various analytic approaches, a "Comparative Clinical Methods Working Group", described in Tuckett et al. (2008), and a "Working
Group on Theoretical Issues", described in Canestri (2006). The Comparative Clinical Methods Working Group wanted to find a way of mapping
the range of contemporary analytic practice in Europe. To this end, they
set up a series of workshops in which analysts presented their current
"best" work in great depth, with time for extensive discussion. The participants and co-ordinators of these workshops were all very experienced
analysts, with many occupying senior positions in their training institutes. What the organizers of the workshops found was similar to what
Victoria Hamilton had described, of presenters tending to remain locked
within their own approach and finding it very difficult to find a way of
listening to the clinical work of other analysts on their own terms. Consequently, many of these initial clinical discussions proved frustrating
and conflict-ridden.

The behaviour of many of these senior analysts is evidence of a
widespread difficulty within the psychoanalytic community when faced
with ways of thinking that are significantly different to one's own.
Instead of trying to find a way of listening to them on their own terms,
what often happens is that a superior attitude is adopted of supervising
the presenter and thereby accounting for the differences in approach in
terms of something the presenter has failed to see or take account of in

their work. Here, for instance, is how Edna O'Shaughnessy deals with a difference of opinion about the centrality of the Oedipus complex within psychoanalysis:

> A current controversy about the Oedipus complex is whether it is indeed universal and of central importance, still to be regarded as "the nuclear complex of development". It is a clinical fact that there are long periods of analysis – possibly, some have suggested, even whole analyses – in which there seem to be little or even no Oedipal material. In trying to account for this fact, analysts have taken different ways. One way, taken by Kohut and his followers, is to set the Oedipus complex aside, posit a theory of self-psychology and advise a new clinical technique, which focuses on deficit and offers restoration. Kleinians take an opposite way. Their approach, when the Oedipus complex is what I am calling "invisible", is that this is so, not because it is unimportant, but because it is so important and felt by the patient (from whatever causes) to be so unnegotiable that he employs psychic means to make and keep it invisible. (1989, p.129)

In this account, Kohut's theoretical ideas, which from O'Shaughnessy's perspective marginalize the idea of the centrality of the Oedipus complex, are not treated as a valid, though different, point of view. Instead they are attributed to a failure on his part and his followers to recognize the strength of resistance on the part of their patients to acknowledging the existence of the Oedipal situation, which, for O'Shaughnessy, is self-evidently present in all analyses.

Part of the problem here may be that O'Shaughnessy assumes that she and Kohut are talking about the same thing, that there is a shared language and common understanding over the meaning of the clinical concepts involved. The organizers of the Comparative Clinical Methods Working Group started out with the same assumption:

> Since the group members mainly used the same technical language, it was assumed that the same terms also meant the same things to different people. It soon turned out that this was not the case. Terminology regarding transference, counter transference, interpretation, frames, setting, perversion, narcissism and so forth turned out to be differently interpreted by different individuals and nationality. (Boehm, 2008, p.63)

And so the organizers concluded that "contrary to what might be expected, psychoanalytic theory and concepts did not provide a common language for communication … especially at the level of clinical examples" (Tuckett, 2008, p.15). David Tuckett calls this the "babelization" of psychoanalytic clinical language:

> The form of theoretical and clinical pluralism to which we have arrived in psychoanalysis is not "disciplined", which is to say that it has not in general been arrived at by an identifiable process of embracing or eliminating approaches and innovations because they do or don't "work" according to some shared empirical criteria, such as agreed outcome. (Ibid. p.18)

A comparative instrument

In order to overcome this difficulty, the organizers encouraged the members of each clinical presentation workshop to shift their attention away from the patient, and their own understanding of the patient and his or her pathology, and onto the clinician, looking in detail at what he or she said in the session and trying to work out what they thought he or she was trying to do. The aim was to try to build a picture of each presenter's particular way of conducting the session, their individual "theory of technique". They devised what they called a "two-step process". In the first step, the organizers of the workshops devised a way of describing the actual interventions made by the presenters. It was important to come up with clinical categorizations which would, as far as possible, be orientation-neutral; that is, general enough to encompass all the different orientations without seeming to favour one over another. At the same time, the categories needed to be specific enough so that they could capture the quality and intent of each intervention. Interestingly (and this is not commented on by the authors), in devising their categorizations, the authors decided not to make use of the traditional psychoanalytic term used to describe what the clinician does, namely "making interpretations", but chose instead the term "intervention", implicitly acknowledging that analysts do much more than make interpretations. After experimenting with a number of different typologies, the Working Group ended up with the following typology of basic interventions used in analytic work (Table 3.1).

These categories were used by the listeners to the clinical presentations, together with input from the presenter, to provide the raw data for the second step of the process. The task for the members, based on their analysis of the types of interventions used and their purpose, was to

Table 3.1: Categories of basic interventions

Basic intervention	Description
1) Maintaining the basic setting	Comments or questions concerned with creating and maintaining the (practical) aspects of the initial contract and therapeutic frame, for example telling the patient about breaks or holidays, or, in a time-limited therapy, reminding the patient about the number of sessions remaining.
2) Adding an element to facilitate unconscious process	These interventions are likely to be brief, either focused or more allusive, aiming to draw attention to something said by the patient which seems to carry unconscious resonances. This could be in the form of an observation, as in "and this happened only two weeks after your mother died", or using emphasis to challenge or suggest something more must be in play, as in "and this happened in the *bedroom*" or "you *never* feel jealous".
3) Interventions aimed at making matters conscious	These interventions are likely to be in the form of questions, observations, clarifications, re-formulations or paraphrases to encourage thinking and/or expression of more immediately experienced affect. They are more discursive and less allusive than the previous category. Examples might be: "what are you thinking?", "what do you mean?", "I have noticed when you speak of your son you often seem sad", "you don't seem comfortable in pursuing this line of thinking."
4) Interventions that address and invite exploration of the therapeutic relationship	These interventions concern the transference, therapeutic relationship and the patient's experience of the therapy, particularly its emotional and fantasy meaning for the patient. They might be comments or more explanatory interpretations *about* the transference or less discursive remarks *in* the transference (see the later section in this chapter: "Speaking 'of' or 'in' the transference?", pp.49–50).
5) Interventions aiming to provide more elaborated meaning	These interventions might be in the form of a formulation, construction or more elaborated interpretation which ties together a number of shared observations in order to provide or introduce a focus or theme to the session. Although put in a discursive form, they are designed to appeal more to the unconscious by bringing disparate areas of experience, affect or thinking together (for instance, the elaborated interpretation given by the therapist in the Milton example in Chapter 2, p.23).
6) Interventions judged to be enactments	All interventions contain elements of the therapist's countertransference reactions, and if too saturated with these, they are likely to push the therapist into making interventions which are not part of their normal way of working with the patient. Once recognized as enactments, these interventions can be cast as "mistakes" and form the basis for exploration with the patient.

Source: Based on Tuckett et al. (2008).

put these categories together in order to produce a detailed description or thumbnail picture of each clinical presenter's typical way of working. This was called the internal clinical template, which was organized along five dimensions (Table 3.2).

The internal clinical template was taken as a representation of the framework of assumptions or "theory of technique" that could be seen to "produce" the particular way of working of any clinician. Once a store of such templates was constructed, the workshop organizers could compare them to each other in order to produce a preliminary "map" of the range of contemporary practice across Europe.

The range of contemporary practice

In a preliminary report, Roberto Basile and his colleagues (Basile et al., 2010) gave a description of the internal clinical template of five clinical presenters from four different European countries. All five analysts are described as senior and experienced clinicians. The descriptions are of the template of each analyst as constructed by the participants of the clinical presentation, with input from the analyst presenter. The templates were chosen to represent as wide a range as possible of contemporary practice.

I have chosen to present each of these descriptions, albeit in highly condensed form, as I think they represent a significant advance in our understanding of analytic practice. They start not from certain assumptions about the correct analytic method, but from using a comparative instrument to produce accounts which are closer to actual practice. Although these accounts rely on the input of the presenter, they bring in the perspectives of the participants to the clinical discussion as well in order to get hold of assumptions and guiding principles of which the presenters themselves may not be able to articulate. Such accounts are thus more likely to describe the basis on which ordinary clinical thinking is carried out and judgements made.

Furthermore, these accounts may pave the way to answering the question that the psychoanalyst Robert Wallerstein put to the analytic community in 1990, namely whether there exists a "common ground" to psychoanalytic practice. Wallerstein claimed that despite the "theory-drenched" language in which clinicians from different theoretical orientations speak, "we do have a common psychoanalytic ground in our shared clinical enterprise" (1990, p.13). This common ground evokes "comparable data of observation" (ibid. p.7), "to which we react with common clinical purpose and understanding" (ibid. p.13).

Table 3.2: Model of the internal clinical template

Dimensions of internal template	Description
1) What is wrong with the patient?	How the patient's history and psychopathology is understood and how these are seen to manifest themselves in the therapy. For instance, does the patient suffer from lack of containment, premature ego development, unresolved Oedipal issues, problems with impulse control, an inability to manage affects or to mentalize and so on?
2) What needs to happen to address/change the patient's psychopathology?	How does the therapist construe the aim(s) of the therapy and how are these aims to be achieved (overall strategy)? For instance, making the unconscious conscious, providing a new emotional experience, facilitating the expression of repressed or split-off affect, recognizing and working through conflicts and so on.
3) What is the listening priority?	What are taken to constitute the most important elements of the patient's unconscious communications, the raw data on which the therapist will construct their interventions? What in particular does the therapist listen out for: memories, affects, stories of events, experiences in the here-and-now, fantasy, dreams, quality of interpersonal relationships and so on? How does the patient's past come into the present: via memories, enactments, expression of buried affects, experiences in the transference, condensed/displaced representations in the material and so on?
4) How is each session conducted?	What needs to happen session-by-session for the aims of the therapy to be realized and the therapeutic process to be furthered? What kinds of tactics need to be adopted (i.e. which particular aspects of the overall strategy need to be employed) and what types of interventions composed?
5) What constitutes the therapeutic setting?	All of the previous elements determine and are determined by the way in which the therapist conceives of the therapeutic setting. The main constitutive elements of the setting can be thought of as: the affective relationship between patient and therapist, a space for playing, a place where past experiences become present, an opportunity to observe how internal object-relationships become actualized, an occasion for starting to mentalize and so on. How does the transference manifest itself: via memories, associations, enactments, the here-and-now relationship with the therapist and so on?

Source: Based on Tuckett et al. (2008).

Descriptions of the internal clinical templates of five analysts

Dennis: "talking directly about a relationship to create a new experience of relationships"

Dennis' theory of technique was to try to make the patient more consciously aware of conflicted feelings, such as longing and depression, in such a way as to make knowing them tolerable rather than anxiety-provoking. He had a view of what is unconscious as an internal pattern of relating and experiencing that is rather fixed and needing to be described and named. His way of working was to make comments to the patient (he presented work with a male patient) about what he was feeling in the session. This was designed to help the patient become curious about his own feelings. In so doing, his aim was to give the patient a new experience, in which an arrested development could be set in motion.

Dennis conceived of the analytic situation in the room "as constructed by forces largely external to it (in the past) which have created fixed patterns of experience and relating that are not really intra-psychically dynamic" (Basile et al., 2010, p.14). And so Dennis considered it very important that the patient he presented was "able to remember and talk emotionally about his traumatic past in the environment of the session which he, Dennis, must keep safe" (ibid. p.14).

Dennis seemed to take up a role "as a parental figure able to encourage and accompany the patient on a difficult journey" (ibid. p.13). It was important for Dennis not to turn into one of the internal figures he believed his patient had in his mind, for example a dominating father or flooding mother. For instance:

> When at one point [the patient] wishes out loud he was more in touch with his feelings, Dennis says "does it scare you if I tell you that you've been touching emotional ground for a long time now?" And when [the patient] denies this, Dennis says, "and if you and I went together once again?" (Ibid. p.13).

Malcolm: "processing an inner relationship to create a new sense of relatedness"

Rather like Dennis, Malcolm's view of his (male) patient's difficulties was that he had an incapacity to digest his emotional states of mind and feared being overwhelmed by them. Like Dennis, Malcolm was very careful to modulate the perceived intrusiveness and intensity of the emotional situation brought about by his interpretations.

But perhaps unlike Dennis, he believed direct interpretation of the wishes, feelings and fears between them (e.g. "you feel this or that") had the potential to thicken his patient's defences and drive him to more of the same quasi-robotic and compliant ways of managing that he already manifested. "Malcolm described to the group how explicit translations from [his patient's] manifest material to latent meanings seem to result in compliant agreement rather than transformation" (ibid. p.15). Instead Malcolm aimed to "allow an experience of unconscious emotional containment and to create at the unconscious level a potential transformation – from sensation to thought" (ibid. p.15). Attending to the patient's associations, Malcolm noticed and even lived inside the pictures his patient projected onto and into him; he was very circumspect about direct interpretation. His interpretations tended to be "open-ended remarks with potential meaning; but unsaturated with specific meaning" (ibid. p.16).

For example, his patient recounted a dream about two aeroplanes dropping bombs, so he had to hide behind a thick wall. Malcolm told the group he noted that this seemed an accurate description in symbolic language of the patient's experience of the previous day's session. He said to the patient, "have I somehow been a bomber who aimed at you?" Later, the patient went on to talk about his mother's lack of hygiene in the food she prepares, and he then recounted eating at a restaurant where he was given indigestible food by an African cook. Malcolm said to him, "So on top of the indigestible food of your mom, you had the food of the African cook? Double dose of heavy food" (ibid. pp.15–16).

"Malcolm thinks in terms of a field of experience between him and [the patient] in which he does not see himself as providing a missing object but more as exemplifying a missing function" (ibid. p.16). By discussing his effect on the patient in this way, he could gradually move the patient to where it is no longer necessary to interpret the disturbing content. His assumption was that if the envisaged transformation took place, the patient would no longer need to evacuate such disturbing content. However, when he felt his patient was sufficiently contained, he would make direct reference to what he thought was going on between them in a session in a more explanatory, although still open-ended way.

Michael: "squiggling to make mental content safer"

Michael described working with a (male) patient whose difficulties, rather like Dennis and Michael, he understood as having his protective shield constantly breached in his childhood. His way of conducting the analysis was to "allow the patient to use or manipulate him to a degree, tolerating a certain degree of enactment to help the patient use the analytic situation" (ibid. p.18). He refrained from direct interpretation of underlying impulses, as he believed this risked flooding the patient. So, for instance, the evident aggression in his patient's lateness in arriving or slowness in departing at the end of the session was not interpreted. His technique was based on Winnicottian ideas of playing with ideas, leaving the patient room, all with the aim of encouraging the patient's "symbolic capacity to represent his impulses and wishes" (ibid. p.18).

The aim of interventions might be said to "leave some shadow" so that the patient can develop ideas but is not forced to confront issues before he is ready. He was against pinning down meaning in his interventions, as he saw it as exactly the foreclosure of the capacity for playful mental capacity that he saw his patient as suffering from. "One could perhaps say that Michael 'feels' linking meanings rather than 'thinking them'" (ibid. p.18). For instance, his patient brought up a dream, which included a scene where, as the boss of a company, he had to put together a sliced-up human body which had its head missing. In another scene, a cleaning lady went by and the patient told the (female) manager that she had more sense than the rest of them put together. A little later in the session, he said he had had his hot water heater fixed. Michael initially commented, "it's the woman who has the head". He later asked the patient what he made of this image, and the patient connected it to something vital missing that was preventing him from finishing his analysis. Michael then remarked, "it seems to be the woman who has the solution".

Michael emphasized the importance of the patient experiencing the analysis as a *rencontre* – a real meeting of two people. The ways his patient makes use of him reveals the quality of his early experiences, but rather than interpreting the details of the situation between them, Michael worked "in" the situation, playing within the role assigned to him. In this way, Michael tried to provide the missing experience his patient had spoken of.

In their description of Michael's way of working, the authors noted that the participants in his clinical presentation found it particularly difficult to pin him down as to what he thought he was trying to do, just as Michael aimed in his work not to provide explicit meanings, as this would inhibit the patient's capacity for play (ibid. p.19).

Alice: "working with emotional conflict as the cause of self-centred and omnipotent sexual relating"

Alice presented work with a (male) patient whom she thought of, rather like the other three analysts, as severely inhibited in managing his emotions. But more than the first three analysts, she focused on these dangerous emotions by drawing attention to the impulses and wishes in the relationship to her. Furthermore, she interpreted these impulses and wishes as the product of past and present inner conflicts around sexuality and aggression rather than as developmental deficit.

For instance, her patient reported a dream of being angry with his mother for being kept waiting in a queue, which Alice interpreted in terms of her forthcoming break over Easter. Further associations of the patient, for example to do with an ex-girlfriend who had betrayed him, were linked to anxiety about the holiday and when he would have to pay the analyst. The patient went on to talk of the impending visit of a girl who had been a chalet girl for him, and related a pleasurable dream of a girl licking his penis. Alice interpreted that he was embarrassed by his wish to be serviced by a devoted servant/analyst, reversing the reality of being abandoned by her over Easter that made him feel weak and angry.

"Alice thinks that verbal interpretation of his inner situation can bring [the patient] into contact with his infantile vulnerable feelings and identity (self) in such a way that he can find this aspect of his life experience acceptable and not overwhelming or humiliating" (ibid. p.22). She aimed to interpret material that was "near the surface" to help her patient connect with it. For this reason, she sometimes offered interpretations that contained both here-and-now and historical elements, allowing the patient to respond at whichever level he felt more bearable.

"Alice sees the analytic situation as driven by the way [her patient's] inner sexual and aggressive conflicts are externalized into his relationship with her as they are into his relations with those around him in his life...She, therefore, observes the way [the patient] feels about her and is very careful to identify it at all times even if she does not speak about it" (ibid. p.23). Her own feelings are an important guide. Her view of the analytic situation in the room is that "she is always conceptualizing the transference situation but not always making it explicit in interpretation" (ibid. p.23).

William: "enacted conflict theories of what's wrong and of the potential of the psychoanalytic situation to produce change"

William viewed his (female) patient's difficulties as having been caused by her being driven unconsciously to conduct her relationships based on defensive and omnipotent phantasies. His main aim was to help her construct or know her unconscious phantasy experience as she has it. He thought of the analytic situation as driven by his patient's conflicting impulses and wishes interacting with her way of managing them. He considered it useful to try to identify and describe the "facts" of their experience together, in other words, the realities of experiences that happen in the session between patient and analyst, so that the origin of what is observed can then be considered a matter for curiosity for them both. For William, his patient's felt awareness of the vicissitudes of the relationship with him was also her awareness of her own mental functioning and capacities: both elements were vital for psychic change. "William's interpretations are aimed at making her aware of this capacity to have realisations of her own in collaboration with him, to be able to tolerate them and to use them and feel good about them" (ibid. p.26).

For instance, his patient talked about seeing a window cleaner outside the consulting room, and of a man she recognized as a heavy drug user who trashed the people in his life as worthless. William thought she was becoming aware of her own sense of her wastefulness in the analysis, which was coming to an end, and said to her, "You sense now that you are terribly frightened to become aware of feeling that without me you have absolutely nothing." After a silence, the patient went on to give an elaborate story about a colleague who had criticized a report of hers, and then stopped, saying she was afraid she had nothing to give the analyst. William said, "but you had dismissed it and I think you've just made it clear why. I should not talk to you about anything you do not expect or do not already know" (ibid. p.24).

His focus was on what the patient was doing and feeling, but not aware of, in the here-and-now. Like Malcolm, he saw the analytic situation as an enacted analytic field, with both patient and analyst on the verge of potentially provoked enactments, where the patient's feelings in the session change how the analyst is experienced and vice versa.

The range of contemporary analytic practices

This preliminary report from the Working Party on Comparative Clinical Methods is of value in demarcating the field of analytic practice. It shows five of the most senior and experienced analysts working in ways which are clearly analytic, and in so doing, sharing a number of key features. At the same time, the descriptions of the inner clinical template of each analyst, that is the working assumptions they each bring to their practice, differ from each other in several ways. If we try to briefly describe these similarities and differences, we will end up with a provisional map of the range of practices that makes up contemporary analytic practice.

Looking for commonalities, for evidence of a common ground of practice, we can see that each analyst has taken it as a fundamental part of their work to create a setting in which the patient can feel safe enough to speak freely and spontaneously. Each analyst is clearly oriented towards the patient's unconscious communications, and their stance embodies the unobtrusiveness of the analytic attitude. Some are more explicit about the use of silence, but they all convey a sense of making a relatively small number of interventions. They each use the patient's early experiences as a template for understanding what went wrong for each patient. They all make use of interventions designed to give understanding and also to give the patient a new experience of some kind. They all work with a notion of transference, whether or not they choose to make it explicit, paying attention to what kind of figure, object or function they represent for the patient.

It is also clear that there are significant differences in the way these analysts work. In some ways, these are clear and explicit, most notably when references are made to particular theorists, as in the invocation of Winnicott in the account of how Michael works. Furthermore, particular ways of practising can also be associated with particular orientations (Alice's way of working, from the surface to the depth, is characteristic of a Freudian approach, whereas William's attempt to identify his patient's unconscious phantasy has the hallmark of a Kleinian approach).

However, the equation of an approach with a particular theoretical orientation can only take us so far. So, for example, both Malcolm and William draw on ideas from Bion – Malcolm refers to his aim of enabling his patient to make a transformation from sensation to thought and William aims to enable his patient to have the capacity to have her own "realization". Yet each clearly has a very different internal template of clinical practice, with Malcolm generally eschewing direct transference interpretations, preferring interventions which are allusive and indirect, unlike William's direct and explanatory focus on his patient's here-and-now experience of the analysis. Indeed, the description of each analyst's way of working conveys a sense that each of them has developed their own very personal and distinctive style and approach, one which resists easy categorization. From this point of view, the idea of a common ground of clinical practice which can evoke common data for observation is more problematic.

Some of the more striking ways in which the internal clinical templates of each analyst seem to differ from each other are as follows:

Deficit or conflict?

One clear difference concerns their view on what is wrong with the patient (the first dimension of the template of practice). For instance, in thinking about what is wrong with the patient, it makes a profound difference as to whether one thinks primarily in terms of deficit (Dennis, Malcolm and Michael), where there is more emphasis on restoring a missing function or experience, or in terms of conflict (Alice and William), where the focus of the work is more on identifying and exploring the particular conflicts in play.

Saturated or unsaturated interventions?

Another striking difference is how each analyst thinks it is better to speak, whether in a way that is more allusive and associative (Malcolm and Michael), keeping the range of possible meanings open, or in a way that values clarity and coherence (William and Alice, and, to a lesser extent, Dennis). Each presupposes a different view of how it is better to help the patient. Using more allusive and unsaturated interventions is designed to avoid imposing ideas onto the patient, relying on the patient's own ability to find meaning in what the analyst says. Whereas the preference for more saturated interventions, that is, more filled with explicit explanation and meaning, is based on the idea that patients will feel more contained the more they are given the means to understand themselves better.

Speaking "of" or "in" the transference?

Another difference, linked to that between saturated and unsaturated interventions, is how each analyst conceives of the analytic situation and in particular how they use the transference. Dennis, Malcolm and Michael make far fewer here-and-now transference interpretations than Alice and William do, with Dennis making use of the transference in linking present and past events, and Malcolm and Michael seeming to make few direct transference comments. Compared to Alice and William, when Dennis, Malcolm and Michael do allude to the transference, they prefer more allusive and indirect references to the analytic situation. Their stance can be described as one in which they speak from within the transference, as though playing a role in it, instead of stepping outside of it and speaking about it, as exemplified in the approach of William and Alice.

Some light can be thrown on the difference between speaking from within the transference and speaking about it by looking at an example given by a French analyst, Evelyne Sechaud. She describes her first analytic session with a young woman patient who said that she had broken off with her first analyst because she could not bear the seductive power she attributed to him, linking it with an image of an overly exciting father. The patient was in a state of great anxiety during the session.

She remained silent for a long time, a heavy and anxiety-laden silence. Then she managed to say: "I am experiencing successive waves of anxiety." I said to her "as if you were in front of the sea (*mer/mère*)?" She answered after a moment: "I chose you to avoid my father and now I realise I am very afraid of meeting my mother in this analysis." (Sechaud, 2008, p.1021)

Sechaud describes this as an interpretation "in" the transference. Its aim is to "put into words that which cannot be verbalized by the analyzand". Such an interpretation "reinforces" the transference, allowing it to develop further. She states that in her own approach this can often be a prelude to interpretations "of" the transference, whose aim is "establishing the gap between the 'here and now' and the original infantile situation". Such interpretations have a different aim, no longer reinforcing the transference, but to "liberate the patient from its grip, and thereby break the cycle of repetition within which the patient is caught" (ibid. p.1023).

Sechaud argues that analytic practice is better if the practitioner can make use of both types of transference interpretation. This is nicely illustrated in the Milton example in Chapter 2 (p.23). The analyst clearly works mainly with saturated and explanatory interpretations "of" the transference. However, at one point, she tells Doug that he felt humiliated by his analyst acting in a "highhanded way" by taking a week's break, as if not recognizing how important the analysis was to him at that moment. By using the word "highhanded", I think Milton is no longer simply speaking to the patient *about* the transference relationship, but speaking from *within* the transference, as if she were really highhanded. This way of speaking demonstrates to Doug that the analyst accepts and understands the "reality" of the transference experience for him, while still conveying at the same time that the analyst "knows" it is the patient's experience and not hers. This suggests to me that the most effective types of transference interpretations are those that can move between speaking "in and of" the transference.

A framework for thinking about practice

One advantage of using the comparative instrument devised by the Working Party on Comparative Clinical Methods is that it gives us a framework in which we can situate different versions of analytic practice. This is a different approach to descriptions of analytic methods such as Milton's, which promote one particular version as the "correct" one. At the same time, this sample of approaches does not support a relativist view that "anything goes". In other words, the number of different versions of analytic practice is not unlimited, and could probably be encapsulated in a few "ideal type" descriptions along the parameters suggested in the previous discussion.

Another gain from using the comparative instrument is that illustrated in my discussion of the difference between interpretations in and of the transference, where I suggested that the best analytic practice probably brings in both types. In other words, in presenting descriptions of some different ways analysts think about what they are doing and how they are doing it, we are also presented with different versions of what constitutes good practice, which we can then compare with each other. This becomes evident when there are clear differences in meaning.

For example, if we look at the debate around the place of "supportive" interventions in psychoanalytic practice discussed in the previous chapter, some of the ways of thinking and interventions in this sample sound as though they are designed to support or reassure. Dennis, for instance, is described as working as if taking up the role "as a parental figure able to encourage and accompany the patient on a difficult journey" (Basile et al., 2010, p.13). This sounds like a supportive approach. However, it may also be the case that all the analysts think that they don't use supportive interventions, but disagree on what they mean by "supportive". What is at stake here is not simply the same word or idea used in a different way, but what version of good practice each clinician holds and how this informs the way they go about their work.

Perhaps the most striking example of different versions of good practice is a brief account given by one of the organizers of the Working Group of a discussion over the meaning of "negative transference". The clinical presenter was felt by the participants in the clinical workshop to be fostering the positive transference and not taking up the negative transference. However, the presenter disagreed and produced the following interpretation given by her to her patient as an example of taking up the negative transference:

> You are telling me that over the last three years of analytical work we have built up a house that you like, you like being there, and it's a valid image of yourself. Now you have to leave it because there isn't room for two and you are sorry, you don't know if you can modulate your times with those of the other person so as to be in sufficient tune with one another. But you've found your own system of freeing yourself from the anxiety of emptiness, of being a woman like a black hole, the washing-machine analysis, where you put these anxieties to get rid of them. (Birksted-Breen, Ferro and Mariotti, 2008, p.191)

What is interesting about this example is that if I came across it in a case description or presentation by one of my students or supervisees, I would think they had simply not understood what negative transference means. This shows how wedded we are to our particular ways of understanding and using analytic concepts. But in the shock of encountering someone who uses a basic analytic term in a very different way – someone who, as a presenter at these clinical discussions is described as an experienced and senior analyst – I have first to articulate what I understand by negative transference if I am to understand how it differs from that of the clinical presenter, which will then enable us to compare our different versions of what constitutes good practice. Here we can see the real value of this comparative instrument in helping each of us articulate the basis of our own practice.

I will illustrate later in the book, in Parts III and IV, how I have incorporated these frameworks into my own practice and thinking. But for the moment, I want to return to a question raised in Chapter 2, namely the relationship between practice and theory. In concentrating so far on practice, we have somewhat neglected the role of theory in how our practice is constituted. The descriptions of practice produced by the comparative instrument suggest that the relationship is not a straightforward one. There are overt references to particular theorists in the descriptions of the templates, which are all written in theoretical language, so we can see that the way we work cannot be separated from our theoretical language and concepts. But how precisely does theory inform practice? This is the question addressed in the next chapter.

4

WHY THEORY DOES NOT INFORM PRACTICE

The gap between practice and theory

When I started out as a practitioner, and, later, when I began teaching psychoanalytic theory and practice, I assumed a very close connection between theory and practice. As a teacher, I saw it as my task to first teach students the main psychoanalytic theories, and then help them "apply" the theories to their practice. But over time, I started to question the value of this way of thinking. What does it mean to "apply" a theoretical construct, concept or framework to a live piece of practice? It is certainly not like applying a coat of paint to a bare wall. Furthermore, what, precisely, was being applied – was it a wholesale theory, or bits of a theory? Probably the latter, but which bits and how would they cohere? These questions led me to doubt the value of this way of thinking about theory and practice. But if theory was not there simply to be applied, what was it meant to be doing?

The idea of a close connection between theory and practice goes back to Freud. It finds its most elegant expression in his idea, in the "Postscript to the Question of Lay Analysis", of there being an "inseparable bond" (*Junktim*) between theoretical knowledge and therapeutic efficacy:

In psychoanalysis there has existed from the very first an inseparable bond between cure and research. Knowledge brought therapeutic success. It was impossible to treat a patient without learning something new; it was impossible to gain fresh insight without perceiving its beneficial results. Our analytic procedure is the only one in which this precious conjunction is assured. (Freud, 1926, p.256)

Freud's argument was that psychoanalytic theories gain their value not from knowing in advance about the patient's behaviour and experience; that is, deducing something from a set of prior principles or theoretical statements. Instead practitioners rely on the observations made in the course of the work itself. So the theorizing happens alongside the observations, or shortly afterwards in the same session or series of sessions. And so it is "impossible to treat a patient without learning something new". Furthermore, the way of determining the correctness of one's theory is not by setting up some form of extra-clinical experiment but by testing in the session or subsequent sessions whether it works – it is "impossible to gain fresh insight without perceiving its beneficial results".

But the idea of an "inseparable" bond between knowledge and cure, theory and practice, assumes that what the practitioner takes to be "knowledge" or "theory" does, in fact, inform their practice. And, as we have seen, this is not what the members of the Comparative Methods Working Party found. So Michael Diercks, based on his experience over more than a dozen years of being a member of the clinical workshops conducted by the Working Group, concluded that it is "illusory" and "dangerous" to assume a "close association between practice and theory":

> Our findings indicate that in nearly all cases there exists a considerable gap between what analysts actually do in clinical practice and what they believe they do...It was also apparent that in most cases what has been called the "explicit public theory" was confused with the "implicit private theory" of the analyst and that this confusion corresponded to a clinical practice that appeared to be only partly connected to theoretical conceptualizations at all. (2013, p.1)

In order to investigate this lack of connection between clinical practice and theoretical conceptualization, the EPF set up another working party, alongside the one investigating clinical methods, called the Working Party on Theoretical Issues (Canestri, 2006). The members of this working party drew on the work already done by Joseph Sandler in positing the existence of implicit private or personal theories which all analytic practitioners use in constructing their own personal way of working with each particular patient.

> With increasing clinical experience the analyst, as he grows more competent, will preconsciously (descriptively speaking, unconsciously) construct a whole variety of theoretical segments which

relate directly to his clinical work. They are the products of unconscious thinking, are very much partial theories, models or schemata, which have the quality of being available in reserve, so to speak, to be called upon whenever necessary. That they may contradict one another is no problem. They coexist happily as long as they are unconscious. They do not appear in consciousness unless they are consonant with what I have called official or public theory, and can be described in suitable words. (Sandler, 1983, p.38)

The Working Party on Theoretical Issues started from the same assumption as Sandler, that, in their actual practice, clinicians use particular elements of theory, adapted to the particular clinical context with each particular patient. Following Sandler, they called these particular elements "intermediate theoretical segments". They argued that these theoretical segments are likely to be in the background while the work progresses smoothly. But whenever a new or unexpected situation is encountered, the clinician will have to construct a new theoretical segment in order to understand and manage the clinical situation (Canestri, 2006, p.2).

The Working Group investigated how these intermediate theoretical segments were composed. They concluded that both elements, public and implicit theory, were essential to the process of theorizing in psychoanalysis. They came up with a formulation of the relationship between the two, as follows:

Theory = public theory-based thinking + private theoretical thinking + interaction of private and explicit thinking (implicit use of public theory). (Ibid. p.29)

This idea now makes sense of why the idea of simply "applying" theory to practice is more problematic than it appears. The parts of theory that belong to theoretical frameworks, public theory, can be applied in this way. However, alongside our "theoretical orientation", we have more personal or private assumptions, images and metaphors which are mixed in with our more explicit theory. These bits of public and private theory combine to give us an overall theoretical picture or series of models which we bring to every encounter with a patient. Werner Bohleber, a member of the Theoretical Issues Working Group, describes this as "an initial preconception with which we listen to and absorb clinical material" (2006, p.64). But then in the course of a session, we also construct partial or mini theories, which we use to guide us in our practice. These "theories" are much closer to practice than the more publicly based theoretical concepts which we also employ. We then have to combine these small-scale bits of constructed theory with our initial preconception.

In this view of theory, it is no longer a massive and static body of knowledge that we apply to a clinical situation. Instead we have a much more complex picture of how each practitioner takes elements from the theory he or she learns in their training and from books and teachers, and then shapes them in order to use them in their everyday practice. In this shaping process, other theoretical ideas or metaphors might be employed. Bohleber calls this a "search and comprehension process".

> The inner cognitive process involved in searching for terms and concepts, and then comparing and evaluating them against clinical material, proceeds associatively, nested in the understanding of that which the patient presents, and in the analyst's ideas and associations, stamped as well by the respective personality-specific strategies involved. (Ibid. p.65)

This way of conceptualizing the relationship between theory and practice makes sense of why it is so difficult to identify the theory or theories used in accounts of good analytic work. Indeed, if the theory is all too evident, it is usually a marker of work done by a beginner or a poor practitioner. But the challenge is then to try to see the operation of implicit theoretical thinking and how it interacts with public theory. In the examples that follow, I have made an attempt to do just that. They can be seen as my own attempts to make sense of these ideas.

Adopting the "splitting and projection" model

Some years ago, in a National Health Service outpatient psychotherapy department, I worked with a patient with whom I frequently felt pushed beyond the bounds of my therapeutic competence. The patient, Mrs. A, had a history of breakdowns which had required admissions to hospital. In the sessions with me, she had periods of profound dissociation, when she appeared to be hearing voices, and was sometimes in a pitiful state of terror and bewilderment.

The most difficult part of the work with her, which led me to question my competence, was that from time to time she would suddenly and without warning change from an attitude of engagement and cooperation to one where she aggressively turned on me, accusing me of doing various things to her. Sometimes my "crime" was that I was trying to force ideas into her, or turn her into someone evil. More often, the accusations were about my manner or demeanour. For instance, on one occasion when she was talking to me about her son, I commented that she seemed to feel sad when he was apart from her. She thought about this and agreed. But then, seemingly out of the blue, her manner completely changed, her face became contorted with rage and contempt, and she snarled at me "what are you fucking looking at?" This happened so quickly that I was completely lost for words. To make matters worse, I had learnt from experience with her that she would become more enraged if I did not find the right response in situations such as this. She would often start shouting at me, threatening to leave the room, which she had done on at least one occasion, continuing to shout down the corridor as she left the building in which I was seeing her.

I took these experiences to my supervisor. Over time, as these occurrences were frequent, he helped me see that these outbursts and attacks followed a pattern. They were usually preceded by some experience where it seemed Mrs. A felt understood by me. We hypothesized that such a state of mind was accompanied by, or ushered in feelings of closeness, vulnerability, perhaps stirring up feelings or recalled situations of longing, sexual attraction and so on. We surmised that these feelings and states of mind were unacceptable to her or, more likely, were experienced as intensely dangerous and threatening, probably setting off feelings of disintegration or going mad.

In supervision, I was helped to become curious about my own reactions instead of being frightened or disturbed by them. Once I became more curious, I could better discriminate between them. I usually had an initial reaction of paralysis, unable to think or access my feelings. Then I would become aware of a wide range of different kinds of reactions: feelings, thoughts, memories, associations, sometimes images or scenarios. Some of these would be felt very intensely and made me feel very uncomfortable. These were usually feelings of shame and exposure (occasionally memories of having been shamed would come to my mind). Other feelings and states of mind were not felt so acutely or intensely but were often present: feeling startled, bewildered, put on the spot, intensely vulnerable, thinking I had done something wrong and had thereby damaged Mrs. A, feeling stupid, incompetent, cornered and so on. Sometimes I was only aware of feelings, typically anger or sadness, later or at the end of the session.

My supervisor's view was that these sudden attacks, and their effect on me, were the product of a powerful process of "splitting and projection". Mrs. A would split off the states of mind and accompanying affects she found intolerable, and then project them into me by means of the attack. So in the example above, feeling close or understood produced feelings or memories of shame and vulnerability which she found intolerable. So she split off both the experience of being understood, and its accompanying affects, and projected them back into me by "inducing" such feelings in me. My paralysis and shock was an indication that such a projection had taken place, and my reactions could be taken as indications of what it was that had been projected into me.

As we went over such experiences again and again, I learnt to incorporate the "splitting and projection" model into my way of thinking. This enabled me to feel more prepared for occasions when Mrs. A seemed to change and turn on me, although their effect on me continued to be massive. But over time, I was able to recover from them more quickly, and so could get in touch with the particular feelings or states of mind which I was aware of in myself. Paying more attention to my own reactions, I became more adept at picking out the dominant feelings or thoughts. I was thus able to put together my understanding of the precursor to the outburst, together with the particular feelings I had noticed in myself, to give me the elements out of which I could compose my interventions. In the situation above, having picked out my dominant reactions as shame and vulnerability, I said to Mrs. A,

> I think you are telling me that you are feeling you have given too much of yourself away to me, that what I just said to you about how you feel sad when your son goes away felt too exposing to you, as though I could see right inside you. (Or words to that effect, I am relying on my memory of the occasion.)

Sometimes, but not always, such comments served to calm her down, or at least give us both a breathing space. Even if they did no more than this, I found them valuable, as they helped me regain my therapeutic balance.

The use of these theoretical terms was not new to me; I had been using them myself for many years. But in these experiences, the concepts came alive for me in a different way. Over the course of my work with Mrs. A, I think this "splitting and projection" model became established as part of my clinical/theoretical repertoire, a kind of second nature, to be called upon in clinical situations which seemed similar or produced comparable reactions in me.

Theory gives an abstract account by bringing in a second context

If we look at what this "splitting and projection" model does, what makes it so effective, we can see that it tells a story about what was happening, a story which made sense to me, and which I could use to regain my therapeutic balance and construct an appropriate intervention. The story was one of experiences and objects in Mrs. A's internal world, what she did with them, and how these affected the relationship between us. In this sense, psychoanalytic theory functions like any theory in the social sciences – "theory means, simply, general and abstract account. A theory of X is a general and abstract account of X" (Schatzki, Cetina and Von Savigny, 2001, p.3).

What is more specific to a psychoanalytic theory is that it gives this general and abstract account by providing another context. What I learnt to do was to transpose the drama in the consulting room to another drama, now located in her mind and between her mind and mine. The theoretical model provided both the framework and the engine by which I could effect this transposition. At first, while I was getting used to using the model, this imagined transposition felt rather awkward and artificial, as I had to go through the steps rather deliberately, silently asking myself: "why is Mrs. A doing this, what is being split off and projected into me?" But this process soon speeded up and, after a time, I hardly noticed what I was doing. Rather like a driver who learns to change gear and glance at the rear mirror while keeping his or her eye on the road in front, I learnt to listen to Mrs. A, think about what she was saying, and still have some awareness that these "theoretical" operations were going on somewhere in the back of my mind.

Finding patterns, extracting and mapping

If we look more closely at how this theoretical model was applied, we can see several operations that needed to take place. Firstly, a particular clinical problem needed to be identified. For me, what this problem was seemed self-evident – I was being subjected to what felt like sudden and massive attacks by my patient which I needed to understand and deal with. However, another practitioner, with a different temperament, may not have found these experiences so problematic, or may have identified other issues as more puzzling or urgent.

A lot of the initial work in supervision was in identifying a "precipitating event" in the therapy to these attacks, which was broadly described as Mrs. A having an experience of feeling understood by me and/or feeling close to me. Once identified, this pattern could be more widely applied. So whereas my initial grasp of the pattern was when a moment of understanding or closeness was immediately followed by the switch in mood and the attack, once I had the pattern firmly in my mind, I could find occasions which might have occurred earlier in the session as also likely to trigger such reactions. Identifying such occasions as potential triggers enabled me to be better prepared if an "attack" came later in the session.

As I have described, I also became more adept at identifying patterns in my affective reactions to such attacks, and learnt to select the ones which would best serve my purpose. In other words, I had to do some work in "selecting" from the range, duration and intensity of my reactions which ones would count as "projections" and therefore form part of the theoretical narrative.

We can thus see that "identifying patterns" means being able to deconstruct or *extract* the salient elements from the clinical event and my own affective reactions. Once I had identified these key elements, I could construct a sequence of events in the consulting room: Mrs. A felt understood/close to me – I felt vulnerable, exposed, ashamed, stupid etc. I could then introduce another context, Mrs. A's internal world, and construct a sequence of events in which Mrs. A split off her feeling understood/being close, together with its accompanying affects, and projected them into me. Finally, I could *map* the events in Mrs. A's mind onto what happened in the consulting room, and my reactions to it, in order to make sense of both the clinical events and my own affective responses. So the "splitting and projection" model can be seen to have created a kind of "fused" reality or domain in which elements from these two contexts – events in the room, events in Mrs. A's mind – were continuously being mapped onto each other.

How consistent do our models have to be?

The "splitting and projection" model was not the only one in my mind. At other times in sessions, Mrs. A would become very depressed. For instance, on occasions she would launch into a series of bitter self-accusations, accusing herself of having done terrible things, such as having murdered a child. Although the "splitting and projection" model could still be applied in such situations, for instance in registering some of my own reactions to her self-abasement and wondering whether these had been split off and projected into me. But I had another model at my disposal which I found to "fit" these clinical situations better.

In this model, the story I told myself became one of her superego viciously and cruelly attacking a part of her ego which had become identified with a disappointing or abandoning object. I had learnt to incorporate this model over the many years of my experience of working with depressed patients. It is graphically described in Freud's "Mourning and Melancholia" (1917), where he reconstructs a series of events to account for the melancholic's self-abasement. Following a disappointment with a loved person in the past, the feelings attached to that person are withdrawn into the ego. A part of the ego then becomes identified with this "abandoned object"; as Freud puts it, "the shadow of the object fell upon the ego". This part of the ego is attacked and vilified by another part of the ego, which Freud would go on to call the superego. And so the previous conflict between the ego and the loved person becomes transformed into "a cleavage between the critical activity of the ego and the ego as altered by identification" (ibid. p.249).

Using this "superego attacking ego" model oriented me in how to "listen" to Mrs. A's accusations against herself, namely that she was in fact attacking "someone else" who had previously rejected or abandoned her and had now become incorporated into a part of her ego. By using the same operations of identifying patterns, extracting salient elements and mapping the two contexts (self-abasement in the room, superego attacking ego in her mind) onto each other, I could use the model to search for the particular experiences and events which might make sense of Mrs. A's behaviour and experience.

So part of my own way of theorizing, and part of my own internal clinical template, was to employ two different models, one in situations where I judged the "affect storms" typical of "borderline" phenomena were more in evidence, the other when more "depressed" features seemed more prominent. The two models are not obviously incompatible with each other; indeed, they can be seen to overlap. But they are also different, employing different concepts which, as we saw in comparing Freud's "unconscious" with Klein's "internal world", carry with them different theoretical assumptions and which will have consequences for practice.

Drawing on theory to solve a particular clinical puzzle

In the clinical example with Mrs. A, I drew on two models which form part of public theory. Both models used theoretical concepts which operate at a high level of abstraction, applicable to a broad range of clinical phenomena. But many clinical situations involve particular problems or puzzles that occur at a more local or specific level, where a particular patient or clinical situation does not seem to fit easily into one's existing models and bits of theory. As Canestri pointed out, if faced with a new or puzzling situation, the clinician is called upon to construct a new "theoretical segment" in order to solve the puzzle or find a way of moving on.

I will now give an example of such a situation, this time occurring in a supervision group I was running. The setting, as in the previous example, was a National Health Service psychotherapy department.

One of the supervisees, a man, was working with a transsexual patient (female to male). His work with him was getting stuck. He said he found it very difficult to know how to think of the change of gender in his patient, and did not know whether to think of the patient as a man or woman. The supervision group was also struggling with this issue, which was threatening to derail our attempt to help the therapist get to grips with what he was trying to achieve in the therapy with his patient. This became particularly evident when the patient, as part of his transition, was due to have further surgery to remove his breasts. One of the members of the group, a woman, said she could not get past thinking that this was a profound piece of self-destructive behaviour on the patient's part, and she wondered whether the therapeutic task was to dissuade him from this action. The therapist himself also felt uncertain. The patient was very clear that the operation was extremely important to him and could brook no questioning of its value. However, the therapist was torn between believing this, and so helping the patient manage the effect of the operation, or thinking, like the female member of the supervision group, that the operation represented a form of mutilation which should be challenged. This problem was compounded by our difficulty in the group of finding a way of referring to the patient's gender which could keep in mind the patient's past life: was "he" simply a "he", or should we find a way of referring to "him" that reminded us that "he" used to be a "she"?

Looking for inspiration, I turned to the analytic literature on working with transsexual patients. One paper in particular, by Danielle Quinodoz (1998) caught my eye. In this paper, Quinodoz described her work with a transsexual patient, who was born as a man and had surgery to become a woman. She discussed the linguistic problem, which she felt was also a transference problem, of whether to speak of the patient as male or female, which made her feel mad. "I could not tell inside whether my patient was a man or a woman, and I always had an inner hesitation when thinking or speaking to her, as I had no spontaneous feeling of the appropriate sex to assign to her" (ibid. p.96). She then described how she found a solution to this transference problem, which was to assume the fantasy role of parents expecting a baby whose sex they did not yet know: "to accept my feeling of not being sure whether I was talking to a man or a woman and to be willing to experience fully the discomfort of this countertransference uncertainty while continuing to hope that one day a certainty would take shape, but without prejudging that shape" (ibid. p.96).

I thought this idea was a simple and elegant position to adopt with such a patient, a way of getting myself out of the dilemma of having to assign the patient to a particular gender. It was also an idea the supervisees found helpful. It allowed us to move on from feeling stuck, and so be of more help to the therapist in gaining a clearer idea of his therapeutic task with this particular patient. The unborn baby metaphor helped him keep the patient's past gender in mind but without compromising the wish to change gender. He was then able to formulate a viable goal of the therapy as to help his patient mourn the loss of the female "side" to his personality which he had had to give up in order to become a man.

I have taken an example from a supervision group rather than clinical practice as this makes clearer the process in which we "search" for concepts when we encounter something that puzzles or disconcerts us. Furthermore, in using a ready-made metaphor, borrowed from someone else, I have tried to make clear what in ordinary clinical practice is a preconscious and intuitive process, that of "fitting" an idea to a clinical situation in a way that enables it to be seen in a different light.

A map of implicit theory

If we return to the distinction between public and private or implicit theory, we can see in the example of the unborn baby metaphor how a particular "theory" was invented or constructed by a clinician to solve a clinical puzzle. This personal theory was then adopted by me as it seemed to fit the clinical situation I was faced with. In this way, it became a form of public theory on which I could draw and it took up a place as part of my theoretical/clinical repertoire. But it can be seen to operate at a much lower level of abstraction, designed to fit very particular clinical situations, than the "splitting and projection" model and "superego attacking ego" model which also form part of my store of theoretical knowledge. But even at this much higher level of abstraction, these two models have to "fit" with particular clinical situations; that is, working with more borderline or depressed features.

So we can think of implicit or private theories in two different ways. One can think of implicit theory as a bank or store of assumptions, models, metaphors, bits of theory, etc. that constitute a backcloth to one's practice. As described by Sandler, these are held in reserve, and can be called upon to construct those theoretical segments which one needs for actual clinical practice. The three models I have described for my own practice all form part of my own implicit theory. The "splitting and projection" and "ego attacking superego" models both draw heavily on public theories, but I have tried to describe the operation of these models in ways that draw attention to the particular ways I use, and thereby adapt these models to particular situations. So in my actual use of these models, at least as far as I can tell in trying to catch myself in action, I can be seen to be bringing in both public theory and implicit theoretical ideas and then combining them in my actual practice.

So one can think of implicit theory to mean not only the *content* of what we hold in reserve in our mind but also the *operations* we employ in evaluating the usefulness of public theories and implementing them in practice. These operations would comprise the cognitive processes we employ whenever we use a bit of theory: identifying patterns, extracting elements and mapping between different contexts, judging when to use one model as opposed to another, determining the level of generality, and combining different models or finding ways of making them consistent with each other. I take these as similar to what Lemma in the "Competency Framework for Psychodynamic Therapy" calls "the procedures used by therapists to guide practice". These procedures are used to "implement higher-order links between theory and practice in order to plan and where necessary adapt therapy to the needs of individual clients" (Lemma, Roth and Pilling, 2010, p.11).

The notion of implicit or private theories remains somewhat elusive, as it is an attempt to describe key elements of our way of organizing our practice that operate mainly at a preconscious level. I have found it helpful to construct a map of this territory, which I have adapted from the descriptions given by members of the Working Party.

The five vectors are an attempt to describe the concepts, assumptions and models that operate at this implicit level (conceptual and developmental vectors), how they manifest themselves in practice (action vector), how coherent and articulated they need to be (coherence vector) and what kind of relationship each clinician has to his or her theories (theories as internal objects). These implicit theories are taken to function at varying degrees of consciousness, some easier to see in operation, and so more conscious, with most elements operating below the surface at a preconscious level, and some elements remaining hidden or

Table 4.1: Vectors of implicit theory

	Conceptual	Assumptions about development & change	Action (clinical thinking and interventions)	Coherence	Theories as internal objects
Conscious level	Clinical concepts used to manage situation (e.g. envy, abandonment) Exemplars of clinical practice (e.g. exemplary cases)	Model of development (e.g. stages, positions, etc.)	Formulations and more thought-out interventions		Placing oneself within psychoanalytic genealogy (influence of training)
Preconscious level	Worldview (e.g. scientific, romantic, tragic) influencing choice of theory Common sense understanding of relationships How clinical concepts combined Clinical generalizations (conceptual and clinical)	Development as linear or more complex (e.g. how regression understood) Theory of change (e.g. importance of insight) Theory of psychopathology (e.g. conflict or deficit?)	Listening: how patient's free associations heard Interpreting: choice of wording Interventions: saturated or unsaturated? Balance of interpretive and supportive interventions How set up and maintained (rules and parameters) What is a psychoanalytical process?	Interventions as internally coherent or patchwork of concepts Use of metaphors or polymorphous concepts	Patterns of affiliation and idealization Bits of implicit theory that contradict one's public affiliations
Unconscious level	Transference to theory, e.g. theory as superego, theory as resistance against engaging with patient		Behaving: personal and cultural factors	Tolerance of ambiguity, contradiction or incoherence	Social and cultural influences Our relationship to theories, e.g. nature of attachment

Source: Based on Canestri (2006, pp.29–43).

repressed to the clinicians themselves, and so probably only accessible in conversation with someone else.

Conscious level

At the more *conscious* level, implicit theories overlap considerably with explicit and public theories. Here, theoretical concepts and models and assumptions about development and change can be articulated, and the more conscious theorizing that takes place in clinical work is likely to happen within one particular theoretical orientation. This is most evident when the clinician makes a *formulation*; that is, puts together a number of elements of the therapy in order to construct a narrative about the patient (as Milton does in her extended interpretation to her patient and as I did with my patient in giving her an account of why she needed to attack me). The store of writings, case descriptions, experiences from supervisors and teachers, etc. which function as ideals or models of good practice constitute each clinician's *exemplars of clinical experience*, and will be fairly explicit at this level, as in my borrowing of Quinodoz's analogy. If asked to describe their theoretical orientation, many practitioners will be able to give some kind of coherent account, drawing on their own genealogical map of the various psychoanalytic schools.

Preconscious level

Most of the elements of implicit theory operate at a lower *preconscious* level, where they are probably not explicitly articulated, but exist in a form where they serve as a guide to the therapy with each particular patient. Along the *conceptual vector*, there are elements which go to determine which theoretical orientation might have been chosen for less conscious reasons and which aspects of it might be highlighted. Each of the different schools carries with it a particular *worldview*, an account of what it is to be human. So, for example, Freud put the Oedipal drama around guilt at the centre of his thinking, Klein saw human existence as an ongoing battle between love and hate, whereas, for Kohut and Winnicott, human existence is more about the vicissitudes around the human need for recognition and affirmation.

In listening to our patients, we draw on a whole range of assumptions and "knowledge", some personal and some cultural, about ordinary living and how people relate to each other. Part of the problem in the supervision group described above was that our "common sense" understanding of gender assignment was being stretched – or challenged. This *common sense understanding* combines with the host of clinical and conceptual concepts we use to understand our patients. Furthermore, clinicians also make use, to a greater or lesser degree, of what Canestri (2006, p.36) calls *clinical generalizations* in their work. These consist firstly of *conceptual generalizations*, which comprise diagnostic concepts (e.g. narcissism), how these might be broken down into different types (e.g. thin- or thick-skinned narcissism) and the kinds of metaphors used in connection with them (e.g. "you have to break through the narcissistic shield").

Technical generalizations refer to the "recipes of clinical practice that are handed down in the transmission of psychoanalysis through supervision" (ibid. p.36). Common examples would be: "treat any dynamic described by the patient as referring implicitly to the analyst", or "avoid asking questions or clarifications as this will interfere with the patient's free association." All clinicians have a store of such technical generalizations which they have taken from (or adapted from) their teachers. Examples of some of my own, each of which I can trace back to a particular teacher, are "confusion is a childish defence", "boredom is a defence" (as opposed to finding things tedious, which may be more to do with the object) and "admission is a way in" (i.e. if the patient admits something, this can be seen as a way in to something important, as opposed to a confession which may be more motivated by shame).

The *assumptions about development and change vector* is where this map most clearly overlaps with the internal template of practice, although at a somewhat more abstract level. *Theories about development* will concern how one sees the relationship between progression and regression in human development, and whether one regards development as a broadly linear process, or one where developmental processes loop back on themselves. *Theories about change* concern the basic aims of therapy: gaining insight ("making the unconscious conscious"), changing the nature of psychic agencies ("reducing the violence of the superego"), putting the patient in touch with repressed or split off feelings, enhancing the patient's capacity to mentalize, reaching the depressive position, gaining a sense of an authentic self and so on. *Theories of psychopathology* concern the way the patient's difficulties are habitually understood, which, as we saw in Chapter 3, normally concerns the balance between thinking in terms of deficit or conflict.

The *action vector* concerns practice. Again there is considerable overlap with the internal template of practice, although here the emphasis is on the more implicit and personal rules, ideas or guidelines each clinician follows in conducting the sessions. In this map of implicit theory, the preconscious elements of this vector concern how the main elements of the internal template of practice (how one listens, how one puts interventions together, what kinds of interventions are used, how the setting is maintained and a psychoanalytic process conceived) relate to the other vectors of the map, particularly in how the clinician judges the quality and effectiveness of his or her actions.

The last two vectors, *coherence* and *theories as internal objects*, concern the relationship of the different bits of theory (public and implicit) to each other, and the clinician's own relationship to or attitude towards his or her theories. Some clinicians can tolerate, or even thrive upon, considerable ambiguity in the theories they adopt, even holding different ideas which seem to contradict each other. Others find it more productive to work with coherent and internally consistent ideas and assumptions. In a similar way, some work best on the basis of a strong and explicit affiliation to one group or school, whereas others prefer to spread or dilute their allegiances to specific theories or groups.

Unconscious level

These last two vectors shade more into areas that are more unconscious, either in the sense of being less available, or as being more repressed. Generally, the *unconscious* level refers to those aspects of implicit theories which bring in more social, cultural, personal and transferential elements. Here, the realm of implicit theory is more distinct from the internal template of practice, which aims to describe the conscious/preconscious levels of practice; that is, those potentially accessible to the clinician. Reference to the unconscious level would include how far we can tolerate ambiguity, how far we use theories defensively and how attached we are to our theories.

Closing the gap between practice and theory

Let us return to the problem we set at the beginning of this chapter, the gap between theory and practice, between what clinicians believe they are doing or ought to be doing, and what they actually do. We can see that this gap arises because of a confusion over what is meant by theory and its level of abstraction, as one commentator, Juan Pablo Jimenez, makes clear:

We psychoanalysts are experts in constructing narratives whose details aim to grasp the singularity of their patients' experiences. It is highly probable that developments of psychoanalytic theory in the course of history stem precisely from the fact that some of these private theories were "made official". The problem is not here but in the unnoticed passage and in a confusion of levels of abstraction. These theoretical fragments, products of inductive inferences that apply quite well to a particular patient, are assigned a universal value that they do not have. (2009, pp.233–234)

So it is essential, when we think of the relationship between practice and theory, that we specify what it is we mean by "theory". Do we mean a theoretical orientation, or specific models which belong to a particular orientation but operate at a high level of abstraction, or models which are more specifically applied to particular situations, or bits of theory which can only be applied to very specific clinical situations?

So we can think of an "inseparable bond" between theory and practice, or as practice as the application of theory, only if we can specify the *level of abstraction* we are talking about. In our day-to-day work, we can think of this inseparable bond not as a given, but as "an ongoing unity, painstakingly constructed by the analyst, in the manner of a craftsman or artisan, day by day in the sessions with the patients" (Jimenez, 2005, p.627).

We can think of this "ongoing unity" as a particular combination of theory and practice, or as a kind of intermediate object which the practitioner will have in mind. Here, we can introduce one more concept which some commentators have found useful in thinking of the relationship between theory and practice, that of the "working model".

Working models

If we go back to Milton's account in Chapter 2, we can see that the only time she makes explicit reference to theoretical ideas is when she speaks of "identifying" with the patient: "on the basis of what she knows about Doug, and what the present situation feels like, she tries to identify with him, and wonder what kind of internal image of the analyst he is reacting to – a parental figure who leaves him, or one who enrages him by reminding him he is not the centre of the universe, or one of a couple flaunting her coupleness?" (Milton, Polmear and Fabricius, 2011, p.10). She uses her identification with him to reconstruct an element from his past: "she found herself thinking what it might have been like for Doug as a small boy when his father had left and his mother had protected herself from her grief with a string of brief affairs, often leaving him in the care of her sister" (ibid. p.11). And again: "recognizing his hurt, his rage and his humiliation at work, she felt sure that he also felt those things towards her at the moment. It was unlike him to come late and not to be interested in what she had to say" (ibid. p.11). Milton is here drawing on common ideas in psychoanalytic practice, often called the capacity for empathy, of getting to know our patient by imaginatively stepping into his or her shoes, trying to see the world through their eyes. Only by drawing on what she knows about her patient, that it is unlike him to come late for a session and not be interested in her contribution, can she identify his lateness and dismissive attitude in the session described as noteworthy. So we can imagine that the analyst has built up some kind of picture of her patient, which can help her guess how he experiences her when she tells him about the cancelled session and which can alert her to when he does not act in accordance with this picture.

Another analyst, Ralph Greenson, makes explicit use of this idea of an inner picture of the patient, which he calls a "working model". He describes what he means by this through the following example.

> I had been treating a woman for several years and usually with good empathic understanding. In one hour she recounted the events of a weekend and focused in particular on a Saturday night party. Suddenly she began to cry. I was puzzled. I was not "with it" – the crying left me cold – I couldn't understand it... Quickly reviewing the events she had recounted, I found no clues. I then shifted from listening from the "outside" to participant listening. I went to the party as if I were the patient. Now something clicked – an "aha" experience. A fleeting event told to me as the outsider had eluded me; now in my empathy this event illuminated the crying. At the party a woman had graciously served the patient with a copious portion of food. To me as the observer, this event was meaningless. But to me as the experiencer, this woman instantly stirred up the picture of the patient's good-hearted and big-breasted nursemaid. The "aha" I experienced was my sudden recognition of this previously anonymous figure. Now I shifted back to the position of observer and analyser. Yes, the longing for the old nursemaid had come up in the last hour. In the meantime the patient herself had begun to talk of the nursemaid. My empathic discovery seemed

to be valid. When the analyst's association precedes and coincides with the patient's, it confirms that the analyst is on the right track. (1960, p.420)

Greenson describes what he means by "working model" as follows:

As I had worked with this patient day by day, I had slowly built up within me a working model of the patient. This consisted of her physical appearance, her affects, her life experiences, her modes of behaviour, her attitudes, defences, values, fantasies, etc. This working model was a counterpart or replica of the patient that I had built up and added to from my new observations and insights. It is this working model which I now shifted into the foreground of my listening. I listened through this model. (Ibid. p.420)

The concept of a "working model" is a useful one, as it allows us to put together the more emotional and visceral experience of the patient with our more localized theoretical and clinical ideas which best "fit" the particular patient at a particular point in the therapy. It is also a way of bringing together aspects of our internal clinical template with our implicit theories. It is the working model or models we have in our mind which we invoke when we feel we "know" our patient and we use this knowledge to guide our practice.

One can then think of working models at various levels of abstraction. The map of the implicit theory and internal clinical template can each be thought of as working models functioning in the background, at a very high level of abstraction. The "splitting and projection" and "superego attacking ego" models I have described earlier can be seen as providing working models, still pitched at a high level of abstraction, but more applicable to particular clinical situations. The more localized and specific working model described by Greenson can be thought of as what Juan Pablo Jimenez calls a "scale model" of the patient, which we construct in our work with each patient.

The value of this more localized scale model is that one can see how its various components fit together:

The working model of the patient that the analyst constructs for himself or herself is a *real* intersubjective experience, through which it is possible to attain an immediate operative knowledge of the functioning of the patient: what matters here are the relationship between the "parts" which in a scale model are immediately intelligible.

In the analytic scale model the analyst looks for isomorphisms between models of early development, transferential models and psychopathological models. (Jimenez, 2005, p.629)

Each clinician will construct these scale models in different ways. So if we compare Greenson's account with that of Milton, we can see that they think of these different elements of the scale model in different ways. For instance, when thinking of his patient's early development, Greenson's spontaneous association is to an affective state, that of longing for a figure in the past which has been reactivated, whereas Milton thinks in terms of a scenario and a particular kind of object-relationship. In Milton's scale model, the transferential model is prominent, whereas for Greenson (at least in this example), his model of early development seems to figure more strongly.

We can also see how these different elements of the working model are constantly being evaluated. Greenson makes clear in his account of how he used his memory of the previous session to "validate" his use of his working model. In this process of evaluation, our working models get revised and updated, as we saw in the Milton session where her view of Doug had to incorporate his new experience of being with someone who was separate and could tolerate his feelings.

Practical and theoretical reasoning

We now have a picture of the practitioner moving back and forth between their experience of the patient in the room and the working model or models in their mind through which they listen to what the patient is saying. We only become more consciously aware of our working models, or the operative elements, when we feel under strain, when the patient's behaviour no longer fits what our working model has told us to expect.

Juan Pablo Jimenez makes a useful distinction between "practical reasoning" and "theoretical reasoning" to describe the different kinds of thinking involved in these two situations. He envisages a constant movement in the practitioner's mind between the two types of reasoning. "Theoretical reasoning" brings in theoretical ideas to ask why something occurred or what an event means. It operates by looking backwards, over the course of the session or sessions so far. By contrast, "practical reasoning" looks forward, trying to gauge on the basis of the present what is likely to happen. In practical reasoning, "the problem is not one of explanation, but of prediction" (Jimenez, 2008, p.589). The kind of question one asks oneself is: how will my patient react if I were to say this to him/her? If he or she reacts in this way, then I might do this, and if in that way, then I will do that. In practical reasoning, one makes judgements: is this the best way to act?

> Practical reasons thus seek, on the basis of a set of alternatives, none of which has yet come about, to answer the question as to which alternative is the best – that is, as to what is to be done. So it is not a matter of questions of fact and their explanation but of issues of value, of what it is desirable to do. (Ibid. p.590)

Of course if we knew "what happened next" our task would be much easier – as is the case in supervision or clinical discussion, where one has the luxury of looking at one part of a session in terms of what happened at a later point or in a subsequent session. This gives us a vantage point to look back and see if we can discern a meaning, pattern or intent which was not visible at the time. And this is what we try to do in theoretical reasoning, which we can employ at any time when we feel we need to gain this intellectual higher ground, and particularly if we meet something puzzling or unexpected. But for most of the time in a session, we are more concerned with keeping an eye on what is going on and how it is going to develop. We have to act without knowing how things will turn out, we have to "venture predictive hypotheses about something that has not yet occurred" (ibid. p.590). A decision is finally taken in the first person, from a subjective point of view in the here-and-now. The clinician takes a risk which, for reasons of principle, can never be wholly covered by theory.

Changing how we think about psychoanalytic work

Jimenez argues that such a conception of analytic practice involves a change in the way we think about our work. It is often taken for granted, as in what I have called the "prevailing view of analytic practice" (see the Introduction to this book, pp.2–3), that analytic work involves uncovering what is in the mind of the patient. This idea is based on comparing psychoanalysis to archaeology, a favourite metaphor of Freud's and one which still exerts a powerful influence on the way analytic practitioners think about their work.

In his paper "Constructions in Analysis", Freud argued that the task of the analyst is "to make out what has been forgotten from the traces which is has left behind or, more correctly, to *reconstruct* it" (1937, p.239, italics in original). This work of reconstruction resembles the work of the archaeologist.

> Just as the archaeologist builds up the walls of the building from the foundations that have remained standing, determines the number and position of the columns from depressions in the floor and reconstructs the mural decorations and paintings from the remains found in the debris, so does the analyst proceed when he draws his inferences from the fragments of memories, from the associations and from the behaviour of the subject of the analysis. (Ibid. p.239)

Indeed, in Freud's view, the analyst has the advantage over the archaeologist, who is dealing with material that has been destroyed, and so can reach conclusions that contain "only a certain degree of probability" (ibid. p.230).

> But it is different with the psychical objects whose early history the analyst is seeking to recover...all of the essentials are preserved; even things that seem completely forgotten are present somehow and somewhere, and have merely been buried and made inaccessible to the subject. Indeed it may, as we know, be doubted whether any psychical structure can really be the victim of total destruction. It depends only upon analytic technique whether we shall succeed in bringing what is concealed completely to light. (Ibid. p.230)

The basic idea in this view of psychoanalysis as a form of archaeology is that the practitioner only discovers what is there to be found. But as we have seen, this misses out the models, frameworks and forms of reasoning we use to guide our work. In this sense, we are not uncovering a "concealed truth". Instead, in the constant interaction between ourselves and our patient, in the way our models of the patient (and their models of us) come into being, get developed, modified and changed, something gets put together which has not previously existed. So rather than the archaeological model, it might be better to think of analytic practice in terms of "an *architectural model*, in which the main concern is the construction of a new house" (Jimenez, 2008, p.593, italics in original).

PART II

Psychoanalytic Practice as a Form of Craft

5

THE CRAFT METAPHOR

Adopting the craft metaphor

The argument of the previous chapters is that if we are to know how to develop as analytic practitioners, we need to know what practitioners do rather than what they think they do or ought to do. In so doing, we have started to think in terms of different images or metaphors to describe psychoanalytic practice, for example in the previous chapter comparing analytic work to the construction of a new house and the practitioner to a craftsman or artisan.

In fact, in my thinking about my own work as a practitioner, I have long had the image of myself as a kind of craftsman, trying to mould the patient's material into a form or shape I can work with. But this was little more than a vague idea in my mind. It took on more substance when I read Richard Sennett's book *The Craftsman* (2008). His description of the basic principles underlying all craft work struck me as a valuable perspective to bring to the issues about psychoanalytic practice I have been describing in the previous chapters.

Sennett's aim in writing the book was to revitalize the idea of craftsmanship or craft (a word that can sound less serious than "craftsmanship" but has the great advantage of removing the gender bias):

> "Craftsmanship" may suggest a way of life that waned with the advent of industrial society – but this is misleading. Craftsmanship names an enduring, basic human impulse, the desire to do a job well for its own sake. (Sennett, 2008, p.9)

He starts with the idea that "all skills, even the most abstract, begin as bodily practices" (ibid. p.11). He argues that this way of thinking can give insight into the practices involved in disciplines which do not involve bodily skills but human relationships. Many of these skills and practices are done intuitively, but this does not mean they cannot be described. So one of the aims of his book is "to take some of the mystery out of intuition" (ibid. p.213).

I have also found Donald Schoen's study of professional practice, in his book *The Reflective Practitioner: How Professionals Think in Action* (1991), to offer ideas that can be useful in thinking about analytic work. He brings in the ideas of implicit and preconscious thinking that we have already explored in the previous chapters:

> The workaday life of the professional depends on tacit knowing-in-action. Every competent practitioner can recognize phenomena – families of symptoms associated with a particular disease, peculiarities of a certain kind of building site, irregularities of materials or structures – for which he cannot give a reasonably accurate or complete description. In his day-to-day practice he makes innumerable judgements of quality for which he cannot state adequate criteria, and he displays skills for which he cannot state the rules and procedures. Even when he makes conscious use of research-based theories and techniques, he is dependent on tacit recognitions, judgements and skilful performances. (pp.49–50)

The rhythm of craft work: An example from architecture

Both Sennett and Schoen speak of a particular "rhythm" of craft and professional work. We began to explore this in the previous chapter by looking at how working models are employed in analytic practice and by introducing the idea of analytic work as a constant movement between practical and theoretical reasoning. Schoen illustrates the rhythm of craft work in a particularly vivid way by describing his observation of a trainee architect, Petra, presenting her initial design of a new school building to an experienced teacher, Quist.

His observation begins with Petra presenting her design to Quist. He immediately identifies a problem. Petra's design may be in accord with what she has learnt about designing, but it does not take account of the fact that the site is on a slope:

> The main problem, in Quist's view, is not that of fitting the shape of the building to the slope; the site is too "screwy" for that. Instead, coherence must be given to the site in the form of a geometry – a "discipline" – that can be imposed upon it. (Ibid. p.85)

Quist goes on to show Petra how her construction needs to flow from her basic design. He tells her, "You should begin with a discipline, even if it is arbitrary" (ibid. p.92). Petra needs to learn to adopt and construct a basic discipline, which will guide all her subsequent moves, but adopt it in such a way that it is open to future revision and modification. Quist does this by helping Petra develop a way of designing that adapts to the site and opens up possibilities rather than closing them off:

> Quist has continually urged Petra to "soften" her "hard" geometric forms and to depart on occasion from the basic geometry – but only after it has been established. (Ibid. p.93)

For instance, Quist redraws Petra's initial design of classrooms so as to fit better into the "screwy" slope. This leads him to suggest some changes to Petra's design of a gallery. He says, "There you might carry the gallery level through – and look down into here – which is nice. Let the land generate some sub-ideas here, which could be very nice" (ibid. p.93).

In the course of their supervision, Quist and Petra use language which conveys the quality and purpose of their design:

> In their appreciation of the situation they are shaping, Quist and Petra employ feelingful or associative terms such as "home base", "nook", and "soft back area". "A kind of a garden" is not liter- ally a garden, and the "soft back area" is not literally soft, but the metaphors of "garden" and "soft" are used to convey particular values of experience. (Ibid. p.97)

Quist takes Petra's design and plays around with it, changing it by mak- ing a series of small changes to the design. Each change seems to lead on to another and another, and by the end, the design has been trans- formed. At times, Quist immerses himself in the design of a particular part of the building, for example, a passageway, so that:

> He becomes so involved in the local development of forms that the design appears to be making itself. But he also steps back from the projected experience of passage through the space to take note of the larger relationships on which the qualities of the whole idea will depend. (Ibid. p.102)

This process of making a whole series of small moves, each of which seems to imply the next one, eventually shifts from "tentative adoption of a strategy to eventual commitment" (ibid. p.102). But these moves are hard to spot:

> In his unfailing virtuosity, he gives no hint of detecting and correcting errors in his own performance. He zeroes in immediately on fundamental schemes and decisions which quickly acquire the status of commitments. He compresses and perhaps masks the process by which designers learn from iterations of moves which lead them to reappreciate, reinvent and redraw. But this may be because he has developed a very good understanding of the feeling for what he calls "the problem of the problem". (Ibid. p.104)

So Quist works like any skilful and experienced practitioner, acting as though he is unaware of what he is doing. The moves he makes which change his design are not made clear in what he says to Petra, but instead are "compressed" and "masked" in his descriptions, just as we saw in Milton's account of her work in Chapter 2.

But Schoen is able to pick out some of the key elements in how Quist thinks of a design and uses it. Quist is clear that one has to start with an initial design or geometry. But as he goes through the various elements of the design, he makes small but significant changes so that it better fits both the site itself and the overall aim of the project. Whereas Petra tends to think in rather rigid and inflexible terms, which are imposed on the design in accord with what she has learnt, Quist shows her how she can use language to open up ideas and think differently about how the different parts of the design can be put together. Rather than simply incorporating the ideas she has learnt, the mark of a beginner, he teaches Petra to initiate a dialogue with the material: "Let the land generate some sub-ideas here, which could be very nice." Finally, we can see how Quist's tentative ideas result in a commitment to the final design.

The situation for the analytic practitioner is, on the face of it, very different. We don't start with a design laid out on a sheet of paper but with a live patient or client in the room. There is no need to let "the land generate its own ideas", as our patient will be telling us their own. So the kind of "dialogue with the material" in analytic work is of a different order. This is the obvious limitation of the craft metaphor.

Nevertheless, I think there are interesting echoes and parallels between the work of the designer and the analytic practitioner. This is clearest when we think of analytic work in terms of the employment of working models.

Problem-solving and problem-setting

Quist sums up what he is trying to do in his design as that of addressing "the problem of the problem" – by which he means all the contingencies that are part and parcel of any design, starting with the "screwy" nature of the site. The accounts of craft and professional work given by Sennett and Schoen converge in giving a picture of the worker engaged in a constant dialogue with their material. Sennett describes this as follows: "every good craftsman conducts a dialogue between concrete practices and thinking; this dialogue evolves into sustaining habits, and these habits establish a rhythm between problem solving and problem finding" (2008, p.9).

Schoen makes the same distinction, using his own terms. He contrasts "knowing-in-action", where the professional relies on their accumulated experience of similar situations to work in a way that feels intuitive and spontaneous and does not require much conscious thinking, with "reflection-in-action":

> When the phenomenon at hand eludes the ordinary categories of knowledge-in-practice, presenting itself as unique or unstable, the practitioner may surface and criticize his initial understanding of the phenomenon, construct a new description of it, and test the new description by an on-the-spot experiment. (1991, pp.62–63)

In this more conscious process of reflection, the professional will reconsider the "problem" they have been trying to solve, to see whether the problem can be approached from a different angle, or a new problem needs to be set. In so doing, the professional will draw on what Schoen calls their stock of "exemplars", by which he means a "repertoire of examples, images, understandings and actions" (ibid. p.138). It may be that what is encountered is not covered by this repertoire, and so a new model or bit of theory may need to be created.

The appreciative system

These descriptions of craft and professional work are clearly similar to the frameworks and ideas introduced in the preceding chapters with the aim of giving a description of analytic practice that reflects how practitioners think, and I take this similarity as giving further weight to the value of these descriptions. Particular attention has been given to the way analytic practitioners conduct ongoing evaluations of their work, for instance in the distinction drawn between practical and theoretical reasoning. Both Schoen and Sennett throw some more light on this process.

Schoen calls the way professionals evaluate their work their "appreciative system". This system "is what makes possible the initial framing of a problematic situation, and what permits reappreciation of the situation in the light of its back talk" (ibid. p.272). This idea is an important part of analytic work. For instance, Ronald Britton and John Steiner, in their paper "Interpretation: Selected Fact or Overvalued Idea?", allude to this process when they write "an experienced analyst continuously monitors the effect his words have in the manner of a violinist who bends his ear towards his instrument to ensure that his intonation is correct" (1994, p.1070). But how this is done is rarely described in any detail.

Some of these appreciations and evaluations are carried out tacitly. Schoen refers to the ordinary demonstrations of skill and judgements of quality of "knowing-in-action" to emphasize the intelligent aspect of this practice. It tends to resist explicit and coherent articulation. However, it often displays elements of a more non-discursive kind of reflection, expressed in such phrases as having a "feel" for the situation or "thinking on one's feet". For instance, a skilled practitioner will often improvise:

> When skilled jazz musicians improvise together, they also manifest a "feel for" their material and they make on-the-spot adjustments to the sounds they hear. Listening to one another, and to themselves, they feel where the music is going and adjust their playing accordingly... Improvisation consists in varying, combining, and recombining a set of figures within the schema which bounds and gives coherence to the performance. (Schoen, 1991, p.55)

But the danger of this non-discursive way of thinking is that it may result in an over-specialized and narrow practice which does not allow anything new to occur. This is where the kind of evaluation and re-evaluation that happens in reflection-in-action is employed, and where it is easier to catch sight of the way the appreciative system functions.

Schoen argues that compared to the judgements that go on in a tacit way in normal work, the testing that occurs in reflection-in-action is much more deliberate and discursive. But it is still a version of on-the-spot experimentation, conducted for practical purposes, unlike the kind of evaluation that goes on in conducting scientific experiments. Whereas the researcher conducting a scientific experiment will have an extended idea of time, and could go on testing indefinitely as long as he or she is able to invent plausible hypotheses, the testing done by the professional "is bounded by the 'action-present', the zone of time in which action can still make a difference to the situation" (ibid. p.62).

Schoen characterizes the hypothesis testing of the professional as not neutral, as in scientific research, but "transactional". The professional:

shapes the situation but in conversation with it, so that his own models and appreciations are also shaped by the situation. The phenomena that he seeks to understand are partly of his own making, he is in the situation that he seeks to understand. (Ibid. pp.150–151)

Finally, Schoen argues that the aims of a scientific experiment and the evaluation of reflection-in-action are different. The experimenter seeks "confirmation" of a particular hypothesis – although this does not rule out other hypotheses that could be brought in to explain the phenomena better. Although this is of interest to the professional, the testing done in professional work is looking more for "affirmation" of a particular idea or theory, namely that it solves the particular problem or demonstrates the value of setting a different problem.

Skill at the live edge

Sennett describes a similar process of on-the-spot testing but uses the language of "resistance". He describes the key craft skill as that of "identifying the most forgiving element in a difficult situation" (2008, p.221). He calls this "skill at the live edge". The edge is "the zone in which people have to deal with difficulty; we need to visualise what is difficult in order to address it" (ibid. p.229).

in hammering a nail, we have to establish that border zone on the hammer shaft in which secure grip interacts with freedom of the elbow; this fulcrum point is our working space...In goldsmithy, the moment of truth in the assay is a border zone both physically and mentally, the fingertips probing the texture of a problematic substance, seeking to name it. (Ibid. p.230)

This is reminiscent of Freud's account of resistance:

One must allow the patient to become more conversant with this resistance...to work through it, to overcome it...only when the resistance is at its height can the analyst, working in common with his patient, discover the repressed instinctual impulses which are feeding the resistance...the doctor has nothing else to do than to wait and let things take their course, a course which cannot be avoided nor always hastened. (1914, p.155)

Sennett fleshes out the steps involved in the process Freud describes. Firstly, there is the need to localize the area of resistance. This is done through the use of probes. Probes serve to identify the areas of resistance, to "specify where something important is happening" (Sennett, 2008, pp.277–278), as in dissection, where the scalpel encounters unexpected hard matter. Secondly, one needs to question this locale, discover its nature and the degree of resistance. Like Freud, Sennett emphasizes the importance of developing "patience", which he defines as "the temporary suspension of the desire for closure" (ibid. p.221).

Finally, the craftsman "opens up" the problem in order to work with it. This may involve adopting a new perspective by "reformatting" or recasting the resistant element. Sennett gives an example from learning to play the piano, where "faced with an intractably difficult chord in one hand, we play it with the other; a change in the fingers used to make the chord, a different hand-protagonist, often provides insight into the problem; frustration is then relieved" (ibid. p.220).

A live edge to craft work is created by a capacity to establish and maintain a frame that is active and fluid. Sennett prefers to use the term "border" rather than "boundaries" to describe this construction of a viable working setting. He compares boundaries to cell walls, which function by exclusion, and tend to be rigidly enforced. By contrast, borders are more like cell membranes, which are more fluid and permit more exchange between inside and outside. He takes an example from city planning, comparing the guarded territory of the boundary, which creates no-go areas, to what he calls the active edge of the border, allowing interchange and movement (ibid. p.227).

Sennett's descriptions in terms of skills are similar to Freud's account of how the psychoanalyst works, but draw a picture of a practitioner more actively thinking and shaping the material. As such, they can give a more fleshed-out account of what might constitute good work. For instance, Sennett identifies the principle of "using minimum force" as a craft skill: "the idea of minimum force as the base line of self-control is expressed in the apocryphal if perfectly logical advice given in ancient Chinese cooking: the good cook must learn first to cleave a grain of boiled rice" (ibid. p.167). This strikes me as an elegant way to think of what makes a good intervention or interpretation.

The craft metaphor offers a different perspective

In introducing the craft metaphor, I am not claiming to be saying anything new. Instead I am proposing a way of thinking that can better incorporate the more recent ideas described in the previous chapters on how analytic practitioners work. Furthermore, as I hope to demonstrate in the next two chapters, adopting this perspective can provide a useful way of thinking about familiar psychoanalytic ideas. But the craft metaphor is not meant to replace the prevailing metaphors used to describe psychoanalytic work.

The two most widely used metaphors are those of science or art. So Freud, while acknowledging the more artistic and aesthetic sides of analytic practice (e.g. in comparing his case studies in *Studies on Hysteria* (1895) to "short stories"), was very clear that psychoanalysis belonged to the discourse and discipline of the sciences. For example, in discussing whether psychoanalysis lends itself to a particular *Weltanschauung*, he was clear that "As a specialist science, a branch of psychology – a depth-psychology or psychology of the unconscious – it is quite unfit to construct a *Weltanschauung* of its own: it must accept the scientific one" (Freud, 1933, pp.158–159). This meant asserting that "there are no sources of knowledge of the universe other than the intellectual working-over of carefully scrutinized observations – in other words, what we call research – and alongside of it no knowledge derived from revelation, intuition or divination" (ibid. p.159).

The metaphor of psychoanalysis as an art functions as a counterpart to the scientific metaphor, bringing in those aspects of practice that do not fit easily into this rational, discursive and coherent way of thinking. Here, for instance, is how Thomas Ogden begins his book *This Art of Psychoanalysis*:

It is the art of psychoanalysis in the making, a process inventing itself as it goes, that is the subject of this chapter. Psychoanalysis is a lived emotional experience. As such, it cannot be translated, recorded, explained, understood or told in words. It is what it is. (2005, p.1)

Each metaphor has its value. The scientific metaphor is important for its ideas on the slow accumulation of knowledge, the reliance on observation and the value of research. Furthermore, as Freud himself was aware, it can be useful in our culture with a prejudice to seeing "scientific" knowledge as the only proper knowledge. The artistic metaphor stresses the creative and intuitive aspects of practice, those that defy the ordinary discursive methods of description.

But each also has its limitations. We have seen that the kind of experimentation carried out in psychoanalytic practice is of a different type to that carried out in scientific research (which is not to decry the value of these ideas for research into psychoanalytic practice). And, as Winnicott rather wittily put it: "An analyst may be a good artist, but (as I have frequently asked): what patient wants to be someone else's poem or picture?" (1954, p.291).

The appeal of the craft metaphor is that it offers a more pragmatic vision of analytic practice than the more scientifically based idea of practice as the application of research-based knowledge. In craft practices, the kind of research carried out is pragmatic in the sense of being localized and oriented to the specific demands of the task in hand. In comparing the craft metaphor to that of the artist, a different understanding of creativity becomes the focus of attention. In distinguishing craft practices from artistic ones, Sennett points out: "art seems to draw attention to work that is unique or at least distinctive, whereas craft names a more anonymous, collective and continued practice" (2008, p.66). So in drawing attention to the uniqueness and distinctiveness of each clinician's way of working, the craft metaphor puts more emphasis on the range of skills and practices which are shared amongst the community of practitioners. The value of the craft metaphor is that it offers a description of these skills and practices which can add to our understanding of how they develop and how they are employed in day-to-day analytic practice.

6

ANALYTIC "RULES" AND CRAFT PRACTICE

One of the biggest sources of the intense and debilitating anxiety of the developing practitioner concerns the application of analytic "rules". That is, practitioners often feel (or so they tell me) that they are not working in accord with these rules. Two in particular are often mentioned. The first is that they should not be imposing their own ideas on the patient, or determining the course of the session by choosing a focus for the work. The second idea, clearly related to the first, is that they should not be trying to "know" something about the patient, as that would seem to contradict the principle of "not-knowing", which they have taken as a fundamental aspect of the analytic approach.

The first "rule", that of not focusing in on anything in the patient's material, goes back to Freud's ideas on the importance of maintaining an attitude of "evenly suspended attention" in analytic work. The notion of evenly suspended attention links in to some of his other ideas that have come to be seen as the "rules" of analytic work, namely neutrality and abstinence. I will argue in this chapter that rather than seeing these ideas as applicable to all situations in analytic work, they were brought in as solutions to particular clinical problems, and that these problems arise in all craft practices. I will take the same point of view in discussing the principle of "not-knowing".

Evenly suspended attention

Freud introduced the idea of "evenly suspended attention" in his paper "Recommendations to Physicians Practising Psycho-Analysis" (1912) in which he gave advice to his fellow psychoanalysts on how they might address particular problems that arise in the course of analytic work. One such problem, encountered as one's practice grows larger, is how to remember the details of each patient, how to keep in mind "all the innumerable names, dates, detailed memories and pathological products which each patient communicates in the course of months and years of treatment" (ibid. p.111). He described a "technique" for solving this problem, one which he had arrived at based on his own experience and temperament – "I do not venture to deny that a physician quite differently constituted might find himself driven to adopt a different attitude to his patients and to the task before him" (ibid. p.111). This technique was simply that of "not directing one's notice to anything in particular and in maintaining the same 'evenly-suspended attention' (as I have called it) in the face of all that one hears" (ibid. p.112).

The aim of using this technique was to "spare a strain on our attention which could not in any case be kept up for several hours daily" (ibid. p.112). But, paradoxically, sparing this strain on our attention enables us to remember better, as we are no longer using our energy in trying to keep things in mind. So Freud concluded that the "rule" can be expressed in the following precept: the psychoanalyst "should withhold all conscious influences from his capacity to attend, and give himself over completely to his unconscious memory" (ibid. p.112).

Freud then identified a further benefit in using the technique of evenly suspended attention, which is that it guards against the imposition of our ideas and suggestions onto the patient. So in keeping to the attitude of evenly suspended attention:

> We avoid a danger which is inseparable from the exercise of deliberate attention. For as soon as anyone deliberately concentrates his attention to a certain degree, he begins to select from the material before him; one point will be fixed in his mind with particular clearness and some other will be correspondingly disregarded, and in making this selection he will be following his expectations or inclinations. This, however, is precisely what must not be done. In making the selection, if he follows his expectations he is in danger of never finding anything but what he already knows; and if he follows his inclinations he will certainly falsify what he may perceive. (Ibid. pp.112–113)

Freud can be seen here to be addressing a major concern about analytic practice – continuously voiced by its critics but also recognized as a danger by practitioners – that psychoanalytic practice operates as a form of suggestion, and that what the practitioner claims to find in the mind of the patient is no more than what he or she has induced through their own expectations. Any competent practitioner needs to find ways of guarding against this danger. Wilfred Bion's comment in this regard, his own version of the principle of evenly suspended attention, has been much quoted:

> The capacity to forget, the ability to eschew desire and understanding, must be regarded as essential discipline for the psycho-analyst. (1970, pp.51–52)

Freud described his technique, or attitude on the part of the psychoanalyst, as the complement to the attitude of "free association" which the analytic patient is encouraged to adopt. Just as the patient needs to learn to put aside his or her critical thinking in order to get in touch with their unconscious thinking and hidden affects, so the analyst needs to give himself over to his "unconscious memory". Freud likened the analyst's unconscious to an instrument which can tune in to the unconscious of the patient:

> To put it in a formula: he must turn his own unconscious like a receptive organ towards the transmitting unconscious of the patient. He must adjust himself to the patient as a telephone receiver is adjusted to the transmitting microphone. Just as the receiver converts back into sound waves the electric oscillations in the telephone line which were set up by sound waves, so the doctor's unconscious is able, from the derivatives of the unconscious which are communicated to him, to reconstruct that unconscious, which has determined the patient's free associations. (1912, p.115)

At first glance, one can see ways in which Freud's account of the value of "evenly suspended attention" seems to support the idea that good analytic practice involves not selecting from the patient's material or focusing on some parts to the exclusion of others. The image of the analyst's unconscious being able to pick up the patient's unconscious communications like a telephone receiver suggests that there can be a form of direct communication between the two minds, and that therefore the practitioner must do nothing that might interfere with this process. However, it is not clear what Freud means when he refers to evenly suspended attention as a "rule" of psychoanalytic practice. This seems to be at odds with how he initially framed his discussion, that he was doing no more than making a recommendation for someone of a similar constitution as himself as to how to solve a particular technical problem.

"Evenly suspended attention" and the capacity to concentrate

We can get a perspective on this issue, and explore what Freud's term "evenly suspended attention" might mean, if we frame the discussion as one about how one learns to develop a skill. Freud's description of "evenly suspended attention" can be seen as a way of helping the beginner learn to find meaning in what he or she hears from the patient. In analytic work, as Freud notes, we have to postpone understanding something until its sense becomes clear – "the things one hears are for the most part things whose meaning is only recognized later on" (ibid. p.112). Listening in an unfocused way means having sufficient trust in the process, and in one's own abilities, that meaning will eventually emerge, rather like someone learning to ride a bicycle has at some point to remove the stabilizers and trust in their own capacity to balance. We saw that Petra, the trainee architect, had to give up relying on her initial design in order to be open to all the irregularities and peculiarities of the particular site (see pp.78–80).

Freud's recommendations, however, although of value for the beginner, are directed towards the developing or experienced practitioner, one who has built up a practice of a number of patients, where the problem of sustaining an alive attention becomes more acute. Let us look at how Richard Sennett considers this issue in his book *The Craftsman* (2008). He states that a key element in the development of any skill is learning how to concentrate. We often think, he argues, that we need first of all to be engaged in order to learn to how to concentrate. But from his study of how physical skills are learnt, Sennett says it is the other way round:

> The ability to concentrate for long periods comes first; only when a person can do so will he or she get involved emotionally or intellectually. The skill of physical concentration follows rules of its own, based on how people learn to practice, to repeat what they do, and to learn from repetition. Concentration, that is, has an inner logic; this logic can, I believe be applied to working steadily for an hour as well as for several years. (Ibid. p.172)

He gives the example of an account by Erin O'Connor of her experience of learning to become a glass-blower. She was particularly taken by the Barolo wines of Italy and wanted to fashion a goblet big and round enough to support the fragrant "nose" of the wine. She learnt that the critical moment in glass blowing is when the molten glass is gathered at the end of an extended narrow pipe. The pipe has to be constantly twirled and turned in a particular way in order to get the desired shape. Getting the right body posture is essential:

> To avoid strain when twirling the pipe, the glass-blower's back must incline forward from the lower rather than the upper torso, like a rower reaching for the beginning of a stroke. (Ibid. p.173)

To do this well involved a form of "absorbed concentration": "she lost awareness of her body making contact with the hot glass and became all-absorbed in the physical material as the end in itself" (ibid. p.174). After many attempts, she gradually became more skilled in going through the various phases. But success still eluded her. Although she succeeded in "gathering the glass into a bubble and forming it into the desired Barolo-friendly shape, the glass, when left to cool, turned out 'lopsided and stout' a thing now dubbed by the master craftsman a 'globlet'" (ibid. p.174).

Sennett argues that she then had to learn to "stretch out" her more absorbed form of concentration.

> The problem, she came to understand, lay in dwelling in that moment of "being in a thing". To work better, she discovered, she needed to anticipate what the material should next become in its next, as-yet nonexistent, stage of evolution. Her instructor called this simply "staying on track"; she, rather more philosophically minded, understood that she was engaged in a process of "corporeal anticipation", always one step ahead of the material as molten liquid, then bubble, then bubble with a stem, then stem with a foot. She had to make such prehension a permanent state of mind, and she learned to do so, whether she succeeded or failed, by blowing the goblet again and again. (Ibid. pp.174–175)

Sennett uses this, and other examples, to show that in learning to concentrate, one also learns to bring together means and ends. So O'Connor's work was about producing an end result, namely a certain kind of wine glass. But in learning to concentrate, she had to become so absorbed in what she was doing, and so "stretched out" in her imagination, as to follow the processes she was trying to create, that her repeated activities become an end in themselves – "this is repetition for its own sake: like a swimmer's strokes, sheer movement repeated becomes a pleasure in itself" (ibid. pp.174–175).

This is why in analytic work good practice is never boring. The sessions we don't remember are those where we feel we have not worked very well; they have no shape or intrinsic pattern to them.

> As skill expands, the capacity to sustain repetition increases. In music this is the so-called Isaac Stern rule, the great violinist declaring that the better your technique, the longer you can practice without becoming bored. (Ibid. p.38)

It is the development of this capacity to concentrate that establishes the distinctive rhythm of any craft practice, for instance in the movement between the more absorbed kind of concentration to the more stretched-out one in the glass-blowing example. These forms of concentration operate at the more intuitive, tacit level of work (what Schoen calls knowing-in-action; see Chapter 5). In order to learn how to concentrate in these different ways, O'Connor had to step back from what she was doing. In so doing, she followed another rhythm in craft work, which is that between the "problem-solving" operation of the form of tacit knowledge employed in these two forms of concentration (absorbed and stretched-out) and the more reflective kind of knowledge when a problem is encountered that requires more deliberate thought. In establishing and moving between these different rhythms in the work, concentration enables self-criticism, the experience in the movements between the different kinds of concentration of studying one's own "ingrained practice" and of "modulating it from within" (ibid. p.38).

Let us now go back to Freud's account. His metaphor of the analyst's unconscious operating like a telephone receiver or recorder of the patient's unconscious communications has been the subject of criticism from some commentators. Helmut Thoma and Horst Kachele, in their textbook *Psychoanalytic Practice*, describe this image as based on a "romantic myth" that "external reality can be perceived directly and correctly" (1987, p.237). From the perspective of this myth, any kind of activity on the part of the therapist would be seen as interfering with this "mystical expectation of fusion and unity". Not surprisingly, such a view is likely to generate enormous anxiety in a practitioner who believes that their task is to become a receiver, in as pure a way as possible, of these communications that come directly from the patient's mind, and that the only way they can do this is by doing nothing at all.

However, one can also see what Freud was saying as not unlike the account given by Sennett. Freud's image of the analyst learning to "turn his own unconscious like a receptive organ towards the transmitting unconscious of the patient" and to "adjust himself" so that he can best receive these transmissions bears some resemblance to Sennett's description of O'Connor's "stretched-out" concentration, where she develops a form of "prehension" in anticipating the various stages of the creation of her wine glass. Although Freud's analogy can be seen to convey the idea of a direct communication between minds, he also refers to the analyst's "reconstruction" of the patient's unconscious based on the "derivatives" of the patient's unconscious. This implies some anticipatory activity on the part of the analyst, which is in fact essential to the whole process. For how is one to know what is "derived" from the patient's unconscious unless one has some idea of what is to count as a derivation?

So from a craft perspective, Freud's notion of "evenly suspended attention" can be seen as his way of addressing the issue of how one learns to concentrate in such a way that the patient's material remains fresh and alive. It is about the establishment of a particular skill, that of becoming engaged and absorbed in the work, which is a necessary step to developing one's own distinctive rhythm of working. His account emphasizes one aspect of this rhythm, the danger of routine and the power of ideas to impose a defining and limiting pattern on the work. Thoma and Kachele see the value of trying to listen in an evenly suspended manner as bringing a "radical openness" to analytic ideas:

> The technique of evenly suspended attention should remind the analyst that every case could turn out differently than one would be led to expect by the general (and always provisional) theory and by one's limited personal experience. (1987, p.236)

Sometimes, they add, being aware of other ways one might have worked means going against the accepted practice of oneself or one's group:

> it is in principle impossible to devote the same attention to everything, and we do not do so in practice. However, it is both possible and necessary to account for our ideas, and for what lies behind them, to ourselves and to the scientific community, and to correct presuppositions in light of observations. The exchange with the patient contains numerous possible occasions for this, especially when assumptions that the analyst has expressed as interpretations are revealed to be erroneous. (Ibid. p.236)

So rather than a "rule" of practice, it would be better to think of evenly suspended attention as the development of a capacity for concentration.

I think Bion means something similar when he refers to the capacity to forget and eschew desire and understanding as a "discipline" which it is necessary to acquire in order to practice well:

> Failure to practice this discipline will lead to a steady deterioration in the powers of observation whose maintenance is essential. The vigilant submission to such discipline will by degrees strengthen the analyst's mental powers just in proportion as lapses in this discipline will debilitate him. (1970, p.52)

The "rules" of neutrality and abstinence

One can apply the same kind of thinking in looking at some other basic "rules" of analytic practice. Probably the most widely quoted rule is that of neutrality, which Laplanche and Pontalis, in their textbook *The Language of Psychoanalysis*, call "one of the defining characteristics of the attitude of the analyst during the treatment" (1980, p.271). Freud introduced the idea of neutrality in the context of recommending that the analyst refrain from imposing his own ideals onto the patient.

> Young and eager psycho-analysts will no doubt be tempted to bring their own individuality freely into the discussion, in order to carry the patient along with them and lift him over the barriers of his own narrow personality... [But] it involves a departure from psycho-analytic principles and verges upon treatment by suggestion... this technique achieves nothing towards the uncovering of what is unconscious to the patient... The doctor should be opaque to his patients and, like a mirror, should show them nothing but what is shown to him. (1912, p.118)

The metaphor of the mirror, and the injunction that the analyst should be "opaque" to his patients, is similar to the metaphor of the analyst as a telephone receiver of the patient's unconscious communications. The emphasis in neutrality is of eliminating anything, such as eagerness on the part of the analyst, which might interfere with the process.

> I cannot advise my colleagues too urgently to model themselves during psycho-analytic treatment on the surgeon, who puts aside all his feelings, even his human sympathy, and concentrates his mental forces on the single aim of performing the operation as skilfully as possible. (Ibid. p.115)

Freud wrote about what has become known as the "rule" of abstinence in a similar way. He introduced the idea in his paper "Observations on Transference-Love" in a consideration of how to handle the erotic transference.

> The treatment must be carried out in *abstinence*. By this I do not mean physical *abstinence* alone, nor yet the deprivation of everything that the patient desires, for perhaps no sick person could tolerate this. Instead, I shall state it as a fundamental principle that the patient's need and longing should be allowed to persist in her, in order that they may serve as forces impelling her to do work and to make changes, and that we must beware of appeasing those by means of surrogates. (1915, p.165)

As with the idea of evenly suspended attention, we are faced with the issue of how to understand these so-called rules. Are they meant to be applied in all situations, or are they designed more to solve particular clinical problems? Thoma and Kachele, for example, argue strongly that to take the "rule" of abstinence as a general precept to be applied in all clinical situations leads to poor practice.

> Wishes that are quite characteristic of resistance in women suffering from hysteria can have completely different meanings in obsessives, phobics, and anxiety neurotics. The analyst's concern that a patient might find secret substitutive gratification in the transference leads to a defensive approach. The function of the rule of abstinence is no longer to produce a favorable tension potential and thus actuate development, but rather to prevent developments which are viewed with apprehension. (1987, p.218)

Finding the live edge

If we take both of these "rules" not as blanket prohibitions but as elements of craft practice, we can see that they address the same question as that of evenly suspended attention, namely how to work at one's best. But here the focus is more on working with resistance. The value of thinking in terms of neutrality or abstinence is that it helps us focus on how best to establish what Sennett calls the "live edge" of the work. As we saw in the previous chapter, this is a zone where there needs to be some resistance, otherwise the work will not be productive. In Freud's words, "only when the resistance is at its height can the analyst, working in common with his patient, discover the repressed instinctual impulses which are feeding the resistance" (1914, p.155). But if the analyst is to work "in common with the patient", the resistance cannot be too strong, or no co-operation with the patient will be achieved. So the task of the practitioner is to be able to identify and work with "the most forgiving element in a difficult situation" (Sennett, 2008, p.221).

We invoke the "rule" of neutrality when we feel under strain in developing or sustaining this zone. This is nicely illustrated in a discussion of the meaning of the concept of enactment by Werner Bohleber and his colleagues. In order to see how the concept of enactment is used in analytic work, they draw on the idea of working models (see pp.69–72).

> From a phenomenological perspective we assume that the patient and analyst both have an intentional representation of each other and their relationship. This is made up of expectations of the thoughts, feelings, beliefs and desires that each anticipates from the other and is founded primarily on the verbal exchanges that occur between the two individuals. (Bohleber et al., 2013, p.510)

They speak of the normal updating process of this model, and that these models remain out of awareness as long as the interaction between patient and therapist is broadly in line with the expectations generated by this model.

> However, these expectations are constantly challenged by both the patient's and the analyst's unconscious phantasies, which, while integral to the process of relating, must be kept in the background if the relationship is to achieve its intended objectives. All psychoanalytic models assume the presence of a constant tension between the analyst's anticipated action and the patient's hope, based on transferential phantasy. The analyst's resistance to this pull is encoded into analytic jargon as "neutrality", which ... actually means very different things to different cultures and different analytic relationships. (Ibid. p.510)

This makes clear that we invoke the idea of neutrality when we feel under pressure, when our normal way of working is in danger of breaking down. In such situations, we need to switch from a "problem-solving" to a "problem-setting" way of thinking, one which can help us reflect on where this pressure is coming from and what we need to do about it. So Freud's descriptions of the "opacity" of the mirror and the putting aside of sympathy of the surgeon can be seen as his ways of describing the kind of attention or concentration needed to identify and sustain the live edge of the work, particularly when it is under strain. In the same way, the idea of abstinence is designed to help the practitioner function and preserve the capacity to think under the intense pressure of an erotic transference.

But if we take adherence to these "rules" as a way of distinguishing "proper" from "improper" practice, then we can see how developing practitioners can learn to persecute themselves for not following them. If they are taken as principles that must be applied to all clinical situations, then they lose their function as craft skills; that is, as ways of thinking of the best way, with each particular patient in each situation, of maintaining and sustaining the live edge or the most forgiving element in the therapy. Furthermore, if the rules are described in such a way that they convey a picture of practice that cannot be attained, then we can see how they can reinforce the already existing anxiety of the developing practitioner.

The idealization of not-knowing

In my experience, it is the idea of "not-knowing" that causes the most anxiety amongst developing practitioners. The idea is really an encapsulation of the principles of evenly suspended attention and neutrality. It owes a debt to John Keats' idea of "negative capability", "when man is capable of being in uncertainties, Mysteries, doubts, without any irritable reaching after fact & reason" (letter to George & Thomas Keats, Casement, 1985, p.223). In analytic textbooks, the idea or principle of "not-knowing" is sometimes quoted as a defining principle of the analytic approach. For example, in his book *On Learning from the Patient*, Patrick Casement describes "the use of not-knowing" as one of the key ideas in the analytic approach:

> Therapists sometimes have to tolerate extended periods during which they may feel ignorant and helpless. In this sense students are privileged; they have licence not to know, though many still succumb to pressures that prompt them to strive to appear certain, as if this were a mark of competence. The experienced therapist or analyst, by contrast, has to make an effort to preserve an adequate state of not knowing if he is to remain open to fresh understanding. (1985, pp.3–4)

Casement is careful to point out that not-knowing does not equate with ignorance, which can lead therapists to "seek refuge in an illusion that they understand".

> But if they can bear the strain of not-knowing they can learn that their competence as therapists includes a capacity to tolerate feeling ignorant or incompetent, and a willingness to wait (and to carry on waiting) until something genuinely relevant and meaningful begins to emerge. (Ibid. p.4)

But how is one to distinguish "striving to appear certain" from taking a risk and claiming to know something, even if one can't really be sure whether one is right or not, which is intrinsic to the operation of practical reasoning (see Chapter 4, pp.72–3). At some point, as we saw in Chapter 5 (pp.79–80), any good practitioner needs to move from tentative hypothesis-making to commitment. How long should one wait before making this move, and how is one to judge this? The idea or principle of not-knowing, just like that of evenly suspended attention, neutrality and abstinence, is a way of talking about what is involved in being able to concentrate, to sustain attention, to prepare the ground for one's eventual commitment to a particular strategy or intervention, and so a way to establish and sustain a live edge to one's work. These are difficult skills to develop, and "not-knowing", in the sense of being prepared to trust one's judgement however provisional it feels, is an important part of this development. But one can only speak of "not-knowing" if one has already acquired some knowledge that one can then put to one side in order to keep a fresh perspective. In other words, trying not to know something is productive only when one has already attained a certain level of skill and then needs to develop the capacity to stand back and reflect on its usefulness. But if, as Casement implies, "not-knowing" is seen as the embodiment of correct analytic practice, as a "privilege" given to the beginner which is then lost as one becomes more competent, it is likely to lend itself to idealization and thereby magnify rather than lessen the anxiety of the developing practitioner.

In sum, learning to develop as a practitioner usually involves a considerable amount of idealization, the tendency to elevate ideas, rules of thumb, clinical generalizations and so on into God-given rules. Here, the craft metaphor can serve as a useful corrective in reminding the practitioner that all such analytic rules started out as specific tools or procedures designed to solve particular clinical or practical puzzles, and that the best way to think of them is as embodying or describing particular forms of craft skills.

7

COUNTERTRANSFERENCE AND CONTAINMENT REVISITED

In the previous chapter, I looked at several so-called rules of analytic practice in terms of the craft skills needed to implement them. In this chapter, I will do the same thing with two of the most widely used clinical concepts, countertransference and containment. Since its introduction in the 1950s as a distinctive way of thinking about certain aspects of practice, the term "countertransference" has now become part of the psychoanalytic canon. It means simply taking one's emotional reactions as a source of knowledge rather than as obstacles to the work. In her seminal paper "On Countertransference", published in 1950, Paula Heimann observed that many analytic students felt the right way to work was to cut themselves off from their feelings, which were perceived as a "source of trouble" in the work: "If an analyst tries to work without consulting his feelings, his interpretations are poor. I have often seen this in the work of beginners, who, out of fear, ignored or stifled their feelings" (ibid. p.81)

Although beginners are often frightened of their feelings, it is now widely acknowledged that in order to practice well, the practitioner needs to engage not just their intellectual understanding, but their emotional understanding as well. In her account of analytic practice, Milton (see Chapter 2) sees countertransference as an essential component of the process. She defines countertransference as the capacity to "be able to receive and register the emotional impact of the patient" (Milton, Polmear and Fabricius, 2011, p.9). Tuning into one's countertransference is a vital part of analytic understanding. By learning to "monitor" and "observe" this registration, the practitioner is able to "understand the patient's patterns of relationships" (ibid. p.9).

The concept of containment, based on the work of Wilfred Bion, was introduced in order to help the practitioner think about what is involved in this process of reception and registration of the patient's feelings. Milton also sees this concept as playing a key role in analytic practice. She defines containment as "the sometimes uncomfortable but often productive process of holding on to the tension, bearing the way the patient is feeling and seeing one, while one finds a helpful way of talking to the patient about it" (ibid. p.10).

The great value of both concepts is that of offering an expanded vocabulary for thinking about the whole range of feelings, thoughts, associations, etc. which are used in one's work. However, as with many other psychoanalytic concepts, their meaning and purpose can prove to be less clear than they seem. I have often found that when I ask my students or supervisees what they mean when they speak of "containing" the patient, or of using their countertransference, they struggle to articulate what it is they are trying to say. They feel these concepts designate an important area of practice, but are often unclear as to what these concepts are meant to be "doing" and so how they inform their practice.

In this chapter, I want to see whether I can make sense of this lack of clarity by looking at both concepts from a craft perspective; that is, to ask: in using these terms, what kind of skill is being invoked, how is it used and what is its purpose?

Countertransference

In her classic paper on countertransference, Paula Heimann proposed using the term "countertransference" in a different way to Freud, for whom "countertransference" referred to the analyst's transference onto the patient, and as such, something to be "overcome" if it was not to get in the way of the work. Instead Heimann used the concept to refer to the importance of the practitioner's "emotional sensibility" as a counterpart to Freud's "evenly suspended attention" (see Chapter 6). By bringing in the affective dimension, the range and quality of the practitioner's "unconscious memory" would thus be expanded.

> I would suggest that the analyst along with this freely working attention needs a freely roused emotional sensibility so as to follow the patient's emotional movements and unconscious phantasies. Our basic assumption is that the analyst's unconscious understands that of his patient. This rapport on the deep level comes to the surface in the form of feelings which the analyst notices in response to his patient, in his "counter-transference". This is the most dynamic way

in which his patient's voice reaches him. In the comparison of feelings roused in himself with his patient's associations and behaviour, the analyst possesses a most valuable means of checking whether he has understood or failed to understand his patient. (Heimann, 1950, p.81)

If one's feelings are in accord with the way one normally understands the patient, they are not normally registered by the practitioner as a problem. However, "often the emotions roused in him are much nearer to the heart of the matter than his reasoning, or, to put it in other words, his unconscious perception of the patient's unconscious is more acute and in advance of his conscious conception of the situation" (ibid. p.82).

Heimann went on to give an example of what she meant:

A recent experience comes to mind. It concerns a patient whom I had taken over from a colleague. The patient was a man in the forties who had originally sought treatment when his marriage broke down. Among his symptoms promiscuity figured prominently. In the third week of his analysis with me he told me, at the beginning of the session, that he was going to marry a woman whom he had met only a short time before.

It was obvious that his wish to get married at this juncture was determined by his resistance against the analysis and his need to act out his transference conflicts. Within a strongly ambivalent attitude the desire for an intimate relation with me had already clearly appeared. I had thus many reasons for doubting the wisdom of his intention and for suspecting his choice. But such an attempt to short-circuit analysis is not infrequent at the beginning of, or at a critical point in, the treatment and usually does not represent too great an obstacle to the work, so that catastrophic conditions need not arise. I was therefore somewhat puzzled to find that I reacted with a sense of apprehension and worry to the patient's remark. I felt that something more was involved in his situation, something beyond the ordinary acting out, which, however, eluded me. (Ibid. p.82)

This example illustrates how Heimann became aware of a discrepancy between her more cognitive understanding, which could assimilate the patient's behaviour into her normal ways of thinking, and her emotional understanding, in the form of her countertransference feelings of apprehension and worry. She took her countertransference feelings as being in advance of her intellectual understanding, a way of alerting her to her puzzlement at the way her patient was behaving. She could then turn her attention to trying to solve this puzzle, by listening out for clues in the patient's material. In the paper, she described how she took elements from the patient's descriptions of and feelings towards the woman he was going to marry, together with his associations to a dream, to make a construction as to the meaning of his behaviour. She deduced that the patient's wish to get married represented a masochistic attempt on his part to repair an object he had injured as a result of his sadistic attacks. She could then see that the wish to get married so quickly was both a destructive attack on the analysis, but also an appeal for help. But the patient himself was not aware of these feelings. Instead they got registered by the analyst in the form of her countertransference feelings of apprehension and worry. Heimann concluded that by paying more attention to our emotional reactions and feelings during a session, we may understand more fully "the way in which the character of the countertransference corresponds to the nature of the patient's unconscious impulses and defences operative at the actual time" (ibid. p.84).

This is a vivid and elegant demonstration of the importance of developing one's emotional sensibility in order to work at one's best. But it is not quite clear in this example what "work" the countertransference is meant to be doing. Let us consider the status of the two feelings Heimann identifies, apprehension and worry. Heimann takes them as manifestations of her own clinical reasoning – "unconsciously I had grasped immediately the seriousness of the situation, hence the sense of worry which I experienced" (ibid. p.82). In fact, her choice of words to describe her countertransference is pertinent. "Apprehension" is a state of mind but also a cognitive judgement. "Worry" also describes a state of mind, but functions as a verb as well, as in dogs "worrying" sheep. So both words are active and incorporate different registers of experience. They serve well to convey a process of evaluation going on in her mind.

Based on the concepts we have employed in previous chapters, we can describe her clinical thinking as follows. Heimann realized that the problem she was trying to solve was not covered by her normal stock of clinical exemplars and generalizations. So she switched from an attitude of "problem-solving" to "problem-setting". In so doing, she brought in more reflective and theoretical reasoning in order to make sense of this unexpected and new situation. This is evident in her paper when she claims that the concept of countertransference "helps the analyst to focus his attention on the most urgent element in the patient's associations and serves as a useful criterion for the selection of interpretations from material which, as we know, is always overdetermined" (ibid. p.84).

In other words, the concept of countertransference, just like the rules of neutrality and abstinence (see Chapter 6), is employed to establish a "live edge" to her work, to identify a zone where the new problem she has set can be identified and grappled with. As we explored in Chapter 6, this involves a certain kind of concentration. In fact Heimann makes an interesting comment on the frame of mind needed in converting raw feelings into countertransference. She points out that "violent emotions of any kind, of love or hate, helpfulness or anger, impel towards action rather than towards contemplation and blur a person's capacity to observe and weigh the evidence correctly" (ibid. p.82). And so "if the analyst's emotional response is intense, it will defeat its object." This means the analyst's emotional sensitivity "needs to be extensive rather than intensive, differentiating and mobile" (ibid. p.82). This description is similar to the "prehension" and "stretched-out" concentration of the glass-blower which we used to make sense of the attitude of evenly suspended attention (see Chapter 6, pp.90–3).

All of this presupposes skilled work on the part of the practitioner. As I illustrated in my account in Chapter 4 (pp.56–60) of how I came to adopt the "splitting and projection" model, I had to learn to discriminate between a wide range of feelings, of different degrees of intensity and duration, in order to pick out the one's which would then "count" as projections. Heimann must have done something similar in order to arrive at the two feelings of apprehension and worry that she describes. Indeed, in the course of her description she alludes to other states of mind. She comments that she had many reasons for "doubting" the wisdom of his plan and for "suspecting" his choice. She is "puzzled", feeling something has "eluded" her. Any of these feelings or states of mind could potentially figure as countertransference feelings.

But there is no reference to such a process of discrimination in her account. I think this is because she also uses the idea of countertransference in a different way, no longer as part of her appreciative system of finding the best way to conduct the session, but as though her feelings have literally come directly from the patient. This is implied in her statement that the character of the countertransference "corresponds to the nature of the patient's unconscious impulses and defences operative at the actual time" (ibid. p.84). At other times, she is more explicit: "from the point of view I am stressing, the analyst's countertransference is not only part and parcel of the analytic relationship, but it is the patient's *creation*, it is part of the patient's personality" (ibid. p.82, italics in original).

In this way of using countertransference, the emphasis is no longer on the work the practitioner needs to do to pick out the most "urgent" feelings as a way of thinking about the patient's material. Indeed, it is not clear the practitioner needs to do any work at all, apart from making sure nothing interferes with their capacity to directly receive these communications from the patient. In this sense Heimann buys into the "romantic myth" of a fusion between two minds identified by Thoma and Kachela in their discussion of the concept of evenly suspended attention (see Chapter 6, pp.92–3). As Thoma and Kachela point out, this form of magical thinking puts the practitioner in a God-like position of knowing everything that is in the patient's mind. They conclude that "whatever the role of the countertransference may be in the recognition of unconscious conflicts, the assumed connection between them has to be made evident" (2007, p.659).

I have found this to be good advice. I know I am deeply affected by my patients, and the concept of countertransference has taught me the value of trying to dig out and monitor these affects. So if I find myself noticing a feeling or state of mind in myself during the course of my session, I find it helpful to wonder where this comes from and what it means. But, if I am alert and working well, I am likely to have a wide range of such feelings during the course of a session, and to assume that all of them have been put there by my patient threatens to turn a clinically useful concept into a form of dogma. In fact, because of this confusion as to the meaning of the term – attention to one's emotional sensibility or direct access to one's patient's unconscious? – I have found that in my own clinical thinking I make much less use of the term than I used to. I prefer to think instead in terms of my practical and theoretical reasoning and how I evaluate my work. Nevertheless, the term "countertransference" has become so much part of our analytic language that students and supervisees need to be able to use the term in an informed way and to see its value. The problem is, rather like the concept of "not-knowing" I looked at in the previous chapter, that the use of the term "countertransference" presupposes a certain level of skill. I illustrated this in my example in Chapter 4 of how I came to adopt the "splitting and projection" model, which involved a lengthy process of learning to discriminate between my various reactions and judging which of these reactions were best suited to "count" as projections. Until the developing practitioner has learnt how to do this, they will not be able to apply the concept with any real understanding or aptitude.

Containment

I will now look at the concept of containment in a similar way, again through the use of a clinical example, this time taken from Patrick Casement's textbook on analytic practice *On Learning from the Patient* (1985). He describes the importance of learning to contain the patient, and defines containment by taking a quotation from Grotstein.

> Bion's conception is of an elaborated primary process activity which acts like a prism to refract the intense hue of the infant's screams into the components of the colour spectrum, so to speak, so as to sort them out and relegate them to a hierarchy of importance and mental action. (Ibid. p.154)

In order to illustrate the use of the concept, he gives an example of a "failure to contain" (ibid. p.154). During the Friday session of a depressed patient whom he was seeing for twice-weekly therapy, Casement describes how he picked up a sense of foreboding in what the patient was saying, even though the patient did not refer explicitly to suicide. Casement told the patient that he was picking up a "suicidal feeling", and the patient started to cry. The patient agreed he was finding it difficult to see any future, and that, without realizing it, he had been brooding on suicide. Casement goes on:

> At this point I misjudged the kind of containment this patient was needing. I found myself thinking about the long break between this Friday session and the next Wednesday. So I offered to see him on Monday if he would like to have an extra session. He asked me if he could think about this and let me know. I later had a telephone message saying he would be coming for the extra session. (Ibid. p.134)

At the extra session, on a Monday, the patient recounted a dream he had had the previous night. One part of it featured the patient rowing a boat, and a man hanging on to the back of the boat in an attempt to help him steer. But the result was that this man actually made it more difficult for the patient to steer the boat himself. The patient identified this man as Casement. The patient told Casement he only came to this extra session because he said he would, but he no longer felt the extra session was necessary. What had happened on Friday, when Casement picked up his suicidal feelings, was sufficient; it had helped him no longer feel alone, so life no longer felt so impossible.

On the basis of this, Casement judges that offering the extra session, which was meant to help the patient, had in fact hindered him. The effect of offering the session indicated to the patient that Casement doubted he had the strength to manage his own feelings, and so had ended up by undermining him.

> The sequence therefore helps to illustrate that trying to reassure, or offering extra support, is often motivated by the helper's own need for reassurance because of the anxiety stirred up by a patient's (or client's) distress. Containment is seldom, if ever, achieved by reassuring the patient. (Ibid. p.135)

Let us look at what the concept of containment does in this example. It starts with an account of an intervention which the patient found very helpful, namely that he was feeling suicidal. The implication is that this was the outcome of successful containment on Casement's part; that is, he had held on to the tension of registering this painful and alarming affect in his emotional sensibility, and was able to use it to good effect to help the patient recognize this. This does indeed seem a good example of how Milton describes containment, "the sometimes uncomfortable but often productive process of holding on to the tension, bearing the way the patient is feeling and seeing one, while one finds a helpful way of talking to the patient about it" (Milton, Polmear and Fabricius, 2011, p.10).

Then Casement decided to offer the patient an extra session. He comes to the conclusion that this was not helpful, and that it was the outcome of a failure to contain his own feelings or reactions through his own anxiety.

We can think of the concept of containment as serving a useful function in helping Casement evaluate his work. He implicitly felt his work was good when he was able to register and manage the patient's "foreboding" and speak to the patient about this feeling. But he then judged himself to have fallen below his own standard of good work by offering a supportive intervention when he was unable to hold on to his anxiety over how the patient was dealing with his suicidal feeling. The supportive intervention offered the patient something he did not need and thus served to undermine his own abilities.

This account of how Casement uses the concept of containment works as far as it goes. But if we turn our attention to the kinds of evaluative judgements employed and how they are used to inform Casement's clinical thinking, the account is much less clear. So if we try to reconstruct how Casement's appreciative system works in this extract, we can see how he gets to his first intervention. It is based on his picking up on his feeling of "foreboding", which he takes as a countertransference feeling that indicates that his emotional sensibility is in advance of his more intellectual understanding, and as a suggestion of what the patient may be feeling, but has suppressed from awareness. We can also see how he tests the correctness or usefulness of his intervention, by implicitly taking as confirmation the patient's crying and the way the patient elaborated on Casement's intervention.

But when Casement goes on to describe himself thinking about the long gap between Friday and Wednesday, we are no longer given this contextual information. All we are told, implicitly, is that he was no longer containing his feelings and so no longer in touch with what his patient needed. Then we are told that, on the basis of this idea, Casement offered the extra session. Compared to his more tentative and exploratory interpretation in the first part of the session, this is now presented as a sudden jump from thought to action. The implication is that this was further evidence of a lack of containment on the part of the analyst. But it seems unlikely that an analyst of Casement's experience and ability would simply come up with an idea and then act on it without having some clinical reasons – whether or not they turn out to be "good" ones – for why he acted as he did. Perhaps the situation activated a working model of the patient which casts him as someone who could not cope with the current situation. We do not know, as Casement tells us nothing about his clinical thinking, simply seeing his "reaction" as the consequence of his "failure to contain".

It would also be very useful, in understanding why Casement acted as he did, to know how he tested his intervention. One might wonder, for instance, why he chose to offer the extra session rather than explore with the patient whether he felt able to manage his suicidal feelings, or simply by asking him whether he felt he needed an extra session. Again, when the patient asked for more time, which does not sound like a full endorsement of the appropriateness of what was offered, we are not told how Casement used this response in his evaluation of his intervention.

Casement does explain how he arrived at the judgement that offering the extra session constituted a failure of containment in his discussion of how he had unwittingly undermined the patient's confidence in his own ability. This is based on the patient's dream and what the patient told him in the extra session, and seems a reasonable clinical judgement to make. This is an example of retrospective theoretical reasoning used to good effect. Casement then goes on to claim that this shows that making a supportive intervention is poor practice. But on the face of it, this sounds like a rather harsh and one-sided judgement on the quality of his own work. In the extra session, the patient told Casement a vivid dream, and seemed able to have used the dream in a thoughtful way. Most practitioners would take a patient remembering and bringing a rich dream to a session as a sign of an analytic process. In the extra session, the patient spoke to Casement in a direct and clear way about how it had not been helpful to offer him the extra session (which does not sound like someone whose strength has been undermined). Furthermore, the patient's behaviour, in coming to a session he did not want out of a sense of obligation or commitment, seemed to offer rich transference material which was available for exploration. In other words, even if his offering the extra session can reasonably be described as a "mistake", as the outcome of a "failure" of containment, it sounds like without this "mistake", the therapy would have been deprived of some productive developments.

The concept of containment can be of value in helping us think about what constitutes analytic competence. A clinician who cannot tolerate strong feelings in his or her clients or patients will never be a good practitioner. The concept, as in the extract from Grotstein quoted by Casement, also offers intriguing parallels between the form of emotional interaction between mother and baby, and therapist and patient. This is why, when I wrote my introductory book on analytic practice, I gave the concept of containment pride of place, describing it as "the basic therapeutic principle" (Spurling, 2009, p.20). However, I would have to now admit that I have not found the concept to have lived up to its promise. I have not found it of much use in helping me think about the nature of good practice and how I evaluate my work. Indeed, as in the Casement example, I have found that thinking in terms of containment can obscure aspects of my clinical thinking and so distract me from this task.

As with the concept of countertransference, thinking of one's work in terms of containment can address aspects of our emotional sensibility and capacity to tolerate powerful and difficult feelings. As such, they are important components of good analytic work. But if they become too removed from the craft skills they are meant to inform, there is a risk that they will be seen as "ends in themselves" rather than as specific tools to be used for specific purposes.

Strengthening the harsh analytic superego

There is another reason I make much less use of the concept of containment than I used to, which is that I have found it can induce an unduly critical attitude towards one's own work. I think this is present in Casement's account. In expecting himself to know what his patient needs through some mental process of containment, he places a very high expectation on himself. How can he know what the patient supposedly needed without testing out his ideas, or having some kind of negotiation with the patient? But Casement writes as though he should know, that he should be able to sort out the different elements in the patient's cry for help. And so he criticizes himself for having picked out and acted upon the wrong element, even though it seemed to have resulted in a very productive period of work with the patient.

Casement then goes on to place a further expectation on himself. Not only is the practitioner expected to recognize what the patient needs and to work in a way that meets these needs; he must also do so in the "right" way, that is, in a way that confirms the "right" analytic method – in this case, one which considers supportive interventions to be "non-analytic".

Now an experienced practitioner would be able to read Casement's account as an example of Casement's particular way of working, an illustration of his appreciative system and how he applies it in his clinical thinking. It can be taken as his own particular way of thinking about and using the concept of containment (Ronald Britton, 1998, for instance, writes about containment in a rather different way). The self-critical tone and the demand he seems to place on himself that his method must exemplify the correct analytic approach can then all be seen as features of his own particular approach that produces his best work (just as Milton's rather ascetic attitude can be taken as a description of the way she works at her best, see Chapter 2).

But for the developing practitioner, accounts such as this can easily serve to reinforce their powerful and critical analytic superego, which gives them the sense that they are constantly failing to live up to some ideal they feel they can never attain. They can feel that they are meant to contain their feelings in such a way as to meet the patient's needs, and if they fail to contain their feelings, and/or offer a supportive intervention, then they are not doing good analytic work. This is why I find it helpful with my students and supervisees, whenever they speak of containment or countertransference, to get them to spell out in ordinary language what they mean. This puts them in touch with their clinical thinking, and we can then get a sense of what they are trying to do with these concepts. They can be used in productive and imaginative ways, as the examples from Heimann and Casement show. But the developing practitioner can only make these judgements once they have attained the level of skill and understanding needed to use these terms to inform their practice rather than obscure it.

PART III

Describing the Craft: Examples from Practice

8

A SESSION FROM AN INTENSIVE THERAPY

In the first two parts of the book, I have argued that many accounts of analytic work miss out an essential part of the process – the implicit clinical thinking that goes on in the background. This is what I shall try to describe in the next two chapters by looking at a piece of my own work in this chapter and the work of a colleague in the next. The question I will address is this: what would a description of ordinary clinical work look like if the practitioner's clinical thinking is foregrounded? This means focusing on what normally remains hidden or obscured: the processes of practical and theoretical reasoning, the invocation of working models, the rhythm of problem-setting and problem-solving, the composing of interventions and all the other operations carried out which "produce" the practitioner's way of working.

The task of this chapter, to write about my own clinical thinking, is clearly an ambitious if not problematic endeavour, as it involves describing features of my own implicit reasoning which operate just on the threshold between conscious and preconscious. So in order to describe or reconstruct them, I will be turning them into discursive thoughts or bits of reasoning that are, of necessity, much more coherent and articulated than they would be as they arise in the course of the work itself.

I have chosen to describe four consecutive sessions of an intensive therapy (three sessions a week), but focusing mainly on the first session in the sequence. In describing the sessions and trying to reconstruct my clinical thinking, I have relied on my memory and on the notes I made immediately after the session. This means working with the inevitable gaps and distortions of what I have remembered. This is bad enough when it comes to remembering what was said in the sessions. But in turning my attention to my clinical thinking, I am trying to get hold of thoughts, associations, resonances, ideas and so on, some of which were fully formed and articulate, some half-formed, some not really formed at all. This is bound to skew the account towards those aspects of my reasoning that resulted in action on my part, that were "validated" or brought into existence by the way my patient responded. Those thoughts, intuitions, images, memories and so on which came to my mind, perhaps only fleetingly or indirectly, during the session which did not find expression in any (conscious) interventions or thought on my part have been lost.

I have written the account of the session with my patient in the following way. In recounting what I and my patient said, I have used direct speech where possible, but sometimes I have had to resort to a narrative account where my memory and/or notes were not specific enough. I have then, at various points in the account of the session, inserted a commentary which tries to describe my clinical thinking. This commentary consists mainly of my *practical reasoning,* the thinking I was doing about how to best conduct the session. This thinking was predominantly forward-looking, tracing out in my mind how the session might pan out and looking for pointers as to what kind of strategy and interventions would be most effective. This part appears in italics. I have then added a further commentary as an attempt to represent my *theoretical reasoning,* a different kind of reflection, drawing more explicitly on models and concepts in order to throw some light on the internal logic of my practical reasoning. This kind of reasoning is more backward-looking, seeking to make sense of what was currently happening in terms of what had already occurred in the session (see Chapter 4, pp.72–3, for the difference between practical and theoretical reasoning). This part of my clinical thinking appears in the text in bold.

Under this section of theoretical reasoning, I have added some further reflections (indicated in the text) concerning the kinds of theoretical assumptions and working models which can be seen to inform my thinking. These reflections were made in the process of writing the chapter. I do not think any of what appears in these further reflections was consciously in my mind at the time of conducting the session, or if it was, it was right at the back of my mind.

In order to preserve confidentiality, I have changed the personal details of the patient and also minor details which occur in the sessions.

Account of a session

The patient, Mr. A, was a middle-aged man who initially sought therapy following the birth of his second child. He had always been anxious and needing to feel in control. But after the birth, he started to have panic attacks, and for the first time in his life he sought help. When he started therapy he had been married for four years and was in a job he found stressful. An only child, his mother had died when he was 12 of a sudden illness. Mr. A felt he and his father had never recovered from this death. He has always felt his father was "weird", but after his mother died, he found his father so bizarre that he left home as soon as he could. In his 20s and early 30s he had a number of short and unsuccessful relationships. He met his wife in his late 30s and found her to be someone he could live with. The birth of his first child, a daughter, was stressful, but managed by largely leaving her care with his wife. But the birth of his second child, a son, seemed to trigger something in him he could not understand.

The session I will describe occurred in the fourth year of Mr. A's three-times-a-week therapy. In the course of the work, his panic attacks had largely subsided, to be replaced by the sudden emergence of new anxiety symptoms (e.g. his fear of harming someone) at times of stress. His self-hatred also became more evident, and his great need to be in control of his own feelings and actions. He struggled to relax sufficiently in the sessions to allow much spontaneity, and if he felt he had "let himself go" in a session, he was likely afterward to berate himself and consequently feel worse. Mr. A had tried using the couch I have in my consulting room, but quickly gave this up and would habitually sit in a chair at an angle to me.

The session I will describe occurred after a bank holiday break.

Mr. A: "I don't want to get all busted up today, I have exams coming up (he is taking a course to gain an additional qualification in his work), I don't have a good feeling about my exams. But I need to make good use of the therapy as my exams are next week. (Pause.) It feels very weird coming today, although we only missed yesterday it feels much longer. (Pause). It's funny, I was talking to Anita [his wife] on Sunday about some of the things we have been talking about in therapy. But now it's all different. When I arrived I was standing outside the door wondering whether I had got the time wrong, I felt really confused. I woke up this morning feeling different, normally I know what is a therapy day and what time it is. But I have come in a bit of a daze. (Pause.) I don't want to start thinking, getting my brain off its tracks. (Mr. A's voice has started to rise, he is now getting agitated and anxious.) Oh no, this is not going well, I've just become a different person, how I feel all weird, panicky. (I come in at this point just to clarify he is meaning right now, in the session, which he confirms. His face has now become harder, it contorts a little; he says more about feeling weird.) Now I know what I have been feeling the last few days was all crap, it wasn't real, I just have to keep running around and not thinking, keep doing things, but if I stop running around and there is just quiet, like now, then this is what is real, all the rest is crap, all the rest is fake. (Pause.) Just grim thoughts. I am going to spend the rest of my life like this."

Clinical thinking (practical reasoning). The session started with Mr. A indicating that he did not want therapy to affect him too much because of his exams. He also spoke of feeling strange, probably because of the cancelled session which has thrown him off his routine. These were familiar themes. I felt no need to say anything; it seemed better to wait and see what happened. But then Mr. A started to become anxious. He had occasionally felt panicky or acutely anxious in a session, but not often, and not for some time, so I was surprised by his rising sense of panic – hence my question about whether he meant he was feeling panicky in the session. I did not feel this was likely to escalate into a full-blown panic attack, which had never happened in a session, nevertheless, his sudden switch into a state of anxiety felt slightly unnerving. I felt I needed to keep an eye on what was happening to try to ensure it did not get out of hand.

But I also did not want to interrupt what was happening. Although it raised my anxiety, I also saw the mini panic attack as a welcome development in the therapy, a chance for me, together with Mr. A, to observe and learn more about his anxiety, how it arose and, hopefully, how he could manage it.

I have also registered that immediately after becoming anxious, Mr. A switched into one of his familiar bouts of self-hatred – "what I have been feeling in the last few days is all crap", and then "grim thoughts". I sometimes respond, semi-automatically by now, by pointing out this critical superego part of him and trying to engage him in thinking about what has activated it. But here I opted to note this, but leave it to one side for the moment, as I was more concerned to track the anxiety state.

Furthermore, I could see that Mr. A was describing, in stark and powerful terms, how he sees much of his life as "fake", the only "real" part being his state of weirdness and self-hatred, a kind of weird centre. This theme, of the split between what is fake and what is real, was a relatively recent development in the therapy. I was aware at some level that this theme was important and needed following up. I was not sure how well I understood it. It came in as part of the depressive discourse, to do with his punishing and critical superego, but it also felt different, more a preoccupation of patients I think of as borderline.

As with the depressive discourse, I tried to keep this in mind but not focus on it for the moment.

My mind was starting to feel full up with too many thoughts to hold on to comfortably, which made me want to say something to Mr. A, to get me into the session. I was also starting to feel he was winding himself up into something, so I decided to come in at this point. I opted for something that was simple, just slightly interrupting him and, hopefully, getting more clarity and perspective on what he was saying.

LS: *"Can you say more about your feelings now?"*

Clinical thinking (theoretical reasoning). By this time in the session, I was already doing a lot of thinking, much more than I would normally be doing with Mr. A. My thinking can be seen to have switched from a "problem-solving mode" – Mr. A brought his own reaction to the cancelled session as a "problem" to be solved – to one where I have set myself a new problem: how to respond to his anxiety state in the session. At this point in the session I had two different, if not contradictory strategies in mind. On the one hand, to try to stop Mr. A's panic from escalating and getting out of hand. I seemed to be thinking of his state of mind as one in which he felt so overwhelmed that he was unable to think about what he was doing or what it meant, so my aim would be to try to introduce more of a reflective state of mind. But on the other hand, I was treating his rising panic as an interesting and welcome development, an opportunity for me to observe and study the natural history of his anxiety as it manifested itself in front of us in the room. I had a vague memory of having noted in a paper by Franco de Masi (2004) on panic attacks that one is only really able to work with the panic when it manifests itself in a session. From this point of view, it would be better to do nothing, to wait and see what developed.

I had registered that I was feeling slightly unnerved, so was aware at some level that anxiety was affecting me, but I judged that it felt at a manageable level and was not interfering too much with my ability to think.

Further reflections. My two conflicting strategies – help Mr. A manage his affective state and frame it, and leave it alone and watch it develop – can be seen to reflect different aspects of a working model, or two different working models, part of my internal clinical template that concerned what I thought was wrong with the patient. Thinking in terms of helping Mr. A manage his panic suggests I was seeing him as someone suffering from a basic defect, an incapacity to regulate his affects, whereas letting the panic develop conveys more belief in Mr. A's capacity to manage his own anxiety. At this point in the session it did not seem the apparent conflict between these two different models concerned me too much.

In thinking about how best to work with Mr. A's panic, I can be seen to be drawing on a working model about working with anxiety. The more conscious theoretical influences and exemplars I am aware of describe the anxious patient as adopting a child-like defence against the fears and conflicts around growing up, and characterize anxiety as the lack of a containing structure which allows one to manage affects (papers such as De Masi, 2004 and Quinodoz, 1990 have particularly influenced my thinking). Another source of influence has been the work of Busch et al. (2012), where the focus is more on anxiety as an inability to manage conflict. My more strategic thinking can be seen to be in line with both approaches. I allude to a second working model around depression and depressive discourse (elements of this working model can be found in Chapter 4 [the "superego attacking ego" model, pp.60–1] and in Chapter 9 [the "ego-destructive superego", pp.148–9]). I also make reference to thinking more in terms of borderline states, in terms of real/fake, but don't elaborate on this. At this point in the session, although focusing on anxiety, I seem to want to keep these other diagnostic models in mind.

My actual choice of intervention – "can you say more…" – can be seen to follow from my strategy at this point of keeping my options open. It functions as an opening move on my part. In terms of the type of intervention (Table 8.1), it can be seen most clearly as an

Table 8.1: Categories of basic interventions (brief version of Table 3.1)

1. Maintaining the basic setting.
2. Adding an element to facilitate unconscious process.
3. Questions, clarifications and re-formulations, aimed at making matters conscious.
4. Designating here-and-now emotional and fantasy reading of the situation with therapist.
5. Constructions directed at providing elaborated meaning.
6. Enactments as deviations from the therapist's normal way of working.

intervention aiming to make matters more conscious, probing to see how much Mr. A could reflect on his state of mind.

In writing this chapter, I am able to look back over the session and see a number of different ways I might have responded. I could have taken up Mr. A's opening remark, about how the missed session affected him, perhaps linking his anxiety state to the cancelled session. I could have focused more on his body, and pointed out to him how his voice was rising, or how his face became contorted. I could have come in with an intervention when he seemed to switch from being anxious to being more depressed. None of these would seem to be at odds with my overall strategies or my working models, and any of these might have been effective, maybe more so than what I actually did in the session. Whether any, some or all of these presented themselves to me as possible forms of intervention during the session I cannot recall. These "what-if" scenarios are always interesting to postulate in reflection after a session. If I had intervened in any of these ways, the session would have turned out differently. But the nature of the ongoing practical reasoning we do in a session is more forward-looking, as in my already anticipating what might happen if Mr A's anxiety were to escalate during the session.

> Mr. A: "It is like a panic, I feel more on my own. I am aware of the silence here. In fact there was a moment like this on Saturday. Anita went out to have lunch with a friend and took the children, I was fine revising in my room, and then suddenly I was aware of being on my own and it was horrible." (He says more about how frightening and disturbing it was to feel on his own like this.)
>
> LS: "How did you feel about Anita and the children going out and you being left on your own?"
>
> Mr. A: "It was fine, I didn't have a problem with them going out, it gave me time to revise, it felt fine."

I had asked Mr. A about this, as I wondered about an Oedipal theme, Mr. A's jealousy of his wife having friends or having a relationship with the children from which he was excluded. I was aware, I think, that there was nothing particular in the material to suggest this, but I had in mind that perhaps this was a new development. However, I felt Mr. A's clear denial was an indication that I was on the wrong track – it did not have the heat or insistence that might have led me to think of it as resistance – so I decided to drop it.

This seems to be an example of an intervention put together to fit in with a theoretical idea. I had somewhere in my mind a memory of Danielle Quinodoz's (1990) paper on "Vertigo", where she distinguishes between a number of stages in her patient's therapy, with Oedipal themes coming up towards the end stages. Perhaps this was wishful thinking on my part that my patient was further on than he was.

One can also see my appreciative system at work here. I took Mr. A's "no" at face value, his denial matched his tone and affect, and I was aware at some level that my intervention was rather forced to fit in with a theoretical idea.

Mr. B: "I was scared."
LS: "Scared of what?"

One of my technical generalizations, or recipes of clinical practice [see Chapter 4, "Vectors of implicit theory", Table 4.1, p.65], can be seen to be operative here, which can be summed up as: "whenever possible, try to match up an affect with an object." So if a patient says, "I am angry", my default response is to ask "angry with whom?" In this case, I asked "scared of what?" when Mr. A said he was scared. I probably had in mind trying to pin down more accurately his affects or state of mind. I could, of course, have asked instead "scared of whom?" This would have made it a slightly different intervention, expecting a different kind of response, indicating that in my mind a person was involved rather than a state of mind. This is another example of the countless clinical "decisions" going on all the time somewhere in a practitioner's mind about how we compose our interventions, what they are designed to do, what kind of response we expect and so on.

Mr. A: "I don't know."
(I urged Mr. A to try to describe his feeling of being scared, but he said he was not able to, he just knew he felt scared of something.)
LS: "I think you are describing a kind of black hole you fall into. It reminds me of the time your mother died, and how that affected you, how suddenly you were on your own. But it is also like being with a mad person, your father I imagine, being with someone who is there but really absent." (I elaborated a bit on all of this.) "Is this right?"

My dilemma about whether to speak in order to help Mr. A with his anxiety, or refrain from speaking to see what happened with his anxiety, now felt more acute. I would have preferred to hold back on any attempt to interpret how Mr. A was feeling in the hope he would find a way himself to try to make sense of his anxiety. Hence my urging him to describe more fully his being scared. I was also aware that linking his panic and anxiety to the time his mother died was something I had done many times before. The link seemed to me so obvious that I hesitated to make it again. So I worried about doing the work for Mr. A when it would be better for him to do it. But was he able to do it? I was concerned that if he was left to carry on in this state, he would get stuck or end up feeling worse. Furthermore, I felt that this was a good opportunity to make the link clearer. I opted for a rather wide-ranging intervention, in the hope that Mr. A would find something in it he could associate to. I ended on an appeal to his own capacity to think – "Is this right?"

Somewhere in the back of my mind was an idea I had come across in the literature in working with very anxious patients, that they often cannot make the links as to the meaning of their anxiety that are staring them in the face. This was the position I found myself in, the link with the time his mother died was obvious to me, and something we had talked about many times before – so why was Mr. A not making this link himself? Here I decided that he was not in a state of mind to think, so it seemed to make sense to come in with an intervention to help him to do so. In making a clear reference to the time his mother died, I could now be seen to be committing myself to a more definite line of approach, making an interpretation as to the meaning and origin of his state of mind on the day described. One can wonder why, at this point, I decided to commit myself more. It followed Mr. A's "I don't know." If I could reconstruct my thinking, it would be that I took this as some form of resistance to thinking, a not wanting to know, which I now wanted to address more directly. If we think of what kind of intervention this was, it could be described as a construction aimed at providing a more elaborated meaning, of linking past and present. It is an attempt to deepen the work. But as an interpretation or construction aiming for more elaborated meaning, it does not seem a very good one. It introduces two different people and scenarios at the same time: his mother, who left him, and his father, who was weird, without providing a link between them. It is perhaps better seen as adding some elements to facilitate unconscious processes, laying out my thoughts to Mr. A and inviting him to choose one which made sense to him.

> *Mr. A:* (Confirmed what I said was right): "It is like they have moved to a different planet." (I am not sure who "they" are but decide not to ask more questions.)

LS: "They have become unavailable, unreachable. And this is what happens here, for the first few minutes it is ok with you, but now everything is different. A session is cancelled and everything is thrown out of joint."

Mr. A used my intervention to speak of people having become unreachable, which I saw as the aspect of my interpretation he found most useful. I wanted to bring this element into the transference, and it felt best to try to describe how things seemed for Mr. A, without commenting on the reality or otherwise of his perception.

My view of Mr. A up to this point of the therapy was that he did not seem to respond well to direct transference interpretations of how he might be experiencing me. Explicit references to what he might be feeling about me or the therapy were usually met with silence, or did not seem to lead anywhere. Up until now, I had found it more productive, rather than making interpretations of or about the transference, to simply try to describe Mr. A's experience of being in the room with me, as though as I was also a player in the game, so speaking "in" the transference (see Chapter 3, pp.48–9).

Mr. A spoke more about how he felt on Saturday, how his sense of alone-ness was not the more normal sense of panic he can feel, but something different. But he struggled to say more. Then, after a short silence, he started to sound desperate again: "It has got all intense again." (He said more on this.) "I am aware of the gap between who I was before I started therapy, and what is happening now." (I ask him to say this again.)

I felt that my speaking "in" the transference and linking this to his experiences on Saturday had helped Mr. A describe the quality of his feelings with more intensity and thought. I therefore wanted to keep open the links between his feelings of aloneness and panic on Saturday, his experiences around the time his mother died and his feelings in the session with me. I also wanted to make mention of the cancelled session and the break, which Mr. A had introduced at the beginning of the session. As usual, Mr. A made no direct reference to my interpretation about the transference, leaving me unclear how useful it was to keep speaking to him about his experience with me. I knew by now that he did not like me to speak directly of his relationship with me, such remarks of mine were usually met with silence. Indeed, in this section, he had gone on to tell me things had got more intense again, that he had become desperate. Perhaps this was his response to my referring to his here-and-now experience of me. But even if this were true, I also felt my speaking "in" the transference to him about how he was experiencing the therapy was making him feel a bit safer in the session and seemed to be helping him get more in touch with his feelings. Furthermore, he then went on to speak of the gap between how he was at the beginning of therapy and how he was now. I took this as a positive response to my speaking about the relationship in the here-and-now, and something to be explored. I didn't really understand what Mr. A meant when he spoke of the gap between who he was and what was happening now, so I asked him to say this again – not something I would normally do, but it felt he was saying something important here and I wanted to understand what it was.

Further reflection. Looking at this section with the benefit of hindsight, I think I missed an opportunity here to explore what was happening in the session which led Mr. A to start feeling more desperate and feel things had become more intense. I took this as an indication he was finding some aspect of the transference difficult, but I did not investigate this further. I can see at least two reasons for my not exploring this. At an affective level, I suspect I was responding to a powerful projection or unconscious communication from Mr. A to keep away from such an exploration. At a more cognitive level, that is, the level of my more conscious clinical reasoning, I became interested in what Mr. A went on to say about the gap between who he was before therapy and who he was now, and saw this as something new being brought into the session, which was worth exploring. My expectation at this point, if I were to reconstruct it, would be that following this tack would throw more light on Mr. A's state of mind.

LS: "So the way you are now is a kind of going back to the way you were before you started therapy."

Mr. A: "Kind of right." (He was clearly getting more anxious, his voice was taking on more of a frightened and slightly whiny quality.) "I just hate the way I was, it was all fake, this is the only reality, the way I am now, this is the only thing that's real, it's the only thing that makes sense." (He says more on this, repeating it several times, speaking with intensity.)

Although Mr. A seemed to agree with my interpretation that the way he was feeling now was like going back to before he started therapy, I took his comment and the rising intensity and despair as an indication that I was on the wrong track here. First of all, he qualified his agreement, "kind of", whereas he was normally more positive when he was in agreement about something. Secondly, I was aware that my remark was influenced by a theoretical idea – that he had regressed in some way. Hearing what he was saying through the lens of this concept, I thought he might be talking about an experience of going back to how he felt before he started therapy. But I was also not sure whether this really fitted what he was saying. When Mr. A went on to speak, with feeling and anxiety, about how fake he felt, and how he hated what was fake, I dropped the idea of regression as throwing no light on what was happening.

When Mr. A said "I hate the way I was", I felt unsure whether to think of this as part of his depressive discourse, and so a way of attacking himself, or whether he was exploring how he feels he has constantly to adapt to other people. In other words, was this an attempt to get to more of a "true self" part of himself? I was not sure, so decided to wait to hear more.

The model of regression, of the need to go back to earlier states of mind in order to progress, is an idea of Winnicott's that used to inform my thinking, but which I have now dropped (see Concluding Remarks, pp.200–1, and Spurling, 2008). Or at least I thought I had. When Mr. A started to speak of a gap between who he was now and who he was when he started therapy, I think the regression model popped into my mind and led me to say what I did about him going back.

Mr. A said more on how fake he feels when he is not like he is now. His way of speaking gradually lost its intensity and took on more of a quiet self-despairing tone. "This is never going to get better, this is the problem with therapy; how can I ever get over these periods, like how I felt on Saturday?" Mr. A spoke more about how he felt dead, not existing and not real on Saturday.

> LS: "When you felt like this on Saturday, what did you actually do? People in this state often try to phone someone or find a way of soothing themselves."

I was starting to feel that we had got as far as we could go with exploring how Mr. A was feeling both on Saturday and in the session. We were now getting near the end of the session and I was still concerned about his state of mind when the session ended. Also, although he kept returning to what had happened on Saturday, I felt there was something I did not quite "get" about what had happened to him. I found myself wondering how he had got out of his state of panic; perhaps there would be something to learn here. My way of framing this intervention, "people in this state often try ... " was rather unprocessed, it being more or less what I was thinking, but I felt it would serve its purpose.

In hindsight, I probably felt more stuck than I realized, and also concerned that Mr. A felt stuck – "this is never going to get better." This kind of despairing discourse was quite familiar with Mr. A, and I normally saw it as his way of dampening himself down. Usually I would have tried to get at what was being suppressed. This could have been an opportunity to explore with Mr. A how his noisier desperation of a few minutes ago had now become a quieter, more hopeless or resigned despair. But this tactic, more evident to me in hindsight, was not in the forefront of my thinking at this point. My change of tack was influenced by my interest in interpersonal therapy (IPT), which involves exploring a depressed person's social network. Hence my rather concrete intervention, which can best be described as a question seeking to make matters more conscious. I was probably asking the question as much to myself as to Mr. A.

> Mr. A: "A waste of time, my friends would also be dead to me, they wouldn't exist."
> LS: "And trying to soothe yourself?"
> Mr. A: "I don't know how to soothe myself, I wouldn't know when I am in that state."

I gave a kind of inward laugh to myself; I felt I was being very nicely supervised by Mr. A, who was telling me I was missing the point in asking him about phoning someone, as when he is in this state of mind, everyone else exists in a different world to him, one which cannot be reached. I found myself thinking here of the Philip Pullman trilogy His Dark Materials *(1995), in which he creates a series of parallel words, but one can only find a way from one world to another if one knows the exact point of entry. And of course he did not know how to soothe himself, or he would not be in the predicament he was in. So this seemed to be going nowhere. Yet, at the same time, I felt Mr. A was being particularly lucid here. Had he somehow recovered his capacity to think? Perhaps my strategy here was not such a bad idea? I decided to persist. During this sequence, I remembered not so long ago that his family had bought a dog, and how, after being initially sceptical, Mr. A had become very attached to the puppy and more than willing to look after it. This felt like something to pursue.*

> LS: "What about your dog?"
> Mr. A: (A bit startled by my question): "The dog was in the garden." (Pause.) "In fact it never occurred for me to look for her."
> (I spoke to Mr. A how he had talked previously about the dog, how having her around made him feel better.)

Mr. A: "Yes, it has, it made a really big difference." (At this point, he started to brighten up, smile, there was a sense of pleasure in his voice, he talked about how important the dog had been to him, having the dog around really had helped, how he liked to cuddle the dog, how cute she was.) "People often say having a pet helps, and it sounds a bit naff, but it really does."

When Mr. A reacted by being startled, and then said, with a sense of realization, that it never occurred to him to look for the dog, my initial feeling was of relief. The strategy in this part of the session was starting to head towards a dead end. I took his being startled by my question, and his own observation that it had not occurred to him to look for the dog, as an engagement of his own curiosity and capacity to think. As he went on to talk about the dog, I started to wonder myself why it had not occurred to him to seek out the dog. There was something here about how he was able to obliterate all his connections, including to the dog, when he got into this state, like moving from one world to another in the Pullman novels.

However, I was also aware of a part of me which was not entirely convinced about what was happening, that my question about the dog, and Mr. A's enthusiastic response, could be seen as a slightly too neat "solution" to his panic in the session. I knew Mr. A hated loose ends and hated feeling dependent. With these thoughts in mind, I was interested in his remarks about how "naff" it might sound to find his dog so cute, and how much he enjoyed cuddling her. His remark brought to mind some recent experiences where two friends of mine had each recently got a dog and told me how much it had changed their life for the better. My own reaction was quite split, I was sceptical, yet they were both people whose opinion I respected. I took my musing as a further indication that I was both sceptical and convinced about Mr. A's recovery in the session.

One of the more recent influences on my thinking has been the work of Antonino Ferro and his colleagues on how the "characters" patients speak about can be seen to embody affects, states of mind or relationships which would otherwise not find expression. By introducing the dog, I was doing what Ferro has called "casting for characters"; that is, trying to find a figure or character which could serve as an "affective hologram" of how Mr. A had been feeling on Saturday and perhaps how he was now feeling in the session (Ferro, 2009, p.226; Spurling, 2012).

LS: (We were now almost at the end of the session.) "How are you feeling now in the session?"

Mr. A: "Rather better."

LS: "Why do you think that might be?"

Mr. A: "I don't know."

LS: "Talking with me about your feelings of anxiety and panic has really helped you, as has us exploring together what it all means."

Mr. A: "I suppose so. I am feeling better. Thank you."

LS: (Ends the session.)

I wanted to end the session with some enquiry about Mr. A's state of mind – was he still feeling panicky? – and to refer to what had happened in the session. I was aware of my interventions here being rather heavy-handed, with me coming over as a teacher wanting acknowledgement of what I have been doing. At some level, I felt a bit stumped, if not irritated, by Mr. A's "I don't know" in reply to my question about why he thought he was feeling better, registering it as a refusal to acknowledge the work he and I had done in the session, and so possibly an attack on the whole process. I decided not to address this, partly because my thoughts here were unformed and unprocessed, and partly because we were now right at the end of the session, never a good time to start opening something up. Instead I opted to spell out to Mr. A that his feeling better was a result of something he and I had done together in the session, and to challenge his deeply held idea that to ask for and seek help was a sign of weakness and failure. His "I suppose so" was a less than wholehearted endorsement of the value of talking about his feelings, but his "I am feeling better", which was said with conviction, seemed an acknowledgement that something important had happened in the session, that he had managed to recover from his state of anxiety. I also had the fleeting thought that his way of speaking could be heard as if the whole point of the session was to make him feel better, as though the therapy was no more than a rather time-consuming and expensive kind of pill he was having to take. He often compared coming to therapy to going to the dentist, something one does not like to do but one needs to go as it will make one better. I had similar thoughts about his "thank you". It was unusual for him to express any gratitude, and I took it as a genuine expression of what he felt towards me. But it also seemed a rather polite way to end the session, as though we had no more than a formal and purely functional relationship to each other.

I ended the session in a somewhat ambivalent state of mind. I felt we had achieved something in the session, that Mr. A had had an experience of recovering from his mini panicky state, and that we had got a little further in understanding a particular quality of the feelings that overwhelm him. This seemed to be a particular kind of aloneness or isolation, when he felt other people were not only absent but actually unreachable, as though on a different planet. He had spoken before of such feelings, but not with such intensity and clarity. I also felt the linking between his feelings in the session, his experience on the previous Saturday, and his experience at the time his mother died were more clearly and firmly established. However, this took considerable activity on my part to make these links and keep them on the table, and I am never entirely happy with this; it is always better if these links are made by the patient.

Looking back at this session in the light of subsequent sessions

I have attempted in this account to distinguish between my practical reasoning (in italics), which is more forward-looking and less processed, from that of my theoretical reasoning (in bold), which looks back over what has occurred, is more articulated and might make direct references to analytic concepts and exemplars. Although this distinction between practical and theoretical reasoning is a useful one, assigning a piece of thinking to one or the other often seems arbitrary, as much of my clinical thinking contains elements of both forms of reasoning. This is particularly true when it comes to evaluating my strategy and interventions, where I seem to be employing both the anticipatory perspective of practical reasoning and the backward-looking view of theoretical reasoning.

The retrospective evaluation carried out in the process of theoretical reasoning does not simply end when the session finishes. It carries over to the next sessions, indeed in some form over the whole of the subsequent therapy. This is particularly true when significant events or experiences occur in a particular session which the clinician may be struggling to understand and may be feeling unsure whether he has adopted the best approach. This was my experience in this session. I was not sure how well I had understood Mr. A's panic at home and in the session, and had mixed feelings about how well I had responded to his anxiety. So I was particularly interested in seeing whether in the next few sessions further light could be thrown on Mr. A's experiences and on the effectiveness of my approach.

We saw in Chapter 5 (p.83) that the time frame of the normal testing and evaluation that goes on in craft work is bounded by the "action-present"; that is, a timescale that can be kept in mind in the course of the work. I made the arbitrary decision to make notes on the next three sessions in the hope this would provide an adequate "action-present". I will present a brief account of these sessions, focusing solely on the material in those sessions where I was consciously looking out for material which would help me evaluate the work done in the session described.

The next three sessions

In the next session, session two, which took place two days later, Mr. A spoke more about the feeling of being alone which he had felt on the Saturday night. He clarified that these feelings were very different to the "grim thoughts" that often paralyze and terrify him; these felt more like going mad (he used the image again of his brain going off its tracks). He said that comparing these feelings to how he had felt when his mother died had been useful, he had been thinking about that, he felt when he was told she was dead his world changed completely, everything before seemed fake and only her death seemed real. He spoke of how he used to wander into her room, which his father had kept as it was before, and even last week had thought about his mother's room before he went to sleep. I remember being surprised to hear that he thought so often about his mother's room; he had never mentioned this before.

In the session after that, session three, which took place four days later, he said the previous session had been helpful, and then spoke at some length about having to deal with a particular incident concerning his father and how helpful Anita had been. I noted that he had never before talked about his wife in this way, usually he felt he had to cope with all of his father's difficulties on his own. I also noted that his father was now starting to see Mr. A and Anita more as a couple – hitherto Mr. A had felt that although his father was polite around Anita and his children, he never felt his father could see him as a proper husband or father. I commented on both of these and Mr. A agreed. He went on to say he had noticed his behaviour around exams was changing. Previously he had never talked to other candidates but now he was initiating conversations with some of the other candidates. He said his exams had in fact been ok. He thought what had helped was that the invigilator he really liked was there, "the one who is really strict, who tells us what we can and can't do", and how good that was; it made him feel better.

In the final session in this sequence, session four, which took place one day after session three, Mr. A described feeling very wound up with his father, who had become ill by neglecting himself, and who had also got into trouble over some dealings with other people. The expectation was that Mr. A had to sort all of these things out. In this session, I focused particularly on how embarrassed Mr. A was in telling me of these incidents, and of the stress he was under. I tried to explore with him the nature of this embarrassment, which he found difficult. The nearest he could get to was: "it's the words coming out of my mouth, I don't want to be talking about them, it's embarrassing...I have to speak these words." In speaking of how his father expected him to solve all his problems, he came up with an image he used to have as a young child, of "my mother and father piled on top of me, I am at the bottom, I can't breathe".

Retrospective understanding and evaluation: Operation of my appreciative system

Trying to reconstruct my clinical thinking in these sessions solely from the point of view of retrospective understanding of what happened previously risks giving a distorted picture. This retrospective understanding would not have been done for its own sake (as in supervision or clinical discussion), but as part of the practical and theoretical reasoning in the session itself. Furthermore, in writing this account, I am presenting the evaluative process as much more deliberate and articulate than it was. Nevertheless, this process of retrospective evaluation is an intrinsic part of the way analytic therapy works, and it is important, whatever the limitations of my method, to try to draw a picture of how such evaluation was carried out.

Looking at this sequence of sessions from this evaluative perspective, I found the next session, session two, to throw further light on the fake/real distinction, and to tie it more closely to Mr. A's depression and grief. I took his telling me about his mother's room, and how he still thought of it, as confirmation of my guiding idea, that his mother's death, and how it was dealt with, was the key experience from his past for understanding his present state of mind, and that it had been useful for me to have pursued it in the session. His statement that he had found the previous session helpful felt like a general endorsement of the direction the therapy was taking.

I took session three as further endorsement of my approach. The more helpful figures of his wife and other exam candidates, and the emerging idea of a couple (Mr. A and his wife in his father's eyes) all seemed to me to herald some new development taking place, with Mr. A, perhaps, starting to move towards a more Oedipal position, and starting to be able to see others as people he could rely on. I remember being struck by his description of the helpful invigilator, and took this as a transference communication and further confirmation he was finding these sessions helpful, that they were enabling him to develop his capacity to think.

I felt the final session in this sequence, session four, continued to build on the work we were doing in teasing out the quality of his different states of mind. In this session, I focused on trying to help Mr. A describe more accurately the nature of his embarrassment in the session in talking about himself. In the course of this exploration, I started to feel there was something about the nature of Mr. A's anxiety, and how it manifested itself in the transference, that I did not understand. His account of how he hated having to speak the words about his father, and in so doing was somehow contaminating himself, struck me forcibly, and I remember playing around with this idea in my mind. Again the childhood image of his parents on top of him, with Mr. A unable to breathe, struck me as a highly resonant image, and I remember thinking this must also be a transference communication of some kind, probably a description of how he sometimes experienced the therapy with me, but I could not quite connect it to the actual session or the previous ones. In speaking of his embarrassment at the words coming out of his mouth, I felt at the time that Mr. A was talking about some kind of very primitive experience, a fusion of physical and emotional experience or word and deed, which was now starting to emerge as his experience in the therapy. This sounded like an important development, one I wanted to track in future sessions.

One of the most interesting features to emerge from this description of the operation of my appreciative system (see Chapter 5, pp.81–3) is how as one problem gets solved, a new one emerges. I took the succeeding three sessions as affirming the correctness of my approach in the session described. In these sessions, Mr. A brought new material and new experiences which signalled a development process. At the same time, my experience in session four was an uncomfortable one that there was some element of the transference that I could not get hold of, and that I had missed in the session described.

Looking at a particular session in the light of what happened next in subsequent sessions is something that happens frequently in supervision and clinical discussion, and provides a valuable retrospective perspective. In this case, we can take the image from Mr. A's childhood that so struck me in session four – "my mother and father piled on top of me, I am at the bottom, I can't breathe" – and look at the session described through its lens. We can speculate that something similar might have occurred in that session that resulted in Mr. A's mini panic attack; that is, Mr. A having an experience of me, or something emanating from me such as my expectations of him, as being on top of him and preventing him from breathing (and, perhaps, also the inverse, of him on top of me or fearing to put himself in that position). Furthermore, this image has clear sexual connotations. It is possible that some of this was picked up in my sense of concern and anxiety over the panic in the session and how it was best managed. But neither my conduct of the session nor my clinical reasoning shows an explicit awareness of this. This illustrates an important feature of analytic work – that our understanding is always trying to catch up with itself, particularly when it comes to appreciating the transference dynamics which usually prove those which are hardest to see.

A view of practice

In writing up this chapter about my work with Mr. A, I am aware of feeling very similar to Joseph's Sandler's description of how practitioners feel when they present their work to their colleagues. He spoke of the "unconscious conviction of many analysts that they do not do 'proper' analysis" (1983, p.38), and therefore expect to be criticized by their colleagues.

It is instructive to think why this might be. Of course it shows that the anxiety of the developing practitioner, that he or she is constantly getting it wrong, never really goes away, and resurfaces in a powerful way when one presents one's work to others. But the anticipation of criticism is also a consequence of something intrinsic to analytic practice, as Sandler describes:

> The conviction that what is actually done in the analytic consulting room is not "kosher", that colleagues would criticize it if they knew about it, comes from the reality that any analyst worth his salt will adapt to specific patients on the basis of his interaction with those patients. He will modify his approach so that he can get as good as possible a working analytic situation developing. To achieve this, he needs to feel relaxed and informal with his patient to an appropriate degree, and at times he might have to depart quite far from "standard" technique. He may be very comfortable with this as long as it is private rather than public, especially in view of the tendency for colleagues to criticize and "supervise" one another in clinical discussions, and the ease with which analytic material can be seen and interpreted in different ways. (Ibid. p.39)

What Sandler calls "the need to adapt to specific patients on the basis of his interaction with them" is something that over the course of any therapy becomes so ingrained in the way we work that it is very hard to describe it without making it sound like one is working in a superficial and clichéd way. The session described with Mr. A can really only be understood in the context of the work we had been doing together over the previous four years. The way I thought about Mr. A and my work with him as described in the session was based on an ongoing series of comparisons between his "normal" way of speaking and behaving and what I saw as modifications of or deviations from what I expected. These expectations and anticipations were contained in my working models, through which I listened to what Mr. A said to me. In my reconstruction of my clinical thinking, both practical and theoretical, I have tried to allude to these working models. I found this to be a difficult task. The models that were more closely tied to theoretical understanding (and so might be seen as the "intermediate theoretical segments" in play in the session; see Chapter 4, p.55) were the easiest to see, as they formed part of my theoretical reasoning. But I have found it very difficult to try to spell out the "scale model", the working model which was closest to my experience of Mr. A in the session (see Chapter 4, pp.71–2). This is why one needs the perspective of other people in order to see more clearly the assumptions that underlie what we "see" in a session. In this case, where this other perspective is lacking, I have chosen to describe a session which was rather unusual, in that Mr. A did not often develop a sense of panic in a session. In having to move from a more "problem-solving" to a "problem-setting" stance, my thinking was more available (and probably more active) than it might otherwise have been.

A further reason for anticipating criticism is that writing in this way brings out the contingent nature of analytic work. The picture that emerges is that any session is constructed out of all the interactions between patient and therapist. If any of my interventions had been different, this would have affected Mr. A's response, which would in turn have impacted on me, and so on. In other words, the session is full of countless "what-ifs". And as soon as one opens the door to alternative ways of conducting the session, one becomes aware of all the things one didn't do which might have produced a different or better outcome. But what emerges clearly in this account is that this constant evaluation of one's work, in the light of the patient's feedback, is a feature of all competent analytic practice. It is a form of self-reflection that is quite different to the anxiety-driven self-criticism of many developing practitioners that they never get it right (see Chapter 1).

9

TWO SESSIONS FROM A BRIEF THERAPY (WITH A COMMENTARY BY DOROTA JAGIELSKA-HALL)

In this chapter, I will attempt to reconstruct the clinical thinking that has informed the work of a colleague, Dorota Jagielska-Hall, who is a qualified and experienced clinical psychologist. I have taken the first two sessions from a 16-session therapy which she conducted under my supervision in a National Health Service specialist psychotherapy out-patient department in which I work. In writing the account of the two sessions, I have relied on Dorota's process notes of the sessions described. All the sessions were taped (apart from the first one) and Dorota wrote her notes after listening to the tape of that session. I have read Dorota's notes from all of the sessions and listened to tapes from three of the sessions (although not of the two sessions described in this chapter). On the basis of this comparison between tapes and notes, I considered the process notes to be a reasonably reliable account of the sessions described, in the sense that they give an account of much of what was actually said between Dorota and her patient (certainly a much more reliable rendition than one dependent solely on memory and ret-rospective notes). Furthermore, the notes are written in a particularly open and transparent way, which leaves many traces and clues for a reconstruction of Dorota's clinical thinking.

I chose this piece of work not only because of the quality of the "data" (Dorota's process notes) but also because I considered it a good example of competent work, and so of value in investigating the relationship between clinical thinking and good practice. My judgement about

Dorota's competence was based partly on my experience of supervising her work and partly on the outcome – the therapy worked. I saw the patient for two initial consultations prior to the therapy with Dorota and I saw the patient again six months after the end of the therapy for a follow-up session. The patient was considerably less depressed in the follow-up meeting, there was something more solid and lively about her, she was appreciative of Dorota and her way of working and could attribute her improvement to the quality of the therapy.

Although I am the author of this chapter, which makes it a monologue, it is the product of a dialogue between Dorota and myself. This collaborative process began in the supervision sessions. Because I only decided to use this therapy in the book after the therapy and supervision of this work had ended, I have not made use of the supervision experience in giving this account. Bringing in material from the supervision, particularly the voices of the other group members, would have added another dimension to this account. Furthermore, in bringing in my own voice as supervisor, it would have made clearer how supervision influenced Dorota's approach. But perhaps one advantage of the decision to use the therapy only after it had been completed is that there was no intrusion of "research interests" in the way the therapy was conducted.

In the chapter, Dorota's voice first comes in with her process notes, which I have reproduced in the account that follows. The material for the chapter was gathered in the following way. After reading the process notes, I wrote a long and detailed commentary on each of the sessions and sent this commentary to Dorota. She sent back to me her commentary on my commentary. I then edited and revised the chapter and sent her this version, to which she made some changes to her own commentary. This is the version reproduced in this chapter.

I had not initially intended to use this therapy as an example in this book as it was not conducted as a psychoanalytic therapy. The model used was that of interpersonal therapy (IPT), and Dorota was doing this piece of work in our department in order to learn this model. The main idea in IPT is that the nature and quality of the depressed person's interpersonal network plays a key role in producing and maintaining depression, so the interpersonal therapist explores this network, helping the patient understand their significant patterns of relating, and trying to help them better manage their relationships and/or develop new ones. IPT draws on psychodynamic ideas as well as those from cognitive behaviour therapy (CBT) and cognitive analytic therapy.

I have trained in IPT and use it in my work. Nevertheless, my psychoanalytic background heavily influences my use of IPT, and

I suspect that the version of IPT I use and teach is much more psychoanalytically oriented than would appear in the IPT manuals (Spurling, 2010, 2012). Furthermore, the kinds of patients we see in our department are normally severely depressed, with many borderline features, which do not easily fit into the classical IPT model for working with depression. In such cases, I have found that it is essential to have an analytic understanding of the depression, especially as it manifests in the transference, and this has influenced how I teach and supervise the IPT approach.

A further complication (another reason I had not initially seen the case as suitable for this book) is that Dorota herself has not undergone a full analytic training. In her commentary for this chapter, she described herself as follows:

> I work in an integrative way, drawing on psychodynamic, CBT (especially third wave) and systemic models in my practice. I have different levels of experience in the various models I use. In respect to the psychodynamic model, I see myself as a developing practitioner, having worked in this model for a year during my training and later developing my knowledge though short courses and seminars.

In reading Dorota's account of her work, the influence of other approaches is sometimes evident, and in her commentary she makes clear that her way of working is informed by trying to apply the model of IPT. Nevertheless, I made the decision to use the material for this chapter as I found her work and her thinking with this patient, as I have reconstructed it, to serve as a good illustration of analytic principles and an analytic way of thinking. This raises interesting questions, which would take me beyond the scope of this book, about the differences in approach and practice between those, like Dorota, who have been trained in a number of different models, and those who have had an exclusively analytic training.

There are other distinctive features of this therapy which I have not explored, as they would take me away from my prime task, the reconstruction of Dorota's clinical thinking. Whereas the therapy described in the previous chapter was part of my private practice as a psychoanalytic psychotherapist, this therapy took place in a public setting, with the therapy offered being part of an overall "treatment plan" made available by the team as a whole. The patient had been assessed by one of the senior members of the team (myself in this case) who also conducted the follow-up meeting after the conclusion of the therapy. In the follow-up, other therapies may be offered as part of the treatment plan. This is a very different way of thinking about therapy to that conducted in one's private practice, where the treatment setting does not extend beyond the therapist–patient dyad.

Also, as happens in all public settings, the therapy described was a time-limited therapy, not an open-ended one as is normal in private practice. This makes a significant difference to the experience of both patient and therapist. The time limit imposes a pattern of beginning, middle and end onto the therapy, and creates clinical experiences, such as arriving at the "half-way" mark of the therapy with its foreshadowing of the ending, that are absent in open-ended work. These features of the setting are important and need to be taken into account in understanding how Dorota has worked with this patient. But they form part of Dorota's overall approach, and I have not attempted to tease out the particular influence of these features as opposed to any others that have impacted on her way of working.

For the purposes of this chapter, I have chosen to write about the first two sessions of the therapy, with a brief reference to sessions three and four. I thought it would be interesting to focus on these sessions as it is in the initial sessions that a therapist usually establishes the aims and approaches that serve to structure the ensuing conduct of the therapy.

Initial consultations

The patient, Ms. B, was a middle-aged woman who presented in her two initial consultations with me as severely depressed, with ongoing thoughts of wanting to die. She led a very isolated and restricted life, telling me she had no friends, and spent her time sleeping or finding ways of amusing herself. She had recently left her country of origin, France, because she had lost her job and the housing that went with it, and was finding it hard to adjust to life in England. Ms. B described herself as having been depressed all her life, and I was very struck by the depth and severity of her depression. She spoke in a very flat and hopeless tone, characterizing her whole life as having been a failure – "I have no job, no husband, no children, I have no future" and so on. At other times, she could become angrily compliant. She told me little about her background, except to say the main event in her childhood had been the death of her mother when was in her early teens. Her mother had died after a long and protracted illness, and during the mother's illness, the patient spent several months staying with relatives. Her father died when the patient was in her 30s. She had a brother and sister, both of whom still lived in France. She had not kept in contact with either of them. She had little hope in therapy working, but felt so desperate she was willing to give it a try.

I remember having some concerns about the depth and severity of Ms. B's depression, and wondering whether any kind of therapy would be able to reach her. There was a danger that if she experienced the therapy as yet another failure, this would simply reinforce her own negativity and hopelessness. But I thought it a risk worth taking, as I had also felt there was a willingness and perhaps determination in her to get help, which might bode well. In view of her social isolation, I talked about group therapy with her, which we offer in our department, but she felt she did not have the resources to contemplate this, so we opted for a plan of individual therapy, either in its own right, or as part of a treatment plan which might involve joining a therapy group at a later stage, to be decided at the follow-up session. I thought she might find the more exploratory nature of a more formal psychodynamic approach difficult initially, so suggested IPT, which she liked the sound of and agreed to.

How the chapter was written

In the following description of the therapy, I begin with an account based on Dorota's notes made after each session. As her notes for each session were quite detailed, I have taken extracts or omitted sections where necessary. The description of each session is written in the first person. This is then followed by my own commentary on the session. This is in turn followed by Dorota's comments on both the sessions and my commentary.

For reasons of confidentiality, all identifying features of the patient have been changed, and any such features which appear in the description of the sessions, or the commentaries, have been omitted. I have made no changes to Dorota's notes or commentary, except where they mention one of these identifying features.

Session one (from Dorota's notes)

Ms. B reported she had been depressed since her teenage years. She spent 17 years seeing a psychiatrist, who prescribed medication and saw her for support. She had had electroconvulsive therapy (ECT) in the past. Prior to her move to England, she had not been happy and had been depressed, but she had had a job, and had friends and had been able to keep going. However, on coming to England, her life had gone downhill.

She said she spent her days listening to the radio; she tries to read but cannot focus. She said her sleep was disturbed, she could sometimes only sleep for a few hours, she was often tired in the afternoon and she said she lies down but does not sleep. She said she did not have much belief in talking therapies or medication, none of it had helped in the past, but was willing to give it a go. She did not have a goal for the therapy, perhaps just to "keep going", perhaps to try to get a job and keep it. I talked about gradual goals.

I asked about suicidal thoughts. She tried to commit suicide in her 20s by taking an overdose, she currently thinks about death and would like to die, but not by killing herself, she would like it to "just happen". She has no suicidal plan as would not like to get it wrong, for example ending up disabled and in a wheelchair. She said she is not afraid of death, she does not see it as something sad, as she can see no point in life, "perhaps we all hang on to life for some reason". I asked whether there was any reason for keeping her here, and she said there was nothing, at least nothing she was consciously aware of. She told me both parents had been high achievers, as are her sister and brother.

She said she did not want to think too much in the therapy. She would prefer to tell me about herself and for me to give her advice on what to do, give her options, she would like to be guided. I asked whether she was interested in taking up the therapy and she said she was. Dates and times were arranged.

Commentary on session one (LS)

The first session sounds to me rather like my own two consultations, with Ms. B displaying the classic picture of a melancholic state of mind, as described by Freud and others: lack of motivation, restlessness, loss of pleasure in living and self-hatred. In line with this, she indicates her wish not to think, not to take the initiative or be anything but a passive and compliant recipient of what therapy might give her. This does not seem like an auspicious start, and it is not easy at this point to see what can possibly be achieved in the remaining 15 sessions.

In terms of what is conveyed in the notes, this session seems to have taken the form of Ms. B talking about her depression and suicidal wishes, her present situation and some aspects of her past. Dorota appears to make few interventions. This is perhaps because she takes this session as a kind of preliminary session, where the contract is established. Ms. B is asked whether she wishes to start the therapy and she says she does.

Looking at the types of basic interventions (see Table 9.1), there is an explicit reference to therapeutic goals, "I talked about gradual goals."

Table 9.1: Categories of basic interventions (brief version of Table 3.1)

1. Maintaining the basic setting.
2. Adding an element to facilitate unconscious process.
3. Questions, clarifications and re-formulations, aimed at making matters conscious.
4. Designating here-and-now emotional and fantasy reading of the situation with therapist.
5. Constructions directed at providing elaborated meaning.
6. Enactments as deviations from the therapist's normal way of working.

This intervention, although having the appearance of a concrete and perhaps rather formulaic comment, may also be seen as a more potent intervention. It appeals to the conscious level, how we will work, but has strong unconscious resonances, conveying an idea of containment, of giving something in manageable doses. Again, "I asked whether she was interested in taking up the therapy" is an intervention consciously setting the contract, but the way it is phrased – invoking interest, drive (taking up), assuming she might be capable of wanting something – can be seen as reaching to unconscious levels by attributing to her a capacity to want something and inviting her to act upon it.

Session one (Dorota's comments on her work and on my commentary on this session)

My preferred practice, even in short-term structured work, is to give more space to clients in the first session. This allows me to observe how they use the session, whether they invite me in, their way of relating to me, etc. I become more active if they find it hard to cope with or organize the space. Contrary to what is conveyed in the notes, I think I was fairly active in this first session, as I felt the need to keep our conversation going. Perhaps my notes bear the marks of "analytic superego" interference, as my activity was mostly restricted to asking questions, rather than "proper" interventions, so it did not feel important enough to mention in the notes.

The first session with Ms. B felt dry and "interview-like". She answered my questions, giving me a factual account of her life, but did not reveal much of herself. She quickly declared a lack of interest and belief in therapy, explaining that she was attending the session only in compliance with her doctor's recommendation. I was concerned about how the treatment was going, until the moment, not strongly picked up in Laurence's commentary, when Ms. B remarked that "perhaps we all hang on to life for some reason". When I asked what her reason for "hanging on here" was, she said there was nothing, but then added "at least nothing that I am consciously aware of". This comment gave me hope, as I heard it as her signalling to me that there is more to her than the compliance and concreteness she presented with, even though she may not have had access to it at that time.

I think this set up the context for the other interventions, my comment on gradual goals and asking Ms. B if she was interested in therapy, which are discussed in Laurence's commentary. Rather than a fully conscious decision on my part to appeal to both the conscious and the unconscious levels of thinking, I heard the patient's comment about hanging on to life as such, and responded in a similar way. Perhaps it was in itself an expression of working in "gradual/manageable chunks". I think my tuning in to the way she chose to communicate and also how much she could manage at the time helped to establish the therapeutic alliance, which emerged in the next session.

Session two (Dorota's notes)

I explained that I wished to record the sessions and she agreed, saying, "I will do as you command." She seemed quieter, less engaged. There were some long silences. When I asked what she was thinking about, she was not able to say. Sometimes she needed me to repeat myself.

She gave no clear answer to whether she had any thoughts about our first meeting. But she did say it had been on her mind, and triggered thoughts about where she sees herself: that she has no life, no friends, she is not sleeping, not eating (she eats once a day, she does not cook, she uses the microwave or has things like yoghurt, sometimes she does not eat for a whole day), she is tired all the time. It makes her feel "what's the point?" I asked whether she planned to act on this and she said no. She said, "I feel bored thinking and talking about myself."

I tried to take up what worried her, but she became silent. I commented on the silence, and she said she felt she was more herself this week. I said perhaps she had more hope than last week, and we tried to think about what had changed between then and now, but she did not know. I wondered about her expectations, perhaps not very conscious ones, about the session making a difference. Ms. B said she knew nothing would change after one or ten sessions, but agreed that perhaps unconsciously she hoped for some change.

I wondered what it would be useful to talk about, and asked Ms. B if there was something she wanted to talk about; she said no. I suggested talking about others, since she was bored of talking about herself; she asked "who?" I asked if anyone came to mind. Ms. B was quiet for a while. I asked if she could tell me about the psychiatrist. Ms. B said she had treated her with medication, she saw her every two to three weeks, but when she lost her job, she lost contact with her. She talked about losing her job, the unfairness of it, how she was picked on. She became more alive here; we talked about how unexpected and unfair it was. She said how when she went to the job centre here she was talked down to and people made it hard for her to make a complaint or find new work. She did not tell her family back in France. I asked about her family, her brother and sister. She feels embarrassed to make contact with them; they do not know she has moved to this country. I asked about each member (I had to ask or she would become silent). When I commented on the fact that she seemed more alone in the session and alone with her thoughts today, she apologized. I explained that there was no need to apologize. We were here to understand what was happening and the more we understood, the more chance we had to change it. Part of this was noticing what was happening in the session. I said that I brought up difficult topics and her reaction was to withdraw, to become silent and lost in her thoughts. Ms. B agreed.

I summarized her story: that not only has she moved countries, to one where she had no links, but all links with her previous life had been taken away. I felt Ms. B was more able to relate to talking about this. She said in her home country it had taken a long time to get her life on track – job, friends – she never expected this to happen. She said it was very difficult to establish a new life, even when one is happy and choosing to come somewhere, but when someone comes over as depressed, the task is enormous. I said perhaps she was now at a stage where she could start reclaiming her life back step by step. I felt I needed to keep hope for her, so I said from where I was sitting, I could see small things we could work towards changing.

I signalled the end of the session and checked times with her over the upcoming Christmas break. Ms. B reported she did not do holidays. I enquired whether it was more difficult over Christmas as that was when she had been sacked; she said maybe, but it did not seem to resonate.

The session ran over by five minutes.

Commentary on session two (LS)

Because of the relative brevity of the notes for session one, it is hard to gauge the quality of the therapeutic alliance that might have been established in that session. Indeed, what is conveyed is the severity of the depression. However, session two starts in a way that suggests some form of therapeutic alliance has been established. Ms. B says the first session had been on her mind and that it had "triggered thoughts" in her. But if there is an alliance, it seems precarious, as these thoughts are depressive and possibly suicidal, and Dorota describes Ms. B as "less engaged". Her compliance is evident in how she responds to Dorota's request to tape the sessions, "I will do as you command", and she goes on to speak of her boredom about trying to speak about herself. Dorota tries to get to what might lie behind her depression, suicidal thoughts and boredom – "I tried to take up what worried her." This is a key move in a psychoanalytic therapy, trying to get at feelings or thought at an unconscious or preconscious level which might account for the patient's particular experience or state of mind. But here, this intervention does not seem to lead anywhere; Ms. B "became silent". The therapist then comments on the patient's silence.

Switch from problem-solving to problem-setting

Dorota does not elaborate on this or why she did so. I take it as an example of what a therapist does when she judges the therapy to have become stuck, the shift from problem-solving, where therapy progresses as usual, to problem-setting, where the patient's response (or lack of response) indicates that the therapy has become unproductive or stuck. In that case, the therapist has to step back and re-define the problem so that the therapy can progress. I think Dorota takes the silence as a form of resistance or withdrawal, and decides to change tack by directly addressing the silence. The "problem" has now been re-set or re-defined. It is no longer "how do I explore with the patient what feelings or thoughts might lie behind her state of mind?" but "how can we understand this silence which seems to deaden or close down the therapy" and, perhaps, "once we have understood this silence, how can the patient be helped to communicate instead of remaining silent?"

The re-definition of the problem and change of approach results in something different happening. Ms. B says she feels more herself this week. I think Dorota takes this comment as a new development, indicating Ms. B now felt more in tune with herself, more relaxed and engaged. On the basis of this, Dorota introduces a new theme, that of Ms. B having expectations of the therapy and hope that she might change, and that something has already changed between this session and the previous one. By this comment, Dorota tries again to make a link with the previous session.

Although this elicits a response that appears to get no further – Ms. B "did not know" and then asserts that she knows nothing will change – Ms. B then agrees with Dorota that, unconsciously, she might hope for change. In describing this part of the session, Dorota uses the phrase "we tried to think", suggesting that now an interchange of some sort has taken place involving Ms. B doing something she has stated she does not want to do, namely think about herself and what is happening in the therapy.

Dorota then "wonders" what it would be useful to talk about, and in the next part of the session, there is some exploration of Ms. B's relationship with other people and of what happened when she moved to England. Dorota notes that Ms. B became more alive at some points in this part of the session. This part of the therapy, and the rest of this session, has a different feel about it. Although there are still periods of silence and withdrawal, Ms. B is now described as engaged in a way she was not at the beginning of the session. Dorota is able to "wonder", which suggests there is now more space for thinking and exploring. This way of conducting the session suggests a change in how Dorota has been thinking about the session. Up until this point, she has conducted the session as though her main task has been that of establishing a therapeutic alliance. I think she now feels, however tentative and precarious this alliance might be, that this has been sufficiently achieved so that a more mutually explorative approach can now be adopted.

Mutual exploration of defences

Indeed, in the next part of the session, Dorota makes a comment that can be imagined as having a powerful effect, and that perhaps she would not have been able to make earlier, namely that Ms. B "seemed more alone in the session". It is interesting to think about the purpose of this simple remark, which like many of Dorota's comments seems an invitation to Ms. B to think on a more conscious level, while at the same time designed to strike chords at a more preconscious or unconscious level. By using the term "alone", Dorota may be suggesting that Ms. B's usual retreats into silence and withdrawal have now changed into an intersubjective experience, along the lines of Winnicott's ideas on the developmental importance for the infant or child of being able to be "alone in the presence of mother". Ms. B's response is to apologize. I think Dorota takes this as confirmation of the correctness of her intervention. She goes on to speak about the purpose of the therapy, which is not to make judgements about what is right or wrong, but to understand what is happening to Ms. B in her life with a view to changing it. She explains how this will be done, by "noticing what was happening in the session", for instance "I said I brought up difficult topics and her reaction was to withdraw, become silent and lost in her thoughts. Ms. B agreed."

Ms. B's defence of withdrawal has now become a topic for mutual exploration. This extended interchange can be seen as building on and perhaps elaborating what happened in the first part of the session, when Dorota "commented" on Ms. B's silence.

How the transference is conceived and addressed

These interventions address the here-and-now in the room. They build on and elaborate Dorota's earlier strategy of commenting directly on Ms. B's silence. Now her silence can more clearly interpreted as a defence. Working with transference is the most distinctive feature of psychoanalytic work. In my reading of this session, it is this opening up the transference dimension, originally by "commenting" on her silence and now elaborated in this sequence, which seems to have been the decisive element in establishing a therapeutic alliance with Ms. B.

We can then consider how Dorota uses the transference. She does not make a transference interpretation about how Ms. B may be experiencing her; that is, speak "of" the transference. To do so would probably involve drawing on the stock of potential transference figures and situations already described by Ms. B: the psychiatrist who stuck with her but with whom she lost contact, or the family members who would be embarrassed by her, or the people in the job centre who looked down on her. Nor is she working "in" the transference, in the sense of speaking as though she has become the particular transference figure Ms. B is responding to, with the aim of elaborating on the nature and characteristics of this transference figure (see Chapter 3, pp.49–50, for an account of this distinction between interpretations "of" and "in" the transference). Dorota's comments are more explanatory, she is speaking to Ms. B "about" the transference and, in so doing, inviting her to explore it. It may be that this more "teachery" quality owes something to Dorota's CBT background, but I think she is also doing something which is essential in any analytic therapy; that is, laying the ground for an exploration of the transference, whether this is done more directly and explicitly (interpretations "of" the transference) or indirectly and allusively (working "in" the transference).

We can get a sense of Dorota's preferred way of exploring transference, at least with Ms. B, by taking an example from the next session. Here is the relevant passage from her notes from session three.

On my asking what else she did over the week, she told me she is reading a book on "self-therapy". I expressed an interest in this, as she told me she did not expect therapy to work. Ms. B smiled, and said it was obvious she was interested, but she prefers to learn things from books, "I trust books more than people." I remarked they may feel more reliable, they don't change their mind or disappear.

I take Dorota's remark as an example of what Thomas Ogden calls "tuning in" to the particular mode of experience of someone operating at the paranoid-schizoid level. Ogden writes:

when working with patients generating experience in a predominantly paranoid-schizoid mode, one must couch one's interventions in language that reflects the concreteness of the patient's experience; otherwise, patient and analyst have the experience of talking in a way that, in the words of one such patient, "completely misses one another". (1992, p.22)

He gives as an example: "one does not talk about the patient's feelings that he is like a robot, one talks with the patient about what it feels like to be a robot" (ibid. p.22). One particularly effective way of tuning in to the patient's experience is by speaking "in" the transference, which is I think what Dorota does here. She accepts Ms. B's assertion that books are more trustworthy than people and elaborates on it by alluding to the transference situation – that she is not a book but a person, and as such has a separate mind to Ms. B, which makes her untrustworthy – in such a way as to leave it open to Ms. B how she takes this remark.

Making an initial formulation

With the opening up of the transference dimension further strengthening the therapeutic alliance, Dorota goes on to make a construction or formulation – "I summarized her story" – in terms of the patient having lost her links to her country of origin and struggling to forge new links and connections to her new home. Ms. B is described as being more able to relate to this story, and, indeed, goes on to elaborate on it, which I think Dorota takes as confirmation of her formulation. The formulation can be seen as a way of establishing with Ms. B an agreed aim of the therapy; that is, to mourn the loss of the links to her former home and life and establish better links with her present life.

The session ends shortly afterwards with some discussion of breaks and dates for subsequent sessions.

Aims, strategies, types of interventions and evaluations

If we look at the session as a whole, we can identify the main aims, strategies and types of interventions used. The overall *aim* of the therapy is taken as helping Ms. B become less depressed, and a more specific aim has been identified as helping her mourn the loss of her old way of life and thereby feel more at home in her new life. A further aim seems to be that of giving her hope, to "keep hope for her". Or perhaps this might be seen as part of Dorota's more *strategic* thinking, as how she might enable Ms. B to mourn her losses and re-establish links. It might also be part of what Dorota states as her main way of achieving her aims, working with "gradual goals".

The notion of working with gradual goals seems to define the particular rhythm of the work with Ms. B. The session can be seen as consisting of a number of segments of intense interaction. These are grouped around particular themes, for example exploring her silence, describing what happened when she moved from France to England, or making contact with other people. Only when Ms. B signals her agreement or understanding of the point being made does the therapist move on.

Looking at Dorota's more specific *interventions* (see Table 9.1), many of them seem to have the aim of making matters conscious. She asks many questions, she clarifies and paraphrases and she gives a number of explanations. Her general style of making interventions is to spell things out as much as she can. But such interventions, such as her "commenting" on Ms. B's silence, can also be seen as "adding an element to facilitate unconscious process", in this case, her defences against engagement, as well as an allusion to the here-and-now experience. My impression overall is that her interventions appear directed at more conscious levels of experience, but in fact are delivered in such a way as to activate resonances at a more unconscious level.

My impression of Dorota's way of working, as conveyed in her writing (and from supervision), is that she makes many on-the-spot *evaluations* about the therapy and her patient's response to her interventions. This is conveyed in the way she notices small changes in Ms. B. In order to track the effect of her interventions, Dorota makes particular use of questions which she uses as probes (see Chapter 5, p.84), for instance when she asks what Ms. B thinks about the previous session, or what she thinks has changed. In this way, she aims to identify the "live edge" of the work.

The affective dimension

So far I have described Dorota's clinical thinking as the outcome of judgements that, although operating largely at a level just below consciousness, can be thought of as mainly based on cognitive and rational thinking. However, this leaves out the question as to how far these judgements are also influenced by emotional and affective factors, what is normally known as the countertransference. This area would bring in features of the therapist's implicit theories, especially at the more preconscious and unconscious levels. These are liable to become activated in terms of the unconscious expectations and phantasies of the patient, as they are experienced in the transference.

To take account of this dimension of clinical experience, the Working Party on Comparative Clinical Methods described one type of intervention as "sudden and apparently glaring reactions not easy to relate to the analyst's normal method". There is one such example in this session, which is that the session overran by five minutes. In her session notes, Dorota does not discuss how or why this happened, but she does in her notes for the next two sessions, which also overran. I will postpone discussing this boundary issue until later in the chapter (pp.151–5), as I want first to address the question of how far the affective dimension of Dorota's work might have influenced the decision-making process.

The ego-destructive superego

One way of gauging how a clinician is responding affectively and emotionally to their patient is to compare their reactions with one's own. I had not only heard about the patient in supervision, but had met her twice myself, and remember being powerfully affected by the flat and toneless quality of the way she sometimes talked, which seemed to suck the life out of the meeting. Reading Dorota's account of these sessions, I wondered whether she was having a similar response, and if so, how this affected her way of working. In order to think more about this, I turned to a theoretical concept which I have found to be of immense help in my own working with very depressed patients, that of the "ego-destructive superego".

This term has been used to describe depressed patients who have a very powerful self-destructive side to their depression which attacks any gain made in the therapy. Edna O'Shaughnessy writes that in many patients, "the superego, even when primitive and strict, is a guiding force, but in others an abnormal form of the superego is a destroyer of the self, its relations and its objects" (1999, p.811). In order to avoid attacks by the ego-destructive superego, the patient will characteristically feel it is better to have no feelings, thoughts or initiative. Richard Lucas describes the start of an analysis with such a particular patient, who sounds rather like Ms. B:

> [Her] opening remark in her analysis was striking, "I want to be a calm sensible person with no feelings"...this statement underlines the central dynamic to understanding depression, for with the desire for identification with an ideal object, there is no room for separate thinking or expression of needy feelings. All tensions related to one's own needs, and how the idealized object is ignoring them, gets projected and then experienced somatically. (2004, p.274)

Is there an ego-destructive superego here? I think the picture is mixed. On the one hand, Ms. B responds and engages with some of the therapist's responses, which does not fit the picture of an ego-destructive superego. On the other hand, her stated wish not to have to think, the deathly quality of Ms. B's depression and her way of breaking into a depressive discourse as a way of bringing the session to a dead end, have some qualities of "a destroyer of the self". It may be that when such features of an ego-destructive superego appear, they have a powerful effect on Dorota's thinking. Taking this idea further, one can speculate whether her active stance in the conduct of the therapy and her persistence in the face of silence or retreat by the patient is designed to forestall the "pull" of an ego-destructive superego as the destroyer of all links and possibilities of communication. It may also play a part in how the therapist formulates for herself her overriding strategy in this session and for the therapy as a whole: "I felt I needed to keep hope for her."

Session two (Dorota's commentary)

Ms. B's depression felt stronger to me in the second session. When she spoke about "being more herself", the picture in my mind was that of her "pulling herself together" for the first session, but not being able, or willing, to continue this level of effort for the second one. This guided my question about her expectations and whether they were let down after the first session. I recall wondering whether, despite her protestations, Ms. B had quite high, if perhaps not entirely conscious, hopes for the first session and felt disappointed when these did not come true. I believe that discussing potential disappointments with therapy is very important for the therapeutic alliance with all patients. Discussing these disappointments with Ms. B was also important from the point of view of the withdrawing pattern that was beginning to emerge.

Problem-solving vs. problem-setting

This is a very accurate reconstruction of my thinking. Since the first session, I was trying to keep the session going by asking questions. However, the silence felt as if I was doing all the work and Ms. B remained in her preferred position of being guided and not thinking about herself too much. I realised that continuing in this way would not move us forward and decided to change strategy. Paying attention to what happens in the room, how the space of the session is used (silence being one aspect of this), is a part of my usual way of working. Therefore, exploring the silence was a natural way to turn, but it was preceded by a conscious decision that something needed to change. Why did I address this particular silence? I am not sure. The feeling of my current tactic not working was growing stronger, and at some point it felt right to change the direction. I hoped that focusing on the silence would give us a better understanding of what was happening in these moments, allowing us to discover a way of working together. Exploring Ms. B's expectations about therapy was a part of trying to understand where the silence, which I did understand as withdrawal and, to an extent, as resistance, was coming from. It appears that after acknowledging that she had some expectations of being helped by therapy, Ms. B could engage more fully in joint work. In a way, it re-defined the problem from a patient who does not engage because they do not believe therapy will work, to the patient who is hesitant to engage due to another emotion or thought, which we needed to understand.

Ego-destructive superego

I was not familiar with this theory before reading this commentary, so although it could not have influenced my thinking at the time, it fits well my experience in the session. I remember how lifeless Ms. B felt to me, and clearly recall a moment when I felt convinced that some vital parts of her life were irrevocably lost, and nothing could be done about it. Only hearing the thoughts of other members of our supervision group about Ms. B's situation allowed me to question this. I also remember holding on to her initial comment about hanging on to life, which for me expressed hope and the possibility of working together. This seems like my preconscious strategy of avoiding hopelessness. Laurence writes about me "counteracting the 'pull' of the abnormal superego" and it feels very appropriate to describe my experience – it did feel that I needed to carry the conversation on, to prevent lifelessness from engulfing both of us.

Probing, looking for a live edge and sessions' structure

I liked the metaphors of *probes* and *live edge* and think it is a very good description of my practice. This links for me with the structure of the entire therapy. I think there is a specific rhythm in the work with every client. With Ms. B, it felt we were working in "bite-sized chunks", having a break after each more intensive piece of work/interaction, and then, as Laurence noticed, moving on when an agreement or understanding was achieved. Conducting the whole therapy as such was not a conscious decision made at some specific point in time, but a result of tracking the results of each intervention and making small adjustments as we went along. The resulting pattern only became transparent afterwards.

Addressing the transference

I think this is an area where the situational and contextual factors of clinical practice, mentioned in the first chapter, play an important role. In my work I use all the ways of working with the transference discussed by Laurence – speaking of, in and about the transference – depending on the therapy model used and the patient. However, working towards an accreditation in IPT, I am trying to stay close to the model. This, perhaps, makes me less inclined to make interpretations *of* the transference, as I see them as more closely linked with analytic work. Speaking *in* the transference feels to me more consistent with how the therapeutic relationship is used in IPT, and I would agree that this was my preferred way of working with Ms. B.

Why were my initial comments on transference more explanatory, or "teachery", as Laurence puts it? I think the experience of working in the CBT framework, which requires the therapist to be transparent and collaborative, may have played a role in this. At the same time, addressing transference in this way allowed me to explain further what IPT involves, while hopefully easing the experience of shame the next time we needed to focus on Ms. B's behaviour in the room.

The management of therapeutic boundaries

One of the key elements in the way each therapist conducts their session is how they manage the boundaries of the therapy. In these two sessions, the issue is not explicitly addressed by Dorota, apart from her allusion to the fact that she allowed this session to overrun by five minutes. She does not discuss her thinking about this issue in her notes from this session. However, the time boundary comes up in Dorota's process notes from the next two sessions, and I quote from the relevant sections of her notes:

> I asked about her life, and Ms. B told me about how her depression started when she dropped out of college. She went on to talk about the death of her parents. But this part of the session felt dry and lifeless. I ended up extending the session as I did not want to end on the moment her mother died. Ms. B continued talking after I switched off the tape recorder, she said she was planning to go shopping and buy an iPad, and asked me for advice as to whether it would be better to wait until after Christmas. She said she did not like shopping. I said this often happens with things we don't do often; they become difficult.
> (Extract from Dorota's notes on the ending of session three)

> We talked more about her time in France; she became engaged then silent. I commented it was easier to talk about facts and much more difficult to share thoughts, opinions or ideas; this was putting her in a more vulnerable position. Ms. B agreed, saying that talking about her childhood made her think about not having children, this was one of her regrets, but it was too late now (this idea, of things now being too late, was repeated several times during the session). She said she did not feel old, in fact she had always wanted to be old as a child, she had wanted to be like her father, who had been successful in his work, but she had failed. She then looked at the clock, which was two minutes past the time. I said talking was becoming easier towards the end, that important things had been said, but we needed to finish.
> (Extract from Dorota's notes on the ending of session four)

Why did Dorota allow these three sessions to overrun? I would reconstruct her clinical thinking as follows. To end these sessions on time, and without engaging in the social conversation in session three, would risk feeling too much like the therapist was allying herself on the side of hopelessness and nullity, of the life-denying part of the patient. Furthermore, it would risk giving the patient another experience of a cold, harsh, rejecting and inflexible object. In giving hope to the patient,

Dorota acted as though she made the judgement that it was important to end these early sessions on a note of connection, even if it meant the session went over time. This could also have informed the judgement to respond to Ms. B's social conversation at the end of the previous session. Indeed, one could argue that the therapist used this occasion as an opportunity to further the work. She had been talking to Ms. B about how she was no longer used to making connections with people, and she brought in the idea that if we stop doing ordinary things, like shopping, they become more difficult.

At the same time, by noting that she "overran" the session time, Dorota indicates that she knows she has breached one of the boundaries that constitute the therapeutic setting. In so doing, the "container" function of the setting, which establishes the therapeutic space as reliable and consistent, is in danger of being compromised (see e.g. Spurling, 2009, pp.26–27). One consequence of this breach of the boundaries is that the therapist may convey to the patient that, she, the therapist, is having difficulty in managing the boundaries of the setting, thereby giving the patient the experience of the therapist as a weak, hypocritical or unreliable object. In addition, patient and therapist are deprived of an opportunity to explore the meaning and impact of the way the therapist maintains the boundaries of the session, which is a fundamental part of analytic work. One could argue that this is particularly important in time-limited work, where the ending of each session foreshadows the ending of the therapy and how this will be managed and survived by both parties.

From this point of view, Dorota's decision, if it was a decision, to allow these sessions to overrun would constitute an *enactment* on her part. An enactment means a deviation from one's normal standard of good practice. It occurs when the working models, or "intentional representations" that the therapist and patient each build up of the other no longer operate in alignment with each other. Instead there is tension between "the analyst's anticipated action and the patient's hope, based on transferential phantasy" (Bohleber et al., 2013, p.510; see Chapter 6, section "Finding the live edge", pp.95–7). So here, we may surmise, when it came to the end of the session, Dorota became acutely aware of this tension, based on Ms. B's hope of finding an object who could give her hope, which became translated into Dorota's decision to end these sessions on a note of hopefulness and connection.

Once the enactment has occurred, and is recognized as such by the therapist, the therapist can try to make sense of what has occurred. The therapist does this by assuming that the gap between their actual behaviour and how they intended to behave can be made to seem complete if the therapist posits that they have "unconsciously acted consistently with the patient's experience of him" (ibid. p.512). The practitioner can then find his or her own way of solving or resolving this discrepancy. Bohleber et al. give two main ways this is normally done in analytic work. The therapist can either interpret the patient's phantasy which has become actualized and would have induced the analyst to act in the way he did. Or the therapist can seek via self-reflection the roots of his own phantasy representation of the patient, or his response to the activation of the patient's phantasy, and interpret to the patient on the basis of this self-analysis.

Dorota's way of resolving the time-boundary issue seems to have elements of both approaches. What she appears to have done in session four, by drawing Ms. B's attention to her having looked at the clock, was to allow the patient to "notice" the end of the session, in fact a two-minute overrun, and then speak to the patient about the ending of the session and how it was being managed. In other words, she seemed to want to make the ending of the session, with all its difficulties, an intersubjective experience, something that could be observed and talked about. She made the clinical judgement – based on the quality of the sessions so far and perhaps on the material that preceded the patient noticing the time, which suggested she was more in touch with her vulnerability and with her sense of time passing – that the patient was now ready to have this boundary drawn. The logic would seem to be that rather than experienced as a "command" – Ms. B's word when asked in session two about the tape recorder – it could instead be experienced as something that could be shared and negotiated. This appears to be a personal, if not elegant "solution" to the enactment, and certainly to the problem of how to draw the time boundary. In fact in Dorota's notes, for the rest of the therapy there is no further mention of sessions overrunning.

Are we then to think of the time overruns in sessions two to four, and the social conversation after the end of the session in session three, as enactments? If so, they could then be seen as enactments based on the "pull" of the ego-destructive superego, with Dorota running over time in accord with the patient's unconscious expectations that she will provide hope and connection. But her way of ending these sessions can also be seen not as something she was pushed into doing, but as a thought-out strategy, an example of her own personal and particular way of establishing boundaries so as to strengthen the therapeutic alliance and maintain a live edge to her work (see Chapter 5, section "Skill at the live edge", pp.83–5).

Extracts from Dorota's commentary on boundaries

Keeping time boundaries and enactment

There are other than psychodynamic models that impact on my style of working and my way of approaching boundaries. It is, for example, normal for clinical psychologists to work at home with clients with obsessive–compulsive disorder (OCD) or agoraphobia. Additionally, in my main work, a psychology service in a medical setting, psychology sessions need to be at times fitted around medical consultations. I share Valerie Sinason's view that ethical and sustainable practice requires us, rather than stiffly following a rule set up by a training institution or therapy model, to make the boundaries our own (Confer, lecture: "Boundaries in ethical and sustainable practice", March 2014). In order to make these boundaries feel right to us, they need to be negotiated with each patient, depending on their personal characteristics, presenting problem and so on.

Allowing the sessions to run over was, each time, a conscious decision. Finishing on time would mean leaving Ms. B in the "flat and lifeless" place of her mother's death and I felt it would mean "letting the depression win"; not responding to social chat about shopping would perpetuate an experience of harsh, rejecting others. At the same time, I was aware this was not what I consider a good practice, and hence I brought this issue to supervision.

Perhaps the ending of this therapy would be easier if the time boundary was kept intact from the beginning. However, I think it would have been a much "drier" and mechanistic therapy and I'm not sure we would have achieved as much as we did. In clinical psychology, we often use "modelling", which refers to learning through observation of others (social learning theory), and means that we not only talk to patients about what is important for their progress, but also try to demonstrate/embody these qualities in the session. Perhaps for someone with such negative views of herself, who considered herself a failure, it was useful to see that I can make mistakes, or do things in a less than perfect way, and that we could talk about it, repair it and learn from it.

The internal clinical template

Looking at these two sessions in depth, and bringing in Dorota's commentary, we can attempt a brief thumbnail account of her way of working by using the categories of the internal clinical template (see

Chapter 3). The main elements of this template are as follows (see Chapter 3, Table 3.2, p.42):

1. What is wrong with the patient?
2. What needs to happen to change? (How does the therapy work?)
3. What is heard? (What is the listening priority?)
4. What kinds of interventions are needed to further the process?
5. What creates the therapeutic situation? How is the setting and transference thought of?

Dorota's view of what is wrong with Ms. B is best captured in her remark that she could "clearly recall a moment when I felt convinced that some vital parts of her life were irrevocably lost, and nothing could be done about it". This describes Ms. B as suffering from a deficit or defect. "What needs to change" is, firstly, to help Ms. B see that she has lost or even destroyed these functions in herself, and, secondly, enable her to restore them. How this is done is through the repair or creation of links between the different parts of her experience. Dorota's listening priority is to see where she can see evidence of the loss of these functions, for example when Ms. B withdraws in the sessions. She also listens out for signs of strength and resilience in Ms. B, particularly in the capacity to have hope, which she aims to build on in the therapy. Her interventions are designed to provide understanding and foster self-exploration. She focuses on affects, current experiences, and in particular on the quality and patterns of interpersonal relationships. Her interventions tend to be aimed at more conscious understanding, through the use of questions, clarifications and elaborations. Some of them also reverberate at more preconscious and unconscious levels. The analytic situation is designed to foster the processes of repair by creating a setting that encourages mutual exploration of events in the patient's daily life, and also in the here-and-now of the therapy itself. To this end, Dorota tries to establish and maintain the boundaries of the setting in a way that involves the patient and thereby makes them as far as possible a joint creation.

What is good practice?

In his book *The Craftsman* (2008), Richard Sennett describes skilled practice in the following way:

> All craftsmanship is founded on skill developed to a high degree. By one commonly used measure, about ten thousand hours of

experience are required to produce a master carpenter or musician. Various studies show that as skill progresses, it becomes more problem-attuned, like the lab technician worrying about procedure, whereas people with primitive levels of skill struggle more exclusively on getting things to work. At its higher reaches, technique is no longer a mechanical activity; people can feel fully and think deeply about what they are doing once they do it well. (p.20)

In this and the previous chapter, I have attempted to illustrate this process of deep thought and feeling in ordinary skilled analytic practice. Strategies and interventions are not determined in a mechanical way but arise out of the clinician's ongoing clinical thinking, their "feel" for the work and what is needed at any particular point. Once the operation of the practitioner's clinical thinking is brought in, particularly in the form of the constant evaluation of the effectiveness of interventions in the light of the patient's feedback, it becomes more and more difficult to separate out the contributions of patient and therapist. This has long been recognized in psychoanalysis, that the best practice is when neither therapist nor patient is fully in control of the analytic process. From the clinician's point of view, this makes it difficult to judge how much their conduct of the therapy is determined by the more thought-out processes of one's clinical thinking, and how much by more affective, counter-transferiental factors, in particular the patient's unconscious hopes, fears and expectations as expressed through the transference onto the therapist. It is not that the skilled practitioner is immune from the effect of the transference. On the contrary, the skilled clinician is likely to be more open and receptive to the patient's transference than the beginner, so encouraging the patient to bring more of their transference experience into the therapy. The difference with the beginner is that he or she is massively affected by the operation of the transference but does not know it. As skill develops, the clinician has more and more respect for how the patient's transference affects their work and learns to incorporate this impact into their thinking. As part of their development, practitioners become better at recognizing what this feels like, so that fine distinctions can be made. We get to know when this feels too much, when we are too much affected by the patient's transference, and so are likely to be pulled into enactments. We learn that if the impact of the patient's transference seems too little, our work is likely to be superficial, flat or directionless. The best analytic work seems to be when one knows oneself to be affected by the transference, and as such one is in tune with the more unconscious communications from the patient, but in a way that still allows one to think fully and feel deeply. At such times, it may well feel we are on the verge of enactment, as we saw in this and the previous chapter. But this is simply a consequence of skill being applied in a way that is not mechanical and "off the peg" but crafted for the particular patient and setting.

PART IV

Developing the Craft: Examples from Clinical Discussion, Supervision and Teaching

10

THINKING ABOUT INTERVENTIONS: AN EXAMPLE FROM A CLINICAL DISCUSSION GROUP

In the two previous chapters, we looked at examples of clinical work over a whole session or group of sessions in an attempt to reconstruct the clinical thinking of the clinician. We drew on the "comparative instrument" designed by the EPF Comparative Methods Working Group in looking at how each clinician's internal clinical template is constructed. This involved looking at each intervention described in the sessions in order to decide on their purpose.

In my own practice and teaching, I have found this focus on each particular intervention to be of great value. In the accounts of clinical work in the analytic literature, the focus tends to be on the particular interpretation or intervention that supposedly made a difference in a session. The danger of such an approach is that the "little" interventions that we make get ignored, the ones that it is all too easy to miss out in any account of our work. This then gives a misleading picture of analytic work. As we have seen in the previous chapters, each intervention made by the therapist plays a part in determining how any given session develops. So a more accurate picture of any clinical session is to see it as the cumulative outcome of each intervention or move on the part of both therapist and patient (and one would need to include all the non-verbal "moves", including silences, to give a more comprehensive account).

Using the typology of basic interventions devised by the Comparative Methods Working Group, it is then possible in a supervision or clinical discussion group to devote considerable time to looking at any particular intervention. It becomes possible to consider its aim and purpose and what part it may play in how the session turned out.

Categories of interventions

The typology of basic interventions devised by the Comparative Methods Group was described in Chapter 3 and illustrated in Table 3.1 (p.40; reproduced here in abbreviated form in Table 10.1).

I have found this model of working of great value in conducting clinical discussions. It keeps the focus on trying to understand the clinical thinking of the presenter and gets away from making more "supervisory-type" comments as to the appropriateness or otherwise of the presenter's approach. By asking the group to consider each intervention in turn, the group is invited to step into the shoes of the clinician presenting, who in the actual session makes his or her intervention without knowing how the patient will respond and what the implications of their intervention will be.

Table 10.1: Category of basic interventions (abbreviated version of Table 3.1)

Basic intervention	Description
1) Maintaining the basic setting	Basic behaviour creating and maintaining setting
2) Adding an element to facilitate unconscious process	Comments likely to be allusive and brief, aiming to encourage more association or linking at unconscious level
3) Questions, clarifications, re-formulations, aimed at making matters conscious	Less ambiguous than 2), aiming more at conscious level; if addresses analytical relationship, likely to be less temporal or personal than 4)
4) Designating here-and-now emotional and fantasy reading of the situation with therapist	Specifically about current session
5) Constructions directed at providing elaborated meaning	Tying observations together
6) Enactments, deviations from the therapist's normal way of working	Capacity to recognize and acknowledge mistakes and enactments

An example from a clinical discussion group

I will give an example from a clinical discussion group for honorary therapists which I conducted in a National Health Service specialist psychotherapy department. Our working session was one and a half hours. The presenter would come with a typed account of a session, distributed to the group members, with an account of each intervention. The presenter would begin by giving a brief background account of the patient and the therapy so far, and then present the particular session. The group would discuss each intervention using the category of basic interventions to help them think about its purpose, and the presenter would speak about their own thinking about what they were trying to do. If possible, on the basis of our discussion, the group might venture a guess about some feature of the presenter's internal clinical template, but this was normally too ambitious for our very limited time available.

One difference with the method described by the EPF is that they were looking at experienced and senior clinicians, not trainees or recently qualified therapists or counsellors, who made up our group of honorary psychotherapists. Furthermore, the EPF participants were asked to present a case in which they felt there was an analytic process, not one where they felt stuck or their work was poor. In other words, they were asked to present their best work. By contrast, as they were working as honoraries in order to develop their learning, the presenters with us were more likely to bring a case which they found particularly difficult or where they felt stuck. So although the aim of the clinical discussion group was to investigate how they were working, as honorary therapists, they were also looking for practical help in working with the patient.

This was the case with Carolyn, who presented a session with a male patient, Mr. C, in the early stages of his once-weekly year-long therapy (for reasons of confidentiality, some identifying features of the patient have been changed). Mr. C had come to therapy because of severe difficulties with depression. He had eating problems and found himself unable to cope in a demanding job. Carolyn described finding the therapy with Mr. C difficult. He was often angry with other people for their failings, such as his girlfriend or colleagues at work, but seemed uninterested or unable to consider his own. In the therapy, he found it both difficult and humiliating to look at himself. He would tend to give long narratives about events which gave little access to his feelings. In the previous session to the one described, he had been very angry with his girlfriend whom he felt had not taken his side over a dispute. However,

Carolyn felt there had been a slight shift, as Mr. C had acknowledged that he felt "flat" and depressed. Carolyn said to the group that she wanted to find a way of building on this.

Looking at one intervention

In the session described by Carolyn, Mr. C was ten minutes late. He apologized several times for being late, saying it was due to the trains. Mr. C then said, "I've had a better week this week" and proceeded to tell Carolyn in detail about an aspect of his work situation.

Carolyn then said: "can you give me some idea of what a better week means for you?"

This is the intervention I will discuss in this chapter. It can be of particular interest to consider the very first intervention made by a therapist, even if it seems of little or no consequence in itself. The group first of all tried to think about what they felt Carolyn was trying to do in terms of the basic categories. The intervention seemed to fit best into category three; that is, trying to make matters conscious. It was given in the form of a question, asking for clarification – what does Mr. C mean by "a better week"? However, there also seemed to be elements which could fit the other categories. In its invocation of what something "means" to Mr. C, some group members felt it could be seen as "adding an element to facilitate unconscious process". One member of the group commented on the form of the intervention, which referred to both Carolyn and Mr. C together ("can you give *me* some idea of what a better week means for *you*?"). So perhaps Carolyn's intervention, although given in such a way as to appeal to more conscious thinking, could also be seen as having elements belonging to category four; that is, referring to the therapeutic relationship, and inviting more elaboration of feelings about this relationship at a more unconscious level.

Another group member felt that what Carolyn was trying to do was to challenge the patient, who seemed determined to keep things at a safe distance, so the aim would be to bring him back to the present situation with Carolyn. The patient began by saying he had had a better week, a clear reference to the previous week, but he did not elaborate on this, speaking instead about an event at work. So Carolyn's intervention could be seen as designed to bring the patient back to where he began the session; that is, that last week he had felt bad, whereas this week he felt better. In this sense, the intervention contains the outline of a potential construction, seeing Mr. C's invocation of a "better week" as a distraction from or covering over of what he was feeling at a deeper level, and trying to keep things at a manageable but superficial level in the therapy.

Generally, the group felt that the purpose of the intervention was to try to engage with Mr. C at a deeper level, to get an analytic process going. In the words of one group member, the intervention was a way of saying: "we need to get started."

There was also discussion about the form of the intervention, asking the patient to give her something. This could be seen as a way of adding an element to facilitate an unconscious process, an implication that Mr. C has more feelings and thoughts than he is saying, and that he might explore these. The group also wondered whether the way of constructing the intervention, "can you...", may have been an expression of a sense of frustration on the part of the therapist, and so perhaps more in category six, a form of enactment, a replay in the transference of some well-established pattern of relationship where Mr. C was not giving what was required of him and probably not getting what he wanted.

Carolyn said she found these comments helpful. She agreed she found Mr. C frustrating to work with, she often felt kept out, and these feelings were heightened in this session because Mr. C had been late. She thought what she was trying to say to him was something like: "I'm asking you to give me something that I can work with, something that is meaningful and real." In particular, it was designed to link up with the previous session and what Mr. C had said about his feelings. But she was not at all sure whether her intervention had been helpful or not in progressing the work.

What happened next

In the clinical discussion group, we were able to move on to the next part of the session. Mr. C said, in response to Carolyn's intervention, "not as flat as before".

Carolyn then referred to the previous session and Mr. C's angry feelings about his girlfriend because he felt she was being dismissive of him, leaving him feeling isolated and angry.

This intervention was met with silence. Then Mr. C spoke at length, with more feeling, about a female friend of his, P, with whom he had argued recently. But in their recent meeting, there was no mention of their argument. Mr. C went on to speak of how the friend spent most of the time talking about herself, only at the end asking about him, and how P dominated the conversation.

Carolyn then said: "can you say more about your relationship with P?" Mr. C then spoke, again at length and with a rising sense of anger, about how he felt P was laughing at him in front of other friends, how once when he phoned P in distress, she had betrayed his confidence. At the end of this, Carolyn made another intervention: "so you felt betrayed by her."

This part of the session was further discussed in the group, in terms of what the group members felt Carolyn was trying to do in each of her interventions. For our purposes, I have brought in what happened next in the session to illustrate how both practitioner and group make sense of each intervention not only by trying to think about it in its own terms, but also by what happens next. Here we can see that the intervention produced a response, which did seem to link Mr. C back to the previous session, so it could be said to have achieved its purpose. Carolyn then made explicit what she thought Mr. C had been feeling in the last session. However, this was met with silence, and Mr. C went on to talk about his relationship with a friend. This produced another intervention, which had a form rather similar to her first one: "can you say a bit more about your relationship with P?" This led to a longer description, told with even more intensity, resulting in Carolyn saying, "so you felt betrayed by her." Whereas with her first intervention Carolyn felt she was trying to get something going in the session, with this intervention, she said she felt concerned about the intensity of Mr. C's feelings, that he was becoming more and more worked up, and felt that what she needed to do was help him feel safe with the intensity of his feelings rather than provoke further escalation of affect.

Carolyn had asked the group for help in thinking about her patient, and in the light of this discussion, the group were able to offer Carolyn some thoughts on how best to proceed. In the story of Mr. C and his friend P, it was clear to the group, as well as to Carolyn, that the material was full of potential references to the transference situation. Discussion then centred on whether it would be therapeutically productive for Carolyn to think of making some here-and-now interpretations, whether these would be experienced as lessening Mr. C's anxiety and escalating feelings, or whether they would have no effect (considering he had met Carolyn's attempt to link back to the previous session with silence), or whether, indeed, they might simply provoke a further escalation of feelings. Alternatively, Carolyn could use her own understanding of what was happening in the transference (e.g. around betrayal) to help Mr. C better understand and access his feelings about P; in other words, only move towards a here-and-now interpretation when a better therapeutic alliance had become established.

The description of this early part of the session and the ensuing discussion took up the full hour and a half and we had no further time to look at the rest of the session and how it unfolded.

Carolyn's comments

I sent Carolyn an early draft of this account, and invited her to comment on it, as well as the method of conducting the clinical seminar. In her reply she wrote: "The model of focusing predominantly on the presenter and her reasons for working in a particular way with a patient, facilitates further understanding of the patient." She said she found this "a very effective thinking model" as it enables the presenter "to go more deeply into the process of understanding the work, the patient and the relationship with the patient; it also deepens her ability to reflect more on herself as a person and in the role of therapist".

She commented on this particular patient that her primary concern was to make the work safe for him. Her first intervention – "can you give me some idea of what a better week means for you?" – was "an attempt to locate him in the room with me by asking him to think about and articulate his better week so it could be thought about and understood by us both". She thought her intervention, "so you felt betrayed by her" "was an attempt to stop his long and impassioned speech about his friend and to think about the possible cause of his distress", namely being betrayed in a relationship where he felt dependent. She found the comment by one member of the group concerning this intervention particularly helpful, namely "that I articulated the betrayal but did not address the underlying primitive feelings that this brought up". This comment "enabled me to identify those primitive feelings in the patient, to think about how they manifest in his behaviour, and to reflect on how best to work with them given the time limit of the therapy and my capacity, albeit developing, as a therapist".

Evaluating the effectiveness of an intervention

In this form of clinical discussion group, unlike a more conventional case discussion group, the focus is more on the presenter than the patient. I think Carolyn's comments show that it was not so much the outcome of the discussion around the purpose or aim of her particular intervention, but the process of considering what she was trying to do from a variety of different perspectives that she found helpful. The discussion enabled Carolyn to spell out to herself what she was trying to do. She was then more able to think about what she then needed to do in order to further the work, which left her feeling that she had a better understanding of her patient.

The example also shows that one cannot evaluate the effectiveness of any intervention without trying to ascertain its purpose. This gets us away from the rather fruitless debate as to whether any particular intervention is "analytic" or not. In discussing Carolyn's first intervention, the group was able to make a case for putting the intervention into several different categories, each with a different purpose. This involved looking in detail at both the content and form of the intervention. In this case, the group found it noteworthy that the intervention was put as a question, and that it contained a reference to both patient and therapist. In discussing the effectiveness of the intervention, Carolyn herself felt it had not really achieved its purpose, as she felt stuck with the patient. But in the light of the group discussion, she was more able to identify why she was stuck and could then plan her strategy – namely focus on the patient's more primitive feelings, particularly as they might arise in the transference – in order to get the therapy moving.

11

How Working Models Inform Practice: An Example from a Supervision Group

Traditionally in psychoanalytic teaching, supervision has been seen as a way of passing on the psychoanalytic tradition and helping the supervisee apply this correctly in their work. However, all too often this can lead to what Juan Pablo Jimenez, writing about clinical discussion groups, calls "a dialogue of the deaf":

> In presentations of material, the persons who present it are not usually concerned about explaining the reasons for which they intervened in the way they did and the discussant is not interested in elucidating the presenters' reasons. Consequently what is produced is a dialogue of the deaf, who never meet on any shared ground, which thus leads to misunderstandings and a growing babelization. (2009, p.235)

But if one shifts perspective to seeing supervision as a way of acquainting the student with their own technique, their way of evaluating their own work and how they come to clinical decisions, the supervisee will then be in a better position to learn to supervise themselves. This positions the supervisor more as a participant in a dialogue than as an authority figure.

In this chapter, I will illustrate what a supervision session looks like when conducted in this manner. I have found that adopting this position, of conducting a dialogue rather than positioning myself as the guardian of the tradition and therefore as the one who knows, is far more satisfying for both myself and my supervisees. However, it is not without its difficulties and points of tension. If one is supervising trainees, one cannot get away from some responsibility for passing on the fruits of one's experience and knowledge. Trainees are entitled to expect instruction as well as dialogue. Another difficulty is that in a dialogue, all normally goes well if both parties are in agreement with each other. But suppose they are not? What then becomes crucial is how differences and conflicts are negotiated. In such situations, the authority invested in the role of supervisor, however much the supervisor favours dialogue, can put him or her in a difficult position.

I will illustrate this by taking an example from a group supervision session conducted in the specialist psychotherapy department I have described in previous chapters. The supervision group consisted of three supervisees (Maha, Sarah and Anne), each working as an honorary therapist. The supervision group was well established and, by common consent, the supervisees felt they had built up a good level of trust with each other and with me.

I will give an account of a part of one supervision session in which one of the honorary therapists, Maha, presented a session with her patient, Teresa. She was a young woman who was suffering from depression, which she would often deal with through brief sexual encounters with men. The salient facts of her history were that she felt she had an over-close relationship with her mother, feeling her mother involved her too much in her own problems. She took on the role of saviour in her family, the one who would sort out any difficulties. She learned to become independent from an early age, for example organizing her own schooling. In her adult life, she struggled to maintain intimacy in relationships and success in her work. Her life seemed to involve periods of strong attachment to a particular institution or social group, followed by periods in which she withdrew from contact.

The session described took place around four months into her one-year therapy, conducted at once-weekly frequency.

Description of the session

For the purposes of this chapter, I have divided the presentation into three sections. In each section, I have put Maha's account of the session in the first person, while her comments directed towards the group are in italics. This is then followed by a description of my thinking about each section. The account is based on my notes made at the time and also a few hours after the end of the supervision session. Identifying features of the patient have been changed to protect confidentiality.

Maha's description: First section of the session

I can always tell when Teresa is down, she looked down today; her expression was sallow and pale. She told me about her trip to America (Teresa had just returned from spending several weeks on a holiday, which meant cancelling several sessions of therapy), saying it was "mostly fine".

Maha: "You weren't feeling good before you went away, and you are not sure whether you could be helped by therapy."
I was trying to bring Teresa back after the break.
Teresa: "Yes, I felt isolated, when I feel down nothing helps. I enjoyed the trip, mostly, for much of the time it felt light and easy, it was good to be away."
I was unconvinced.
Maha: "You feel down."
Teresa: "Yes, I was fine when in America but I did have some anxious and panicky moments, but it felt like a distraction, removed from the real environment. I needed to come back to everyday, and to therapy, so in a way I'm glad to come back. But when I came back I felt lost and disappointed in myself, and did not know what to do."
Maha: "You have said you enjoyed some of the time being away, you felt light and easy, and lively (*I deliberately added the word 'lively' to link with the idea of the life instincts*), so part of you can find pleasure and enjoy yourself, but then you also felt anxious and stuck, there is this part of you that devalues the experience of being lively and attacks it, as if it were a distraction."
It was important to get hold of the two parts of her, the sabotaging and destructive side and the healthier parts of her, I wanted to help her see the two sides and how she sabotages her enjoyment or pleasure.
Teresa: "When I came back I felt paralyzed, full of uncertainty, I felt disappointed, ashamed of myself. I thought I could change but instead felt stiffness and heaviness. (*I noted the phrase 'stiffness and heaviness', which I felt was opposed to the 'light and easy' of being on holiday*). I felt I had to hide myself away. When I meet someone I imagine myself in their eyes, what they see, and this leads me to feel ashamed. So I have been staying at home and distracting myself."

My thoughts as supervisor on this section

Listening to Maha's account of this part of the session, I was aware, as supervisor, of a growing sense of discomfort. We had discussed previously in the supervision group Teresa's decision to take a holiday, and I knew Maha felt this represented a flight from therapy and that she had said this to Teresa, but Teresa would not be dissuaded. When Maha said she was "unconvinced" by Teresa's account of the holiday as a good experience, so was I. But I was then unconvinced myself about what followed. I did not see Teresa's enjoyment of herself on holiday as evidence of liveliness, as Maha did, and so a part of the life instincts or the capacity for enjoyment which had to be preserved from the destructive part of her personality. I thought Maha's choice of this theoretical framework was a good one for Teresa, but I could not see how it fitted this particular situation. I saw the "lightness and easiness" of the holiday as a sign of a manic or magical flight from reality and the "stuckness and heaviness" on her return as a crashing back to reality, or a return of the depressive part of a manic cycle. Maha's approach here felt wrong to me. I could not reconcile it with her having been "unconvinced" by Teresa only a few minutes earlier.

The issue was not that Maha thought she was floundering or did not know what she was doing. If that had been the case, I would not have felt uncomfortable. In fact, in her comments to the supervision group, Maha showed she had a well-worked-out appreciative system in place. She added the word "lively" to "light and easy", and saw Teresa's description of how she felt "stuck and heavy" as a direct reference to her previous state of mind. But Maha was thinking of these two states of mind in ways that were at odds with how I was experiencing them. I wondered whether Maha might be feeling somewhat at odds with herself here, as she had started off this section feeling "unconvinced" by Teresa's account, yet now seemed to be taking what Teresa was saying at face value.

Maha's description: Second section of the session

There was a pause, then Teresa spoke in a quieter voice, as though she was slightly ashamed.

Teresa: "I met a guy earlier this week."
She tends to tell me she met someone earlier in the week, as a way of distancing me, as if "don't ask me about it" – I don't want to scrutinize

her, this would be too much like her mother. Teresa went on to say more
about her "encounter", and described it as "neither horrible nor great".

Maha: "You seek relationships that are nothing remarkable, as if you want them to be doomed to fail, and to remain in control, keep the status quo."

Teresa: "Yes, so I can erase them from my mind."

Maha: "Your trip was similar, a distraction, so no need to remember it. You don't bring much to the session about your encounters or your trip – *she only allows me a glimpse of what happens* – as if you want to keep something hidden, from you or from both of us. In therapy it is similar, so you can erase it and I become the mother who fails you."

Teresa: "What you say makes sense, I can understand it, but I am not doing it consciously. When I am not feeling like this, I sabotage myself less."

Maha: "Can you tolerate taking a risk, otherwise you keep yourself safe in a bubble."

Teresa: "Yes, I am petrified of trying anything."

Maha: "Going to America was a flight, from my invading your private space."

Teresa: "I felt positive coming back, I don't think my trip was a flight from therapy – *she denied this strongly*. But while I was on holiday, I did wonder about continuing therapy, what it would be like."

My thoughts as supervisor on the second section of the session

In this section, by contrast, I felt differently, in tune with what Maha was saying and the way she was conducting the therapy. Whereas in the first section of the session I felt she was not hearing the manic flight, in this section, I thought she had "got" her patient and made some pertinent and effective interventions. Her comment, that Teresa's relationships were "nothing remarkable" was an interesting intervention, seeming to find a way of pricking her narcissistic bubble in a matter-of-fact and sensitive way, in a way she could tolerate. Maha was now clear that her trip abroad was a flight from therapy, unlike in the first section where she seemed more open to thinking that Teresa also used the holiday as a time when she could relax and enjoy herself. Maha went on to identify how Teresa keeps herself hidden, how she blanks out what she does not want to remember. In particular, she brought out a key aspect of the transference, that she becomes the mother who fails her. This attention to how the patient distances and blanks herself in order to avoid connection and relationship, and how she might be experiencing Maha in the transference, seemed to allow Teresa to get to how frightened she was about trying anything new, a significant admission. I felt more comfortable hearing this part of the therapy, in the sense that my evaluation of what was happening in the therapy was close to Maha's, as evidenced by what she said to Teresa and her comments to us (in italics) about why she said what she did. I felt Teresa was more engaged in this part of the session and there was some shared understanding between patient and therapist.

However, I could not put this part of the session together with the first part. Furthermore, my earlier sense of discomfort and incongruity had not entirely gone away. I was still not sure about how Maha was taking some of Teresa's comments. For instance, her remark apparently agreeing with what Maha said about her having taken flight, but that "she was not doing it consciously", felt to me like a way of buying Maha off rather than taking in what Maha was saying. In other words, I was not wholly convinced about how far Teresa was fully engaged.

Maha's description: Third section of the session

Maha: "There is a constant struggle between your destructive and healthy parts. *I elaborated on this.* I feel a need to challenge you, if not you can become indulgent."

Teresa: "I am up for that. *She became more alive, there was colour in her cheeks.* I feel as if there's a bit of wind in my sails now. The trip was a breath of fresh air. I feel I am an able traveller." *Teresa said more on this.*

Maha: "You are resourceful and part of you is able to take risks."

Teresa then talked about a leaflet she saw in reception, about asking for people to volunteer to become an adviser to other service users, and how she thought she would put in an application to become a volunteer.

Maha: "Part of you tries to rob yourself of the wind in your sails."

Teresa: "When I was young I was fearless. I feel like I could make baby steps. *This felt moving.* And I sense I can get to a little island of achievement, then I could really flourish."

Maha: "I like the way you are describing this, it sounds like a rebirth – but there is a constant battle in your mind between your destructive and healthy parts." *I said a bit more about this struggle. I felt a glimmer of hope here.*

Maha ended the session.

My thoughts as supervisor on this section

My feeling of discomfort returned when Maha went on to tell Teresa of her need to challenge otherwise she would become indulgent. I felt suspicious about Teresa's ensuing animation and could not relate to Maha's comments about Teresa being resourceful. Whereas Maha heard Teresa's wish to become a volunteer as a sign of her drive and courage, I saw this as Teresa's attempt to take over Maha's function as therapist, by taking up the role of therapist to other service users, adopting a pseudo-position of maturity. I felt uncomfortable when Maha reported feeling moved by Teresa at this point; I did not. And the same with the "island of achievement", which I associated to a psychic retreat, not to Maha's place of re-birth.

My usual practice in group supervision, after the therapist has presented a session, is to turn to the other group members and invite their thoughts and comments. In this case, I was particularly glad to do so, partly to buy me a bit of time, but more as I hoped their contributions might help me gain more perspective on my own thinking, and help me make sense of my own feelings and put them together in a more thought-out way.

Group discussion

Sara: "I thought you got hold of something in this session, it felt she was on the edge of things with you. I was interested in what she said about other people being a mirror where she sees herself through their eyes. I wondered what she does see when she sees herself reflected like this."

Maha: "It is interesting you say that. There was this friend, whom she had met some time ago, who came to stay with her, but she felt more depressed as she felt this friend saw her as a failure."

I found Sara's remark interesting. Sara's sense that Maha had got hold of something was what I felt in the middle bit, and her phrase that Teresa was "on the edge of things" felt right, at least in the middle section. I had not paid particular attention to Teresa's remark about being concerned about what image people had of her, but it provided another useful perspective for the session. The story of the friend who came to stay but left her feeling more depressed also seemed like a useful commentary on the dynamics of the therapy, which did not seem to be helping her with her depression. To my mind, it confirmed Maha's transference interpretation of herself as a mother who failed her.

Anne: "I found it hard to get a clear sense of what was going on in the session, or of Teresa, hard to get to grips with her. I felt she was distancing. She does come alive when she was challenged by you. I felt her island of achievement was also a way of distancing, like being in a bubble."

Both Sara and Anne commented on the importance of the idea of Teresa erasing memories.

Maha agreed with these comments, and said she could easily lose Teresa in the session, "she is like a baby who could slip through my hands."

I thought the comments from both Sara and Anne had usefully opened out the discussion, and had each provoked comments from Maha which threw more light on her clinical thinking. In particular, her agreement with Anne that the "island of achievement" could be seen as a bubble significantly lessened my sense of discomfort about the discrepancy between my thinking and the thinking that seemed to have informed Maha's approach in the first and third parts of the session. Her comments to the group seemed to show her holding more than one view of Teresa in her mind. I found her description of Teresa telling: "she is like a baby who could slip through my hands." To my mind, this comment made more sense of how Maha was working, namely trying to get hold of someone who is elusive and slippery. This married up more with the picture I had built up of Teresa in my mind.

I felt ready to give my own thoughts of the session. I said I felt Maha's comments in the middle part of the session were effective and seemed to help Teresa understand herself more. However, I saw things differently in the early part of the session, seeing Teresa's "light and easy" as a manic flight, an emptying of herself. And in the later part, when challenged, when Teresa spoke of life having been breathed into her and she became animated, I felt she was acting like a parasite, who was feeding off Maha's energy, or that it was a kind of seduction – a repetition of something with her mother. I wondered if the therapy at this point had become like one of her sexual encounters, with a release of tension in a kind of orgasm. I also pointed out how things get erased.

There was more discussion in the session. At one point I asked the group what they made of Teresa's metaphor of an island of achievement, saying it sounded to me more like a psychic retreat. Anne agreed, Sara said it made her think more of a secure base, Maha felt open to both possibilities.

Towards the end of the discussion of this session, I tried to sum up where we had got to, and which also represented my understanding at that point of what Maha was trying to do in the session. I said Maha's approach was to ally herself with Teresa's healthy side, her life instincts. This was why she felt it important to frame what Teresa was doing, for example in wishing to become a volunteer, as taking "baby steps", and hence also her introduction of the analogy of a re-birth. Maha said she agreed, adding this is how she sees therapy in general and in particular working with Teresa, "I don't want to drown with her, rather to give her a lifeline."

I went on to say (here more clearly taking on the more teaching aspect of being a supervisor) that Maha might think instead, or as well, of following the theme of how Teresa erases parts of herself. I said I felt Maha had been spot on with how she seeks nothing remarkable in relationships so she can then erase them. She erases them to make sure they don't become remarkable. I wondered if this could be a thread for Maha to follow in subsequent sessions. But, I added, I could see from Maha's point of view that she wanted not just to keep the destructive in view, but also to find a place for the healthy part of Teresa.

The role of supervisor: Practical and theoretical reasoning

My position as supervisor gives me a different perspective to the clinical presenter. I do not have access to the emotional and affective quality of the session, nor to Maha's clinical thinking except through what she tells us of the session and the manner of her presentation. As I listen to Maha's account of the session, I am bringing in my own processes of practical reasoning. I am putting myself in Maha's shoes, trying to listen with her ear as she reports what Teresa says in the session. So, when Maha describes to us a particular intervention, I am aware of my own expectations of how I think Teresa will respond. And, when Teresa speaks, I might imagine what Maha will then say. As such, I am trying to build up a picture of how Maha thinks and also how she evaluates her own work. At the same time, this is all mixed in with what I imagine I might have done and what I might have said. In other words, as someone listening to another clinician present their work, I rely on my own appreciative system, my own assumptions of how psychoanalytic work is done, in order to gain a perspective on what is being presented.

In listening as a supervisor as well as using my own processes of practical reasoning in order to anticipate how the session will pan out, I will also be employing more theoretical ideas in order to make sense of what is happening. That is, I will be looking backwards, over the session, as well as forwards, anticipating what is to come. This process of looking back over what has happened, and then forwards again to the presenter's account of where she has got to in the session, takes concrete form in the written notes I make during a supervision session. I note down the interventions, even if in abbreviated form, and then flip back and forth between the present session and my notes of previous sessions, going right back to the first session. I always make notes on some key aspects of a patient's family background and early life, and will often glance back at this information to help me think about the transference dynamics that might be in play in any particular session.

This process of moving back and forth between my notes is a rather concrete demonstration of how theoretical reasoning works. It makes sense of what is happening in terms of what has gone before, bringing the elements together into a larger context of meaning. Maha also uses theoretical reasoning, explicitly so in her use of the distinction between healthy and destructive parts of the personality, but her thinking in the session is more in the form of practical reasoning as she designs her particular interventions and tracks their impact and meaning. It is this reasoning which becomes the main focus of the supervision session.

Working models of presenter and supervisor

I have presented this supervision session in terms of my oscillation between at times feeling in accord with Maha's thinking and approach and at other times feeling her understanding was different, if not in conflict with my own. In order to make sense of this phenomenon, it is useful to bring in the notion of working models.

Maha can be seen to draw on two versions of Teresa, each of which can be thought of as a working model. The first, that of the conflict between her healthy and destructive sides, is explicitly used by Maha at various times in her presentation. The second, that of a slippery baby she is trying to keep hold of, only appears in her discussion in the group, but I think is a description of another version of Teresa which informs Maha's work.

By her own account, Maha draws on her understanding of the work of Herbert Rosenfeld in making use of the healthy/destructive parts in conflict. In writing this chapter, I looked again at Rosenfeld's paper "A Clinical Approach to the Psychoanalytic Theory of the Life and Death Instincts: An Investigation into the Aggressive Aspects of Narcissism", and came across his striking clinical description of the consequences for a patient caught up in the deadly conflict between the healthy and destructive sides of his personality:

> One narcissistic patient, who kept relations to external objects and the analyst dead and empty by constantly deadening any part of his self that attempted object relations, dreamt of a small boy who was in a comatose condition, dying from some kind of poisoning. He was lying on a bed in the courtyard and was endangered by the hot midday sun which was beginning to shine on him. The patient was standing near to the boy but did nothing to move or protect him. He only felt critical and superior to the doctor treating the child, since it was he who should have seen that the child was moved into the shade. The patient's previous behaviour and associations made it clear that the dying boy stood for his dependent libidinal self which he kept in a dying condition by preventing it from getting help and nourishment from the analyst. I showed him that even when he came close to realizing the seriousness of his mental state, experienced as a dying condition, he did not lift a finger to help himself or to help the analyst to make a move towards saving him, because he was using the killing of his infantile dependent self to triumph over the analyst and to show him up as a failure. The dream illustrates clearly that the destructive narcissistic state is maintained in power by keeping the libidinal infantile self in a constant dead or dying condition. (1988, p.248)

I think this extract captures something of how Maha thinks about her patient Teresa. She acts as though she sees Teresa keeping her libidinal self in a dying condition, and that her task as her therapist is to make Teresa aware of what she is doing and elicit her help in nourishing this part of her. Her view of her therapeutic task as one of giving her a "lifeline" seems to fit with this view.

Her other working model, with Teresa as a baby and herself as a mother trying to hold her as she slips through her fingers, seems to refer back to a figure such as Winnicott. Maha has spoken at other times in supervision about how she sees herself as a mother figure to her patients. With this model, the therapeutic task would be directed towards holding the patient so as to facilitate her own maturational processes.

Having identified these two working models – each of which seems to provide a lens through which Maha sees Teresa's experience and behaviour in the session, and so could be thought of as a "scale model" which informs her thinking (see Chapter 4, section "Working models", pp.71–2) – we can then wonder how well they fit together. The two working models seem to imply different ideas on what is wrong with the patient and what to do about it. In the healthy/destructive parts model, the aim of the therapist is clearly to be on the side of the healthy part and to speak to the patient about this battle between the two sides of her personality. It is based on a notion of conflict, with the aim of helping Teresa see and acknowledge this conflict, and, hopefully, find her own way of managing or resolving it. By contrast, the model of therapist as mother and patient as baby is a developmental model, seeing what Teresa does in terms of her "making baby steps" towards functioning in a more adult and mature way. What has gone wrong would be seen more in terms of a "deficit" or "failure" of the holding environment. The aim of the therapy would be more about facilitating development rather than giving the patient insight into her conflicts.

These views are different, but not incompatible. I think that Maha's invocation of the baby as "slippery" could be seen as her own way of bringing these two working models together. Teresa is a baby who needs holding by a benign mother. But she is also a slippery baby, one who can fall through one's hands, because she can be elusive, hiding herself. When she makes herself unavailable in this way, she can be seen to be acting in accord with her destructive part.

Thinking in terms of the working models that become activated in the session introduces an illuminating perspective both on the session itself and on my reactions as supervisor. In terms of the two working models identified, we can look at how Maha managed the relationship between them, and speculate that Maha's work was better (in my evaluation of her work) when these two models were aligned with each other. In my reconstruction of the session, this happened in the second part of the session when I felt Maha was more in touch with herself as a failing mother in the transference, which then enabled her to better pinpoint the way Teresa was evading contact. I thought in this part of the session Maha succeeded in getting hold of Teresa's destructive side and was able to show her how it impeded and spoilt her growth. But, in my view, this did not work so well in the first and third parts of the session. This may be because in these sections only one of these working models was operative, or perhaps they no longer worked well together.

A further perspective on my reactions as supervisor to Maha's work can be gained by thinking about my own working models which became activated in the supervision session. While listening to Maha's presentation, I recalled a paper I had recently re-read (as part of my preparation for teaching a session on "narcissism" to my own students), one called "The Identificate" by Leslie Sohn. In this paper, Sohn describes a part of the personality which develops in certain patients and which takes over some of the functions of the ego. It is similar to Rosenfeld's description of the destructive part of the personality. But whereas Rosenfeld tends to emphasize the dominating, controlling and hateful aspects of the "destructive" part of the personality, in Sohn's paper, the emphasis is more on the seductive, tricky and covert nature of this identificate. This part of the personality "mimics a variety of apparently positive situations" (1988, p.278). Sohn writes that

> the commonest version seen in an analysis is where it suddenly takes up a collusive pseudo-alliance in the analytic work with an analyst, and criticises the hated dependent aspects of the personality which are felt to be ill, and helps in the enquiry into the illness, as if it were a crime, but with complete callow hypocritical indifference to the fate of the ill part. (ibid. p.278)

Sohn goes on to say that "in the working through various problems with the patient, one is always aware of an undercurrent" (ibid. p.278).

> Although insightful conclusions appear to be reached there is a covert sabotaging process at work which dislocates and disrupts progress. It is as if a pied piper process is at hand, with the dependent parts of the personality constantly being led away to disappear, leaving the personality like the crippled boy who survived in the story. (ibid. p.279)

The pied piper analogy expresses nicely some of what I was thinking, that Maha was being led away in the beginning and end sections by the pseudo-growth of the patient, and that what was left of the therapy suffered as a result. This way of thinking about the therapy with Teresa felt to me to be at odds with how Maha seemed to be thinking about her patient, particularly in the first and third sections of the session. However, in the course of the group discussion, it became clear that Maha was herself aware of such an "undercurrent" in her work with Teresa, in her view of Teresa as a "slippery baby". I think this allowed for the supervision session to be a productive experience, in which the group members were able to find ways of speaking about their different views and reactions to the clinical material in a way that we could all learn from the discussion and, hopefully, find ways of being helpful to the presenter in her ongoing work with the patient.

Looking at a supervision session or any form of clinical discussion from this perspective, thinking of how each member of the group "listens" to the clinical material according to their own working models, changes the way one thinks about the work. What becomes of interest is not so much that of determining the "right" way to listen to the clinical material, but to find ways of talking about the different views of what the "right" way is. The supervisory process works best when differences of perspective can be articulated and then explored, allowing for the possibility of negotiation between them. The result is that supervision becomes a learning experience for the supervisor as well as supervisees.

12

DEVELOPING ONE'S OWN WAY OF WORKING: AN EXAMPLE FROM TEACHING

If we think of the capacity to become more aware of one's implicit clinical thinking and how this informs our practice as a key part of developing as a psychoanalytic practitioner, what might the implications be for the formal teaching of psychoanalytic practice? Traditionally, psychoanalytic trainings have emphasized the importance of *unlearning*. This means the student, especially at the beginning of their training, needs to give up on all previously acquired knowledge or methods of doing therapy which involve leading the patient towards any pre-determined ends. Only then will the trainee be in a position to acquire and maintain an analytic attitude, the capacity to listen in an unfocused way to the patient's unconscious communications and to the unfolding of the transference (see Introduction, "The prevailing view of analytic practice", pp.2–3).

A consequence of this view is that what each trainee brings to their training – their previously acquired knowledge, experience and skill – tends to be seen as something to be jettisoned if the trainee is to develop into a "proper" psychoanalytic practitioner. The best student is then seen as one who can form themselves into an empty vessel, with nothing in them which might contaminate their ability to tune in to the patient's unconscious communications as well as being receptive to the new psychoanalytic ideas which they will need to absorb.

In my experience, a student's past experience and knowledge *can* get in the way of learning new psychoanalytic ideas. But I have also found that what a student brings to their training can also be the repository of a host of actual or potential elements for their clinical thinking, especially those aspects which go to make up their implicit theories and internal clinical template. In order to better understand these elements, the student needs to be encouraged to sift through their past experience and learning in order to see which parts can be built on, which may need to become modified and which are better put aside.

This sifting process continues throughout the student's training. Students are constantly faced with the problem of how to integrate what they are taught into their existing way of thinking and working. This also involves knowing what to do with those elements of their learning for which they can find no place. This process goes on at various levels. Students learn not only from what they are explicitly taught. They are also influenced by and absorb their teachers' own tacit ideas and assumptions, just as we saw in Chapter 1 how medical students learn to practice by becoming able to recognize and implement the "logic of practice" of the ward or consultant team in which they are based.

In this chapter, I will give a simple illustration from my own teaching of how students can learn to become interested in their own way of thinking and working and how these develop. I teach on the third and final year of a training in psychodynamic counselling/psychotherapy. Normally, I use the final individual tutorial with the students in my tutorial group to conduct a review of their learning over the three years of their training on this course. I then decided to try something different, in an attempt to put into practice the ideas in this book. I asked each student to write a brief account (I suggested three paragraphs) on how they work. I left it to each of them to decide how they went about this task. We then used this final tutorial, which would normally last between 20 minutes and half an hour, to discuss the ideas they had brought. My aim was to produce an outline or thumbnail sketch of each student's developing way of working, based on what they brought to the tutorial (what they had prepared in written form or not) and the ensuing discussion between us. In writing these accounts, I have relied on the student's own written preparation (when available) together with my notes of the tutorial, taken both during the tutorial itself and shortly afterwards.

Sometimes in the tutorial, the discussion became quite personal, as the student related their clinical practice to their own life and experience. For reasons of confidentiality I have omitted these more personal aspects from the accounts that follow.

Bola

Bola approached this task by sending me five paragraphs of text in advance. Her document began as follows:

The first patient that I saw, in session one, started out by saying, "There is a being that climbs into the front of my head and takes over me." My first feeling was fear and my first thought was run! But after a few minutes I thought, "How am I going to proceed with this? This man is here because he wants to gain some kind of understanding as to why he is the way he is. Maybe get some help, maybe relief, how can I foster that?" My first plan of action was not to show or feel fear and to realise that maybe what I was feeling was actually what he was feeling.

In her written account, Bola went on to describe this patient as "detached from his feelings". Sometimes "he would go blank in mid-sentence and say that he had lost the train of thought and was unable to 'get a thread to connect to it'". Her approach with this patient, as well as her second patient, was to "get him in touch with his feelings"; that is, identify his feelings and the effect they had on him. She gave an example of him feeling sadness and that he "cried for the first time since he was a child".

In her written account, she then went on to identify John Steiner's theory of psychic retreats as having been particularly useful. It helped her understand what the patient was doing when detached; that is, retreat psychically to somewhere safe and familiar. It also helped her formulate to herself her therapeutic task, as this phantasy position of retreat "could not be sustained if a therapeutic alliance was to be formed". She saw that while her patient remained withdrawn in this way, "nothing [would] change for him", and so her approach was "to attempt to challenge him gently to try and [help him] explain to me his thinking behind this".

In working with her second patient, she described how the patient used to "retreat into constant floods of tears where she would reside for the first 15 minutes of a session". She described how she came to realize that this constant crying was a "defence" to avoid the greater anxiety she was feeling in the room. Her approach was to "give her time to hide in her defences", but she would also "put it to her that I wondered why she found it so difficult to speak in the room". These "promptings" enabled the patient to "open up a little" to tell Bola what she was thinking and feeling without crying.

In the tutorial, I commented on how working with affects seems central to her approach. Bola agreed. I also commented on how the concept of projection (although not mentioned explicitly) seemed important in her thinking. It enabled her to take up a viable stance as the therapist, by seeing her reactions as ways of gaining access to what her patient was feeling. We then talked about the adoption of Steiner's concept of psychic retreat. She described Steiner as a "hero" and how important reading his book had been to her (she also mentioned Bion's paper "Attacks on Linking").

I commented that she seemed to be using the idea of a "retreat" as a way of thinking about what her clients did with their feelings. In the first patient, she used the idea of a retreat to see how the patient got away from feelings by having none, whereas in the case of the second patient, it was more about a person who had too many feelings. Bola spoke about how, with the patient who would go into floods of tears, she would have to physically stop herself from getting up from her chair in order to comfort her. This seemed to illustrate how thinking in terms of retreat helped her manage her own feelings and also get a clearer idea of her therapeutic task.

We talked about how thinking in terms of place seemed a progression from thinking in terms of feelings. Bola said in the first year of the course she would formulate "my client is detached", but in the second year, she introduced the idea of a retreat, and this enabled her to see what the detachment was. She could think to herself: where is it that you actually go when you detach? It helped her think of the place in her mind that the client retreats to and to formulate the cost of such a retreat. Furthermore, it enabled her to make a link to the transference. Thinking of the function of the retreat led her to wonder what it was that was happening in the therapeutic relationship that the patient wanted to retreat from. There was no time to explore this further, but this seems to be a description of the formation of two different kinds of working models, one based primarily on feelings and their intensity, the other on a notion of place in the mind.

I asked Bola whether the concept of retreat had helped her think about herself, that in her description of how she began with her first client she was not just detached, but had herself gone into a kind of retreat at some points in the sessions described. Bola agreed. She said that she had learnt about detachment from her therapist, who had told her that she detaches herself, and she was able to apply this to her clinical work.

There was also little time to look at how Bola used the model of "psychic retreat". Bola's description of the first patient's way of withdrawing fits with how I would expect the model to be used, whereas her description of the second patient who cried is a more idiosyncratic use of the concept. She seems to be playing with the idea that this patient's way of flooding the session with her crying was a manifestation of a retreat, and that if she could get hold of this retreat, she would understand the function of her crying. So this might be an example of how Bola was in the process of shaping (or creatively misusing?) Steiner's original idea into a tool or working model of her own.

Susan

Susan had written three short paragraphs which she brought to the tutorial. She described her way of working "to be influenced by my use of empathy and my belief that empathy is an essential component of the therapeutic alliance". She wrote about the importance of maintaining the boundaries of the work. She thought that "much of my working is instinctual and relies on many years of life experiences" which helped her "to maintain an inner truth". She described herself as having a "tenacious nature", allowing her to stick with difficult clients. She said she had worked with many client cases involving severe trauma, and that she had the ability to contain such clients, holding the therapeutic space and "returning to them something palatable while also communicating unconditional positive regard". In her final paragraph, she commented that she had felt psychodynamic terms like transference and countertransference were familiar concepts to her, but she was now experiencing them "at a far deeper level" with her clients as she was also broadening her "personal way of working".

In our discussion, we talked about Susan's previous training in person-centred therapy and how she had worked hard to bring together this approach with her analytic learning. I picked on her use of the concept of trauma, and wondered whether this served as a nodal point or organizing concept for her, a way of bringing both forms of psychotherapy together. She agreed, adding that the concept of trauma also brought together psychological and social for her. I asked her to say more about how she felt she worked with trauma, and she spoke of the need to "get stuff out into the therapeutic space" so that she and the client could start to "sort it out". She felt her approach (influenced by her person-centred background) was to help her clients recognize their strengths so that they could "heal inwardly". I suggested that her view of working with trauma led to her thinking of what was wrong with her clients in terms of deficit rather than conflict, and she agreed.

I asked about the difference in her thinking between empathy and containment; she spoke about the concept of containment going hand in hand with her increasing use of the ideas of transference and countertransference. There was no time to explore this more. Perhaps for Susan, just as the concept of "trauma" served to bring together her person-centred past and psychoanalytic present, the notion of "containment" performed a similar function to describe her own attitude as therapist, bringing ideas of depth, discrimination (sorting things out) and the therapeutic relationship to the concept of "empathy" which she had inherited from her previous training.

Perhaps because of her person-centred background, or perhaps more to do with the kind of person she is, Susan's way of describing her approach has a strong personal and ethical feel to it. This finds expression in her notion of an "inner truth", which she puts at the centre of her work. It would seem to follow from this that for Susan it would be difficult to describe her work simply in terms of what she says or does with her clients. To do so would miss out the key dimension, her own capacity for truthfulness, achieved by using her psychoanalytic skill and knowledge in accord with her personal experience and ethical sensibility, thereby giving her clients an experience of being healed.

Jan

Jan approached this task by bringing a short account of her work with three patients she was working with in her clinical placement, a public health setting which sees highly complex patients. She described the first patient as having "an overwhelming need to be told what to do". Being able to follow instructions gave this patient a kind of anchor in "the swirling sea of her mind". Jan felt that in the therapy, when the patient was compliant in this way, she (Jan) became "a very distant, shadowy figure to her". She gave an example of the patient telling her about her wish that the police tell her what to do with her abusive boyfriend. Jan said to her, "it seems to me that you ask various organizations and people what they think and sometimes the advice makes sense but you can't take it in, can't believe it almost", and the patient agreed – "no I can't" and "smiled ruefully".

She described her approach as trying with the patient "to make sense for her of what is happening to her – what she actually wants is for me to tell her what to do", but that her attempts to elucidate this were "invariably met with another request for instructions". In talking with me about working with this patient, she talked about feeling that there was "nothing to get hold of", the patient seeming to have "no mind of her own".

She described her work with a second patient, who would tell her over and over again in an angry and upset way about a time when he had been raped. Jan said to him, "and perhaps you are angry with here, with me, for poking in the wound". The patient agreed, saying he had lost all trust in her. Jan continued, "perhaps I was supposed to be caring and motherly, make it better, make it go away?" The patient again agreed, saying he would have liked her to phone his place of work to explain what he had been going through. In describing her approach with this patient, she said she was "anxious not to make him any more angry than he was already". She thought she was "attempting to show I understood by using the transference to me as idealised mother as we have frequently talked about previously".

In talking about the work with this patient, she felt they had made a "tiny bit" of progress. She felt she had tightened up on boundaries with him which had been important for both the patient and herself. We talked about her conscious wish not to make him angrier, whether it was a countertransference fear that was inhibiting her or whether it was more about a conscious goal of affect regulation. Jan felt both elements were present. She saw her patient's fixation on one point, having being raped, as the main difficulty in the work. She has found writings on narcissism (Britton and Klein) particularly helpful.

In her written account, Jan described the beginning of a session with a third patient, who began by apologizing for not having come to the previous session as he had forgotten about it. Jan said to him, "that's interesting, perhaps we can think about it", and when the patient asked, "why?", Jan went on, "it seems odd, we have been meeting every Monday for over a year and you forgot." Jan wondered with him how important he found the therapy. He replied that it was nice to have someone to talk to, but therapy was not important, he felt no different – neither better nor worse.

In her commentary on this short extract, Jan acknowledged she felt irritated and angry with him, but was able to be "much more direct" with him than with the previous patient, and that, in the face of the constant challenges around boundaries, she felt it was important to keep him "on task". In the discussion with me, she talked about this patient as her most difficult one, and that she has had to "develop courage" to bring herself "into the room".

In our discussion, Jan talked about how much the reading on narcissism and working with borderline patients had helped her, particularly the notion of the patient as a blank wall. The patients were clearly very testing, but she felt now she had a belief in the psychoanalytic method. We talked about her approach, which is about elucidating – both for herself and then with the patient – what she sees as the "facts" of the transference. She aimed to talk directly and simply about the transference situation and sees this as the key in working with these patients, the best, or perhaps only way to reach them at a deep level. She seems to take this as a baseline, even if it did not in itself result in change, but unless this is done, she seems to feel there would be no way forward.

There was no time in the tutorial to elaborate more on how Jan uses the transference, but her examples can be seen to be of two types. Her main aim was to be able to use the transference directly in her work, as with her second and third patients. Here, she can be seen as making interpretations *of* the transference – "perhaps I was supposed to be caring and motherly?" – with the aim of helping the patient see how their experience of the therapy was determined by their phantasy and expectation of what should be happening. She can also be seen as working *in* the transference – "and perhaps you are angry with me for poking in the wound", which positions her as more of a player in the drama (someone poking in his wound) than as a commentator about it (see Chapter 3, section "Speaking 'of' or 'in' the transference?", pp.49–50).

In our discussion, she raised a concern, "do I need to see some neurotic patients as well as the borderline patients I am working with?" She could see that because of their challenging nature, she liked working with this patient group and felt she was developing some skill in this area. Indeed, she found the work quite exciting. As we discussed this further, she formulated the issue for herself as: "are my interests too narrow and my methods too specific?" Jan's question concerns how far a particular method can be generalized. Some practitioners work best with one particular way of working that they apply, more or less, to all the types of patients they see (with appropriate flexibility and modifications to take account of each unique clinical situation). Others think of themselves more as using different approaches with different types of patients. Jan's question seems to be motivated by a wish to know which camp best describes her approach, something she recognizes she is not yet in a position to know.

It can be seen that all of Jan's examples concern speaking about the transference to her patients. She makes clear that this way of working has now become an essential part of her approach, perhaps what she sees as what makes her work distinctive. The clinical examples she gives are not all of one type, and it is perhaps difficult to discern a clear line of thinking. I have supplied one of my own by bringing in the distinction between thinking of and in the transference. But this already risks imposing a pattern on her use of the transference which she is in the process of developing herself. Her examples can be seen as her way of trying out using a new tool in a variety of different clinical situations; indeed, in situations where it seems her interpretations are sometimes not welcomed by her patients, or seem to have little effect. But Jan does not appear to be put off; these experiences all seem to be part of her learning how to work with the transference, what its purpose might be, how she might judge its effectiveness and how to become more skilled in its application.

Jane

Rather than come with a prepared piece of writing, Jane preferred to speak about how she worked. She came to the course with considerable previous experience of working as a counsellor. She said she was influenced by Winnicott's ideas on the baby and the good enough mother, and in her work, tried to create boundaries and a holding environment. She found Klein's ideas on projective identification and Bion's on containment important. With clients she focuses on feelings, sometimes asking directly "what are you feeling?", sometimes linking to other feelings they have expressed or shown. She pays attention to the transference, and in particular to attacks on herself or on the therapy. She feels she has developed in becoming more aware of and in exploring the negative transference. She describes herself as working in a "slow-paced" way, thinking before she responds.

She gave an example of how she feels she has developed as a practitioner by recounting what happened recently on her clinical placement in a public health setting. Her patient arrived half an hour early for her session. In the waiting room, the patient curled herself up like a foetus and started to howl. One of the receptionists came into Jane's room and asked her to do something. Jane said, "we don't need to do anything." The receptionist asked her to see the patient early, but Jane said no, saying to the receptionist that the patient needed to stay in the waiting room. The patient was moved to a quieter part of the waiting room. In explaining her decision to me, Jane said it would not have been holding to intervene or see the patient earlier. Based on what she knew of the patient, she believed the patient would recover on her own, and that it might even be good for her to do so. The important thing, Jane felt, was that she "managed not to get caught up in the panic". In the session, Jane talked to the patient about what had happened. The patient had seen Jane arrive early and did not understand why she had not come out early to start the session. This opened up an exploration of how the patient dealt with the experience of having to wait. In discussing this example, Jane emphasized the importance of keeping to the frame and making it "my frame".

In her work, Jane has always focused on feelings, but during her training, she has learnt to create more space to think. She feels she now works in a more informed way; she is more aware of what she does, what she needs to do or not do. When I asked her how she would describe the difference between her work prior to the training and her work now, she thought about it and then said, "I do what I did before but the difference is that I do it more." We discussed what this meant: that she now feels she can work with more determination and intensity as she is clearer about what it is she is doing.

Jane's description of her way of working puts the idea of "holding" at the centre of her approach. This idea encapsulates for her the key aspects of her way of working: keeping to the frame and boundaries, keeping her in touch with her patient's feelings and giving herself time to think. The idea of holding is closely linked to her ability to sustain and process feelings, which gives her the capacity to wait. Waiting gives her patient time to allow an experience to develop, even if this experience is unpleasant and frightening. Once the patient has been able to fully experience something, Jane can talk to her about it and help her understand its meaning.

Jane thinks of her work in terms of the time dimension, for example working in a "slow-paced way" (unlike Bola, for example, who thinks more in terms of space) and in terms of intensity – "I do what I did before but the difference is that I do it more." Jane's account seems to be a way of describing a particular rhythm in her way of working that she is developing, one which both slows the process down so that both she and the patient have time to experience events more intensely, and then have time in which to think about what has happened.

Greta

Greta also preferred to come without anything prepared. She began by saying she didn't really know how she worked. When she began in her training she was not sure how she worked, beyond a sense that "I like to take my time to feel things." Sometimes she felt quite "adamant" about how she worked. She told me how, in a clinical seminar, I had once described her approach as "rudderless" in a piece of clinical work she had presented, saying she felt I had gone to another extreme. Instead of "rudderless", she preferred "diffuseness" (this was a word we both came to) or "polyphony" (her preferred word), having a wide spectrum of notes.

She said over the course of her training she had started off not seeing meaning, now she sees so many meanings it can feel "psychotic". She commented on her own musical background as giving her the concepts and experiences from which she draws. So, in elucidating this experience, she compared it to how she used to listen to the tune of a song but now she also listens to the lyrics, and then she hears them everywhere; it becomes overwhelming. We discussed what kind of experience this was. It could be seen as now being able to see patterns in meanings and then being able to apply this understanding to other experiences. So as understanding becomes more articulated, it is easier to generalize and apply it to different contexts. Greta agreed with this. But, she added, it can also mean that one loses perspective, that one can end up feeling all over the place and seeing so much meaning in everything that one loses one's bearings.

Greta characterized her way of working as: "I lose myself in diffuseness, then slowly bring things together." She gave the example of having worked with a client for a year, the sense that the client and her were "in something together", "we were waiting..." By "waiting", Greta meant waiting for meaning to emerge or for things to take on a shape so that they could then be talked about.

She brought in two authors who had influenced her thinking. From Jessica Benjamin, she had taken the idea of mutual recognition between client and therapist, of therapy being an intersubjective experience, of the danger of therapy becoming an experience of domination and submission. And from Enid Balint, she had taken the idea of waiting; that both therapist and patient need to wait before they can be released from the prison of fixed meanings and expectations. She could see how she has developed into becoming less rigid herself in her thinking and her work, allowing herself to become more flexible. Her aim in her work was to say something that "triggers something" for the client. I suggested to her that she preferred interventions that were "allusive" rather than explicit, and she agreed. She has an idea of therapy as enabling the client to give birth to something new.

I commented that the two authors she had mentioned were not taught on the course, and she had not mentioned any authors we do teach. She acknowledged this, and we got to the idea that Greta learns best by finding her own way of doing things, which may place her in opposition to the way other people do things or tell her to do things. But she added that she has drawn on what she learnt on the course; for example, she finds Winnicott's ideas on playing and potential space of great value. I commented that she did not mention Winnicott's ideas on development and asked about that, and Greta acknowledged she did not make use of these ideas. I was intrigued by this, and wondered whether she would find a developmental model too rigid or restricting, putting someone on a map, whereas she preferred things to remain less defined. She felt there was something in this.

In trying to describe her way of working, Greta faced a problem similar to Michael, the analyst described in Chapter 3 (pp.44–5) who used Winnicott's idea of "squiggling" to characterize his approach. That is, in trying to articulate or define an approach that is based on working without fixed meanings, but instead on a "polyphony" of meanings, one risks distorting it and making it look as though it has no internal logic or form (so Greta's complaint to me that I had once characterized her approach in a tutorial as "rudderless"). This is not an easy position for a student to be in, as it may lead to those in authority, who have the power to assess her work, not understanding what she is trying to do.

Greta is able to articulate for herself what she sees as the danger in her approach, that in losing herself among the multiplicity of meanings, she is in danger of never finding her bearings. This is an issue that all psychoanalytic practitioners have to face, that analytic ideas are very powerful and persuasive, but there is then a danger that they consume everything in their path. This is a feature of all skilled practice. In his book *The Craftsman* (2008), Richard Sennett remarks, "the pursuit of quality entails learning how to use obsessional energy well" (p.243). In the psychoanalytic literature, obsession has usually been described as the need to guard against theories and interpretations turning into "overvalued ideas" (Britton and Steiner, 1994). We have seen one version of this danger in Jan's account when she spoke of this concern in terms of whether her own way of working had become too narrow. Greta articulates the risk of a different kind of obsessive thinking, one where her way of working has become too wide. She can then be seen as indicating that one of her developmental tasks might then be to know when to stop assigning meaning, when it is best to put polyphony to one side and commit oneself to one particular approach (see Chapter 5, section "The rhythm of craft work: An example from architecture", p.80).

Kiran

Kiran also chose to talk rather than write about her way of working. She described what she tries to do as creating a safe environment. To do this, she listens, paraphrases and reflects back "so the client knows they are being listened to". She described how, when she started seeing clients, she would try to link something from one session to another session. She noticed that when she did this, her clients felt "remembered and thought about" and this taught her that this was "a good thing to do".

Over the time of her training she has learnt to use transference interpretations. I asked her about this and she said she tried to bring a greater awareness through the transference. Her way of going about this was to start with relationships outside and then link these to the client's behaviour with her in the counselling room. For example, if she noticed that the client was agitated, she would say, "I can see your agitation, perhaps that's because I left you during the break."

I commented on her word "perhaps" in this example. Kiran said she tends not to be so definite. She thought that was partly down to her lack of confidence, but also that it was her preferred style, to put an idea as a hypothesis to be shared with the client.

Kiran said she found the concept of the Oedipus complex useful in enabling her to think developmentally about her clients, and this helped her think about the kind of trauma they had experienced. She gave an example of one of her clients who felt invisible to her father. Kiran wondered whether the client had always felt like this with her father or whether it had started at a certain point in her life, for example as an early child or later in her adolescence.

This developmental perspective allowed Kiran to focus on the client's need for "individuation" and "separation", the aim of therapy being to help her client function as an independent person. I pointed out the concept of "individuation" was a Jungian idea, not something we taught on the course. Kiran said she had come across the term in a paper she had read about mothers and daughters, and she had used the concept in her case study the year before about a client whom she thought had the experience of merging with her. We discussed this some more, and the concept of "identity" came up as a guiding idea for Kiran. As in the example of the client who felt invisible, we articulated her aim of therapy as one of allowing her clients to become visible in their own way. Kiran tied this in with her experience of being a student on the course, allowing herself to become more visible.

She went on to say that she was now working with a borderline client, who identified with the different labels given to her by other people. In the counselling, she was starting to get to know herself – but she did not like who she was. This has proved very challenging for Kiran. Her guiding idea, to help the client know who they are by becoming more visible, was no longer adequate, as she was now coming across clients who do not like what they see when they start to see themselves as they are. She was therefore in the process of revising her ideas on the aim of counselling.

I asked about theory. Kiran said she was most influenced at present by Kleinian theory. I was a little surprised by this, as her way of describing her approach did not sound very Kleinian. Kiran said this was because of working with her borderline client. She found the readings on narcissism, envy and the client's destructive parts by such writers as Rosenfeld very helpful. She felt earlier in her development she had been more Freudian, in the sense of thinking in terms of separation between mother and daughter. But she now wondered whether she was being pushed into working in a different way with her borderline client. She was finding that her usual transference interpretations had not been welcomed by the client. I said that I understood her to be saying that her guiding concepts up until now, visibility and identity, were now being revisited through her experiences with this client, together with her reading on narcissism, where having a sense of identity was no longer something to be welcomed, but had now become a form of alienation, finding oneself fixed in an identity from which one cannot escape – and, furthermore, an identity which one does not like or recognize. Kiran's take on this was that working with her borderline patient was pushing her back to the beginning of the course to the concept of containment, which she was re-visiting. She felt she was having to "de-skill" herself, by which she meant "use myself more, think more about how I go about doing the work".

Kiran's account is an example of how, over the course of development, working models can change when faced with clinical situations which no longer fit one's assumptions and expectations. She seems to be right in the middle of this change of model, where her old way of working was no longer adequate, but she had not yet developed a new way (or, if she had, she was not yet able to articulate this to herself). This experience, never an easy one, took her to the literature, where she found theoretical and clinical descriptions that now matched her own experience with her clients. It also took her back to a concept she had learnt previously, namely "containment", which she described as enabling her to think in a different way and "use" herself more as an object to her client. We did not have time in the tutorial to clarify this further. It may be that Kiran was describing a different use of the term "containment", one which rendered her more active and involved in the work, and thereby more open to the transference, particularly the negative transference which she was indicating was now a feature of her work with her borderline client. Or perhaps, in "re-visiting" the concept of containment she was describing how she was using the concept with more skill, that she now understood better what kind of tool it was and how it could be used in a particular way with her borderline client to make sense of her own affective experiences and turn them into material she could use in her interventions.

Analytic ideas as tools

What do these accounts tell us about how analytic practitioners develop? My first answer to this question is: not enough! It is evident, from the many times I have had to admit defeat and acknowledge "there was not time to develop these ideas further", that the exploration of how each student develops their own way of working over the course of a training needs much more systematic attention than can be given in a brief, final tutorial.

Nevertheless, even in this brief exploration I am struck by how different these accounts are from each other. Compared to the five analysts from the Comparative Clinical Methods Working Group, who were chosen to represent the range of contemporary analytic practice in Europe (see Chapter 3, "Descriptions of the internal clinical templates of five analysts", pp.43–7), this group of students all came from the same training, which teaches one particular psychoanalytic orientation ("object-relations") and, to cap it all, all shared the same tutor (although only for their final year, and they were exposed to the influence of all the other tutors on the course as well as their placement supervisor and personal therapist). And yet these students can been seen to differ among themselves in ways that are broadly similar to the five analysts. For instance, there are those students who aim to speak in a clear and articulated manner (Jan), whereas others prefer a more indirect and allusive style (Greta). Some emphasize containment (Susan, Jane, Greta), others rely more on making interpretations or interventions (Jan, Bola, Kiran). Some aim to work directly in the transference (Bola, Jan), others prefer to work with experiences in the client's current life before bringing them into the transference (Kiran). Some think of what is wrong with the client or patient mainly in terms of deficit (Susan), others have ideas which might be closer to thinking in terms of conflict (Jan, Kiran).

How can we account for the same training seeming to produce such different students? It is likely that what each student brings to their training plays an important role in determining each student's particular way of working. In terms of the training itself, it suggests that whatever the formal or "official" version of psychoanalysis and psychoanalytic practice the teachers of a training believe themselves to be teaching, it is their implicit theories and the elements of their internal clinical template that are conveyed in their teaching and from which students learn. As we have seen, a major task for each student on a training is to learn how to put together and negotiate between these different inputs, explicit and implicit.

This is what we get to see in these accounts, more clearly than in the more worked-out and sophisticated descriptions of the internal clinical templates of the five senior analysts. In the students' accounts, we can see them trying to make sense of analytic concepts, models and techniques by testing them out, seeing how they can be used as tools for specific purposes with certain kinds of clients or patients. This may mean a period when they are not sure how they work, or, indeed, whether they work at all. In order to get them working, it may mean using concepts in ways that are different to how they were originally described. So although these students have all learnt the same concepts, and therefore speak a common psychoanalytic language, on closer examination it emerges that this language is used by each student in quite different ways.

We can see also in these accounts a variety of ways in which the students describe how they shape and put together the different elements that make up their way of working. Some make use of theory or theorists to help them articulate what they think they do in their work, enabling them to locate themselves in terms of the different psychoanalytic schools. Others write about their work drawing more on their own personal experience or values. Some use particular analytic concepts – trauma, containment, the facts of the transference. Other prefer metaphors – becoming more visible, finding an inner truth, practice as polyphony. Some refer to the challenge to their thinking of encountering a different group of clients or patients. Some describe a new capacity or skill developing, others of a change in the quality of what they are doing (as in Jane's: "I do what I did before but the difference is that I do it more"). Some look to the future (Jan wondering whether she needs to work with more neurotic clients), others back to an earlier stage in their learning (Kiran re-visiting her understanding of containment), or to the learning done before the course (Susan and Jane). Some allude to qualities from other registers of experience and behaviour (Susan's ethical and Greta's artistic dimensions), and some bring in their relationship to the training in general or to particular tutors (Greta's challenge to my perception of how she works).

The value of these accounts is that they give us a glimpse of how the different elements of one's implicit theorizing and internal clinical template are formed. For these students, at this early stage in their career, it may be hard to know which elements will find a permanent place and which will prove to be more temporary. For instance, there is a contrast between those students who present their way of working as having attained a coherence and equilibrium (Susan, Jane), and those who describe their approach as in a state of transition (Kiran). Does this mean those with a more well-worked-out approach are further on in their development? Or is this more to do with the "coherence" vector of their implicit thinking; that is, their tolerance for ambiguity, incoherence and contradiction (see Chapter 4, Table 4.1, p.65)? It is likely that this, and other questions about their thinking, will only become clear to each student after they have finished their training and when they have accumulated sufficient experience, theoretical understanding and confidence so that the work-in-progress starts to take on a more definite shape.

CONCLUDING REMARKS

Honouring our teachers while freeing ourselves from them

In a paper called "On Becoming a Psychoanalyst", Glen Gabbard and Thomas Ogden reflect on the developmental task of how to become an analyst "in one's own terms". They remark that few analysts feel they know what they are doing when they complete their formal training: "we strive to find our 'voice', our own 'style', a feeling that we are engaging in the practice of psychoanalysis in a way that bears our own watermark" (2009, p.311). In order to illustrate this, Thomas Ogden describes how he came to notice, for a period in his work with one particular patient, that he would preface his remarks with the word "well". When he thought about this, he realized he had adopted this mannerism from his first analyst. This led him to reflect on his relationship to authority and tradition. Gabbard and Ogden describe this relationship as one of tension between "inventing oneself freshly" and "creatively using one's emotional ancestry":

> In the process of becoming an analyst, we must "dream up" for ourselves an authentic way of speaking that involves disentangling ourselves from our own analyst(s) as well as past supervisors, teachers and writers we admire, while also drawing on what we have learned from them. (ibid. p.315)

This tension between honouring our ancestors and teachers while at the same time trying to free ourselves from their influence is a task facing all psychoanalytic practitioners. In my own case, an important milestone in my own development was when I was able to disentangle my own thinking from that of Winnicott, who was the psychoanalytic figure who at that period of my career had influenced me the most. In this process, I found it helpful to think of Winnicott not only as a real person, but also as a "transference object", a figure who embodied for me the ideals of analytic practice to which I aspired. It was only when I was able to begin the task of dismantling my transference that I could look more critically at his ideas. This no longer meant trying to fit what I did to Winnicott's version of psychoanalysis. Instead I was able to look to my own developing practice and see which of his theoretical and clinical concepts continued to inform and enrich my practice, and which ones did not (see Spurling, 2003 and 2008 for an account of this process).

In this course of interrogating Winnicott's ideas and trying to match them up with my own work, I was forced to articulate to myself what it was I thought I was doing. In this way, I got a clearer sense of who I was as a practitioner. My sense of identity was a function of how I practised, and only became clearer and more substantial as my work started to take on a distinctive shape and direction.

A practice-based view of practice

In writing in this way about my own development, I am drawing on a view of practice espoused in this book, which might be called a practice-based view of practice. I only felt I had become a psychotherapist when my own work reached a certain level of competence, when I felt I knew what I was doing well enough to feel my work was my own. My sense of identity resides in my work. If I were to wonder where this sense of identity is located, where the particular "watermark" of who I am can be found, I would look to the actual words I speak to my patients and the way I speak them. In a similar way, if one were to ask where the self or identity of a painter is to be located, the best place to look would be in the work that they do, the way their hand co-ordinates with their paintbrush to produce the particular brushstrokes that create their painting. This is a craft view of practice. In a craft perspective, identity is always embodied, traceable to the exercise of particular skills which can be seen as extensions of bodily practices (Sennett, 2008).

However, there is a well-established tradition within psychoanalytic thinking of seeing good psychoanalytic work as being something more or other than its practice. Sometimes, as we have seen, this "more than practice" is seen to reside in adopting or acquiring the correct attitude. At other times, the notion of a "self" which is separate from practice is invoked. Gabbard and Ogden, for instance, quote approvingly from Bion:

It is only after you have qualified [as an analyst] that you have a chance of becoming an analyst. The analyst you become is you and you alone; you have to respect the uniqueness of your personality – this is what you use, not all these interpretations [these theories that you use to combat the feeling that you are not really an analyst and do not know how to become one]. (2009, p.310)

Bion is writing here about the defensive use of interpretation and theory (see the more unconscious elements concerning our relationship and transference to theory in the map of implicit theory in Chapter 4, p.65). But in his evocation of the "uniqueness of your personality" as being something separate from if not opposed to how we use theories and make interpretations, Bion draws on this tendency to see the essence of good practice to reside in some part of ourselves which is distinct from our practice – "who we are" rather than "what we do".

Here is another example, this time from an analyst expressing his distrust of any attempt to categorize analytic practice or think of it in terms of a tick-box list of "competencies":

There is a risk of losing what is essential in psychoanalysis by hoping to sum it up in lists of particular competencies, and a risk that we will try to specify excellence as a psychoanalyst too much in terms of skill and technique, thus leaving out crucial personal qualities such as courage, tenacity, negative capability, imagination, integrity, willingness to confront, sensitivity and ongoing efforts to limit our own narcissism as analysts. The analyst has to work with the "telos" or aim of the work implicitly in mind, and if he or she can do this then many technical problems will find answers naturally. All this requires balance, tact and a delicate judgment in the psychoanalyst. (Brierly, 2010, p.5)

One can agree with Michael Brierly's sentiment about the dangers of reducing analytic work to any kind of politically driven framework which has the aim of standardizing analytic practice or forcing it to conform to some narrow notion of "evidence-based practice". But his way of doing this is to define good practice not as what the analyst does ("skills and techniques"), but as a function of who they are, their "personal attributes". These manifestations of our unique personality are characterized as though they reside in a special region which renders them immune from the normal demands we make for our practice: that it can be articulated, compared to other practices, evaluated against standards of competence and so on.

By contrast, a craft perspective would put the acquisition of skill at the centre of analytic practice. In this view, acquiring skill is not seen as a mechanical operation, reducible to a "list of competencies", but as a lengthy and complex process of combining intellectual, practical, affective, aesthetic and personal qualities. Doing something skillfully is an expression of who we are. If one has not attained a sufficient degree of the qualities identified by Brierly – courage, tenacity, imagination, acknowledgement of our narcissism, tact, balance, delicate judgement and so on – one will not be able to practice in a skilled way.

If we foreground "practices" rather than notions of correct attitude or unique self, and so look at all a practitioner does in a session – the strategies adopted, interventions composed, evaluations made – Brierly's contention, "if we have the aim or 'telos' of the work implicitly in mind...many technical problems will find answers naturally", does not give an adequate description of good analytic work (at least without extensively unpacking what this means). Furthermore, one might even wonder whether Gabbard and Ogden's resonant metaphor of the need to find one's "authentic voice" does justice to the complexity of what we normally do. Looking at practice as I have done in terms of the implicit clinical thinking that goes on all the time, what comes over is the *contingency* of what we say to our patients or clients. What actually goes on in a session, what we choose to say to them, represents only a small proportion of what we might have said. What was thought but not said, or what was thought but then forgotten or discarded, or what was imagined but in such a way that it could not at the time find expression in words – all of these constitute a vast backdrop of possible interventions which never found the light of day. We could then think of our actual speaking voice as composed of several potential voices, only one of which has become actualized in any particular session or therapy.

The period when one is developing as a practitioner could perhaps best be characterized as one when this movement between actual and potential speaking voices is at its most intense. It is a time when two different but complementary operations take place. It is an opportunity for a number of different possible speaking voices to be explored and tried out. It is also a time when these potential voices become crystallized into one (or possibly more than one) predominant or overriding voice, which comes to characterize one's particular style. One can then wonder what happens to these potential approaches or voices that get dropped from one's clinical repertoire. Do they disappear, never to return? Or do they re-surface in a particular guise, as Ogden illustrates in his elegant example of having incorporated a particular way of speaking into his practice which was derived from his former analyst. Or do these redundant or forgotten voices and practices get "relegated to limbo", as Winnicott so aptly describes the fate of transitional objects that have lost their appeal, perhaps to serve in some minor region in our store of implicit theories or internal clinical template?

REFERENCES

Basile, R., Birksted Breen, D., Bonard, O., Denis, P., Diercks, M., Ferro, A., Hebbrecht, M., Hinze, E., Jackson, D., Mariotti, P., Hanke A., Tuckett, D. (2010) "How do psychoanalysts work? The work of the EPF Working Party on Comparative Clinical Methods 2003–2009", *Psychoanalysis in Europe, Bulletin of the European Psychoanalytic Federation,* Bulletin 64, Year 2010, Supplement.

Bion, W. (1970) *Attention and Interpretation,* London: Tavistock.

Bion, W. (1984) *Second Thoughts: selected papers on psycho-analysis.* London: Karnac.

Birksted-Breen, D., Ferro, A., Mariotti, P. (2008) "Work in progress: Using the two-step method", in *Psychoanalysis Comparable and Incomparable,* ed. Tuckett, D. et al., London: Routledge.

Boehm, T. (2008) "Before the method, underestimating the problem and the meeting in Prague", in *Psychoanalysis Comparable and Incomparable,* ed. Tuckett, D. et al., London: Routledge.

Bohleber, W. (2006) "Discussion of public and implicit theory in Peter Fonagy's case presentation", in *Psychoanalysis: From Practice to Theory,* ed. Canestri, J. Chichester: Whurr.

Bohleber, W., Fonagy, P., Jimenez, J., Scarfone, D., Varvin, S., Zysman, S. (2013) "Towards a better use of psychoanalytic concepts: A model illustrated using the concept of enactment", *International Journal of Psychoanalysis* 94: 501–530.

Brierly, M. (2010) "Rendering unto Caesar the things that are Caesar's and unto God the things that are God's", *Psychoanalytic Psychotherapy* 24: 3–7.

Britton, R., Steiner, J. (1994) "Interpretation: Selected fact or overvalued idea?", *International Journal of Psychoanalysis* 75: 1069–1078.

Britton, R. (1998) "Naming and containing", Chapter 2 of *Belief and Imagination,* London: Routledge,19–28.

Britton, R. (2003) *Sex, Death and the Superego: Experiences in Psychoanalysis,* London: Karnac.

Busch, F., Milrod, B., Singer, M., Arsonson, A. (2012) *Manual of Panic Focused Psychodynamic Psychotherapy – Extended Range,* London: Routledge.

Canestri, J. (ed.) (2006) *Psychoanalysis: From Practice to Theory,* Chichester: Whurr.

Casement, P. (1985) *On Learning from the Patient,* London: Tavistock.

De Masi, F. (2004) "The psychodynamic of panic attacks: A useful integration of psychoanalysis and neuroscience", *International Journal of Psychoanalysis* 85: 311–336.

Diercks, M. (2013) "Freud's 'transference': Claim and reality, theory and practice", unpublished paper presented at University College London conference: "Transference, countertransference and enactment", 13–15 December 2013.

Ferro, A. (2009) "Transformations in dreaming and characters in the psychoanalytic field", *International Journal of Psychoanalysis* 90: 209–230.

Fonagy, P. (2006) "The failure of practice to inform theory and the role of implicit theory in bridging the transmission gap", in *Psychoanalysis: From Practice to Theory,* ed. Canestri, J., Chichester: Whurr.

Freud, S. (1895) "Studies on Hysteria", *The Standard Edition of the Complete Psychoanalytic Works of Sigmund Freud,* SE 11: 19–307, London: Hogarth.

Freud, S. (1912) "Recommendations to physicians practising psycho-analysis", *SE* X11: 109–120.

Freud, S. (1914) "Remembering, repeating and working-through", *SE* X11: 145–156.

Freud, S. (1915) "Observations on transference-love", *SE* X11: 157–171.

Freud, S. (1917) "Mourning and melancholia", *SE* XIV: 237–258.

Freud, S. (1926) "The question of lay analysis", *SE* XX: 179–258.

Freud, S. (1933) "The question of a 'Weltanschauung' ", *New Introductory Lectures SE* XX11: 158–184.

Freud, S. (1937) "Constructions in analysis", *SE* XXIII: 255–270.

Frosh, S. (2012) *A Brief Introduction to Psychoanalytic Theory,* London: Palgrave Macmillan.

Gabbard, G., Westen, D. (2003) "Re-thinking therapeutic action", *International Journal of Psychoanalysis* 84: 823–841.

Gabbard, G., Ogden, T. (2009) "On becoming a psychoanalyst", *International Journal of Psychoanalysis* 90: 311–327.

Greenson, R. (1960) "Empathy and its vicissitudes", *International Journal of Psychoanalysis* 41: 418–424.

Hamilton, V. (1993) "Truth and reality in psychoanalytic discourse", *International Journal of Psychoanalysis* 74, 63–79.

Heimann, P. (1950) "On counter-transference", *International Journal of Psychoanalysis* 30: 81–84.

Jimenez, J. (2005) "The search for integration or how to work as a pluralist psychoanalyst", *Psychoanalytic Inquiry* 25: 602–634.

Jimenez, J. (2008) "Theoretical plurality and pluralism in psychoanalytic practice", *International Journal of Psychoanalysis* 89: 579–599.

Jimenez, J. (2009) "Grasping psychoanalyst's practice in its own merits", *International Journal of Psychoanalysis* 90: 231–248.

Keats, John. Letter to George and Thomas Keats, quoted in Casement, 1985, 223.

Kilminster, S., Zukas, M., Roberts, T., Quinton, N. (2011) "Preparedness is not enough: Understanding transitions as critically intensive learning periods", *Medical Education* 45: 1006–1015.

Laplanche, J., Pontalis, J.-B. (1980) *The Language of Psychoanalysis*, London: Hogarth.

Lemma, A. (1993) *Introduction to the Practice of Psychoanalytic Psychotherapy*, Chichester: Wiley.

Lemma, A., Roth A., Pilling, S. (2010) "The competencies required to deliver effective psychoanalytic/psychodynamic therapy", available at: http://www.ucl.ac.uk/clinical-psychology/CORE/Psychodynamic_Competences/Background_Paper.pdf.

Lemma, A. (2012) "Some reflections on the 'teaching attitude' and its application to teaching about the use of the transference: A British view", *British Journal of Psychotherapy* 28: 454–473.

Lucas, R. (2004) "The management of depression – analytic, antidepressants or both?", *Psychoanalytic Psychotherapy* 18: 268–284.

Milton, J., Polmear, C., Fabricius, J. (2011) *A Short Introduction to Psychoanalysis*, London: Sage.

Mitchell, J. (1986) *The Selected Melanie Klein*, Harmondsworth: Penguin.

Ogden, T. (1992) *The Primitive Edge of Experience*, London: Karnac.

Ogden, T. (2005) *This Art of Psychoanalysis: Dreaming Undreamt Dreams and Interrupted Cries*, London: Routledge.

O'Shaughnessy, E. (1989) "The invisible Oedipus complex", in *The Oedipus Complex Today*, ed. Britton, R. et al., London: Karnac.

O'Shaughnessy, E. (1999) "Relating to the superego", *International Journal of Psychoanalysis* 80: 861–870.

Quinodoz, D. (1990) "Vertigo and object relationship", *International Journal of Psychoanalysis* 71: 53–63.

Quinodoz, D. (1998) "A Fe/Male transsexual patient in psychoanalysis", *International Journal of Psychoanalysis* 79: 95–111.

Pullman, P. (1995) *Northern Lights: His Dark Materials 1*, London: Scholastic.

Ronnestad, M., Skovholt, T. (1993) "Supervision of beginning and advanced graduate students of counselling and psychotherapy", *Journal of Counselling and Development* 71: 396–405.

Rosenfeld, H. (1988) "A clinical approach to the psychoanalytic theory of the life and death instincts: An investigation into the aggressive aspects of narcissism", in *Melanie Klein Today, Volume 1: Mainly Theory*, ed. Bott Spillius, E., London: Tavistock.

Sandler, J. (1983) "Reflections on some relations between psychoanalytic concepts and psychoanalytic practice", *International Journal of Psychoanalysis* 64: 35–45.

Schatzki, T., Cetina, K., Von Savigny, E. (2001) *The Practice Turn in Contemporary Theory*, London: Routledge.

Schoen, D. (1991) *The Reflective Practitioner: How Professionals Think in Action*, Farnham: Ashgate.

Sechaud, E. (2008) "The handling of the transference in French psychoanalysis", *International Journal of Psychoanalysis* 89: 1011–1028.

Sennett, R. (2008) *The Craftsman*, London: Allen Lane.

REFERENCES

Sinason, V. (2014) "Boundaries in ethical and sustainable practice", lecture given as part of Confer series on "The Impossible Profession: a series of talks examining the experienced clinicians' most difficult dilemmas", 24th March, 2014: Tavistock Centre, London.

Sohn, L. (1988) "Narcissistic organizations, projective identification and the formation of the identificate", in *Melanie Klein Today: Volume 1: Mainly Theory*, ed. Bott Spillius, E., London: Tavistock.

Spurling, L. (2003) "On psychoanalytic figures as transference objects", *International Journal of Psychoanalysis* 84: 31–43.

Spurling, L. (2008) "Is there still a place for the concept of therapeutic regression in psychoanalysis?", *International Journal of Psychoanalysis* 89: 523–540.

Spurling, L. (2009) *An Introduction to Psychodynamic Counselling* (2nd edition), London: Palgrave Macmillan.

Spurling, L. (2010) "Can there be an analytic practice of a non-analytic therapy?", *Psychodynamic Psychotherapy* 16: 45–59.

Spurling, L. (2012) "Characters in interpersonal and psychoanalytic therapy: A comparison", *Psychoanalytic Psychotherapy* 26: 230–244.

Thoma, H., Kachele, H. (1987) *Psychoanalytic Practice 1: Principles,* Berlin: Springer-Verlag (available online on PEP-WEB).

Thoma, H., Kachele, H. (2007) "Comparative psychoanalysis on the basis of a new form of treatment report", *Psychoanalytic Inquiry* 27: 650–689.

Tuckett, D. (2006) "The search to define and describe how psychoanalysts work: Preliminary report on the project of the EPF Working Party on Comparative Clinical Methods", in *Psychoanalysis: From Practice to Theory*, ed. Canestri, J., Chichester: Wiley.

Tuckett, D., Basile, R., Birksted-Breen, D., Bohm, T., Denis, P., Ferro, A., Hinz, H., Jemstedt, A., Mariotti, P., Schubert, J. (2008) *Psychoanalysis Comparable and Incomparable: The Evolution of a Method to Describe and Compare Psychoanalytic Approaches,* London: Routledge.

Tuckett, D. (2008) "On difference, discussing difference and comparison", in ibid. Tuckett et al. (2008).

Wallerstein, R. (1990) "Psychoanalysis: The common ground", *International Journal of Psychoanalysis* 71: 3–20.

Winnicott, D. (1954) "Metapsychological and clinical aspects of regression within the psycho-analytical set-up", in *Through Psychoanalysis to Paediatrics*, 1978, London: Hogarth.

INDEX